Production Ready OpenStack - Recipes for Successful Environments

Over 90 practical and highly applicable recipes to successfully deploy various OpenStack configurations in production

Arthur Berezin

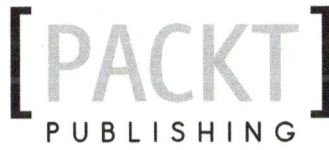

[PACKT] PUBLISHING
open source
community experience distilled

BIRMINGHAM - MUMBAI

Production Ready OpenStack - Recipes for Successful Environments

Copyright © 2015 Packt Publishing

All rights reserved. No part of this book may be reproduced, stored in a retrieval system, or transmitted in any form or by any means, without the prior written permission of the publisher, except in the case of brief quotations embedded in critical articles or reviews.

Every effort has been made in the preparation of this book to ensure the accuracy of the information presented. However, the information contained in this book is sold without warranty, either express or implied. Neither the author nor Packt Publishing, and its dealers and distributors will be held liable for any damages caused or alleged to be caused directly or indirectly by this book.

Packt Publishing has endeavored to provide trademark information about all of the companies and products mentioned in this book by the appropriate use of capitals. However, Packt Publishing cannot guarantee the accuracy of this information.

First published: September 2015

Production reference: 1280915

Published by Packt Publishing Ltd.
Livery Place
35 Livery Street
Birmingham B3 2PB, UK.

ISBN 978-1-78398-690-3

www.packtpub.com

Credits

Author
Arthur Berezin

Reviewers
Chad P. Lung
Nilesh Pawar
Adam Stokes

Commissioning Editor
Andrew Duckworth

Acquisition Editor
Sonali Vernekar

Content Development Editor
Shubhangi Dhamgaye

Technical Editor
Mitali Somaiya

Copy Editor
Dipti Mankameh

Project Coordinator
Harshal Ved

Proofreader
Safis Editing

Indexer
Hemangini Bari

Graphics
Disha Haria

Production Coordinator
Komal Ramchandani

Cover Work
Komal Ramchandani

About the Author

Arthur Berezin is an active member of the OpenStack community and a hands-on OpenStacker since the early Essex release of OpenStack in 2012. During this time Arthur has built multiple production data centers based on OpenStack, helped dozens of organizations in planning their OpenStack environments, and in executing their software defined data center strategy. Prior to OpenStack, Arthur worked on KVM virtualization management project oVirt/RHEV and open source virtualization management technologies for production mission critical environments.

Arthur is the Director of Product for Cloudify at GigaSpaces. He works on open-source and open-standard cloud application orchestration platform with cloud aware applications in mind that run natively on OpenStack and other private and public clouds. Prior to Cloudify, Arthur was a Senior Technical Product Manager for OpenStack at Red Hat, Product Owner of Keystone, Heat, Horizon, RHEL OpenStack Platform Installer (Foreman/Puppet based Project Staypuft), Packstack, and OpenStack High Availability.

In the past 14 years, Arthur has served in various management and technical positions in the high-tech industry, including working as a founder and technical lead of a start up, a product line lead, Linux consultant, technical pre/post sales, and as a Linux Instructor, where he prepared students to pass the Red Hat Certified Engineer (RHCE) exams. You can find Arthur on Twitter as `@ArthurBerezin` or on his blog at `www.Berezins.com`.

> I would like to dedicate this book to my parents, Bella and Arkady Berezin, who allowed me to explore the world and learn from my own experiences. My beautiful spouse, Elizabeth, who supported me fully in the process of writing this book, encouraging me at tough moments and supporting me through countless sleepless nights and many of my good friends at GigaSpaces, Red Hat, and the OpenStack and DevOps communities, without you guys this book wouldn't have happened.
>
> I hope you find this book educating, informative, interesting, and fun to read.

About the Reviewers

Chad Lung is a Cloud engineer working with the EMC Cloud Services Group. He is also an active OpenStack core contributor and has over 18 years of industry experience in various roles.

Originally born in Canada, he moved to the United States in 1997 and began his software engineering career. He has worked with various technologies and also with large cloud orientated companies, such as Rackspace and EMC.

Chad has three sons and lives with his wife in San Antonio, TX.

Nilesh Pawar has worked in the field of Information Technology since 2008. After graduating with a bachelor's degree in Information Technology he has worked in various positions, such as a developer in .NET, Linux administration, virtualization admin, technical consultant, and so on. He is currently associated with upcoming new technologies in Telecom industries, such as C-SDN, vCPE, and vEPC. He can be reached on `nilesh56@gmail.com`.

Adam Stokes has been an open source evangelist for a long time. Currently, he's working for Canonical Ltd as a technical lead for their Solutions Engineering team and is the lead developer for Ubuntu OpenStack Installer. He's been in a direct relation with all the components that make up OpenStack in order to provide the most streamlined and simple approach to deploy private clouds. He has worked for 7 years at Red Hat in the Cloud Research and Development department, where he worked on service discovery and management applications.

www.PacktPub.com

Support files, eBooks, discount offers, and more

For support files and downloads related to your book, please visit www.PacktPub.com.

Did you know that Packt offers eBook versions of every book published, with PDF and ePub files available? You can upgrade to the eBook version at www.PacktPub.com and as a print book customer, you are entitled to a discount on the eBook copy. Get in touch with us at service@packtpub.com for more details.

At www.PacktPub.com, you can also read a collection of free technical articles, sign up for a range of free newsletters and receive exclusive discounts and offers on Packt books and eBooks.

https://www2.packtpub.com/books/subscription/packtlib

Do you need instant solutions to your IT questions? PacktLib is Packt's online digital book library. Here, you can search, access, and read Packt's entire library of books.

Why subscribe?

- Fully searchable across every book published by Packt
- Copy and paste, print, and bookmark content
- On demand and accessible via a web browser

Free access for Packt account holders

If you have an account with Packt at www.PacktPub.com, you can use this to access PacktLib today and view 9 entirely free books. Simply use your login credentials for immediate access.

Table of Contents

Preface   v

Chapter 1: Introduction to OpenStack and its Deployment Using Packages   1
- Introduction   2
- Configuring hosts prerequisites   10
- Installing MariaDB database   12
- Installing RabbitMQ   14
- Installing Keystone – Identity service   15
- Generating and configuring tokens PKIs   17
- Installing Glance – images service   21
- Installing Nova – Compute service   26
- Installing Neutron – networking service   31
- Configuring Neutron network node   36
- Configuring compute node for Neutron   40
- Installing Horizon – web user interface dashboard   45

Chapter 2: Deploying OpenStack Using Staypuft OpenStack Installer   47
- Introduction   47
- Setting up the environment   48
- Installing Staypuft packages   51
- Discovering hosts for provisioning   55
- Creating a new OpenStack deployment   58
- Configuring a network   60
- Allocating hosts to roles   65
- Configuring host networking   66
- Deploying OpenStack   68

Table of Contents

Chapter 3: Deploying Highly Available OpenStack — 71
- Introduction — 71
- Installing Pacemaker — 73
- Installing HAProxy — 74
- Configuring Galera cluster for MariaDB — 78
- Installing RabbitMQ with mirrored queues — 81
- Configuring highly available OpenStack services — 83

Chapter 4: Keystone Identity Service — 89
- Introduction — 89
- Configuring Keystone with the MariaDB backend — 91
- Generating and configuring tokens PKIs — 93
- Configuring Keystone with Microsoft Active Directory and LDAP — 97
- Configuring Keystone caching with Memcached — 100
- Securing Keystone with SSL — 102

Chapter 5: Glance Image Service — 107
- Introduction — 107
- Configuring Glance with the local file backend — 108
- Configuring Glance with the NFS backend — 110
- Configuring Glance with the Swift backend — 111
- Configuring Glance with the Ceph backend — 113
- Configuring Glance image caching — 115
- Configuring the Glance image size limit and storage quota — 117

Chapter 6: Cinder Block Storage Service — 119
- Introduction — 119
- Configuring Cinder with the logical volume management backend driver — 120
- Configuring Cinder with the Ceph RADOS block device backend driver — 123
- Configuring Cinder with the Network File System (NFS) backend driver — 125
- Configuring Cinder with the Ceph RBD backup driver — 127
- Configuring Cinder with multiple backends — 129
- Configuring Cinder scheduler filters and weighers — 132

Chapter 7: Neutron Networking Service — 135
- Introduction — 135
- Configuring Neutron VLAN provider network with ML2 and LinuxBridge — 139
- Configuring Neutron VXLAN and GRE tenant networks using Open vSwitch — 144
- Configuring the L3 agent with Open vSwitch — 148
- Configuring the DHCP service agent — 151
- Configuring LoadBalancer as a service — 152
- Configuring Firewall as a Service — 155

Chapter 8: Nova-Compute Service — 157
Introduction — 157
Configuring Nova Hypervisors — 159
Configuring Nova-compute with KVM Hypervisor — 160
Configuring Nova-compute with a QEMU Hypervisor emulation — 161
Configuring Nova scheduler filters — 163
Configuring Nova host aggregates — 168
Configuring Nova host aggregates filters — 171
Configuring Nova scheduler weights — 174

Chapter 9: Horizon Dashboard Service — 179
Introduction — 179
Securing Horizon with Secure Socket Layer — 180
Configuring Horizon caching with memcached — 184
Customizing Horizon dashboard appearance — 185

Index — 187

Preface

OpenStack is an operating system that allows administrators and developers to consolidate and control pools of computer (memory and so on), networking and storage resources with a centralized dashboard and administration panel to enable the large scale development of cloud services.

The purpose of this book is to provide a comprehensive guide to set up and configure OpenStack. The book will show the reader how to manage and optimize their deployment so that it provides the solution that fits their situation and requirements the best. This book will focus on topics such as the correct storage configuration, image cache configuration, security, and access permissions. It will also cover essential and important areas for any OpenStack configuration and will therefore cover: compute, networking, image services, identity services, object storage, and block storage.

What this book covers

Chapter 1, *Introduction to OpenStack and its Deployment Using Packages*, describes the prerequisites and how to set up the environment for OpenStack deployment. It also shows how to check whether OpenStack was installed successfully or not.

Chapter 2, *Deploying OpenStack Using Staypuft OpenStack Installer*, describes how to install Staypuft packages, verify them, and also gives an overview on how to troubleshoot during the deployment process.

Chapter 3, *Deploying Highly Available OpenStack*, expands OpenStack services configuration and discusses how to configure each of the OpenStack services, database, and message broker in a highly available configuration.

Chapter 4, *Keystone Identity Service*, introduces the Keystone service and its role in OpenStack. It includes how to secure Keystone using SSL.

Chapter 5, *Glance Image Service*, introduces Glance's role with OpenStack. Here, you will learn how to configure the Swift Object storage as a backend for Glance.

Preface

Chapter 6, *Cinder Block Storage Service*, describes how to set up and configure Ceph as a volume backend for Cinder.

Chapter 7, *Neutron Networking Service*, describes the various networking models that can be used with Neutron.

Chapter 8, *Nova-Compute Service*, introduces Nova services, its role, and possible uses. It also explains how to secure Nova with authentication and authorization.

Chapter 9, *Horizon Dashboard Service*, describes how to configure Horizon to use Apache HTTPD, how to secure horizon with SSL/TLS, and also how to customize Horizon's user interface.

What you need for this book

The recipes and examples covered in this book use Red Hat's community based OpenStack distribution RDO, which can be downloaded freely from http://rdoproject.org, running on latest version of CentOS7, can be downloaded from http://www.centos.org. It is recommended to obtain 4 physical machines with visualization capabilities (Intel VT-d or AMD svm), or use virtual machine with nested virtualization enabled.

Who this book is for

If you have a basic understanding of Linux and Cloud computing and want to learn about configurations that OpenStack supports, this is the book for you. A prior knowledge of virtualization and managing Linux environments is assumed. A prior knowledge or experience of OpenStack is not required, although it is beneficial.

Conventions

In this book, you will find a number of styles of text that distinguish between different kinds of information. Here are some examples of these styles, and an explanation of their meaning.

Code words in text, database table names, folder names, filenames, file extensions, pathnames, dummy URLs, user input, and Twitter handles are shown as follows: "The search method has a similar format to the `knife` command."

A block of code is set as follows:

```
all_users = search(:users, 'id:*')
users_s = search(:users, 'id:s*')
all_nodes = search(:node, '*')
```

Preface

Any command-line input or output is written as follows:

```
$ knife data bag show credentials aws
```

New terms and **important words** are shown in bold. Words that you see on the screen, in menus or dialog boxes for example, appear in the text like this: "Once there, a tab labeled **Chef Server** will be present at the top of the page".

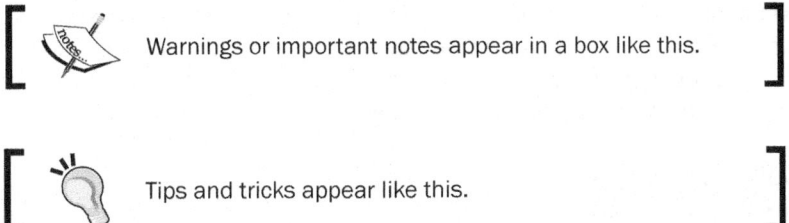

> Warnings or important notes appear in a box like this.

> Tips and tricks appear like this.

Reader feedback

Feedback from our readers is always welcome. Let us know what you think about this book—what you liked or may have disliked. Reader feedback is important for us to develop titles that you really get the most out of.

To send us general feedback, simply send an e-mail to feedback@packtpub.com, and mention the book title via the subject of your message.

If there is a topic that you have expertise in and you are interested in either writing or contributing to a book, see our author guide on www.packtpub.com/authors.

Customer support

Now that you are the proud owner of a Packt book, we have a number of things to help you to get the most from your purchase.

Downloading the example code

You can download the example code files for all Packt books you have purchased from your account at http://www.packtpub.com. If you purchased this book elsewhere, you can visit http://www.packtpub.com/support and register to have the files e-mailed directly to you.

Preface

Errata

Although we have taken every care to ensure the accuracy of our content, mistakes do happen. If you find a mistake in one of our books—maybe a mistake in the text or the code—we would be grateful if you would report this to us. By doing so, you can save other readers from frustration and help us improve subsequent versions of this book. If you find any errata, please report them by visiting http://www.packtpub.com/submit-errata, selecting your book, clicking on the **errata submission form** link, and entering the details of your errata. Once your errata are verified, your submission will be accepted and the errata will be uploaded on our website, or added to any list of existing errata, under the Errata section of that title. Any existing errata can be viewed by selecting your title from http://www.packtpub.com/support.

Piracy

Piracy of copyright material on the Internet is an ongoing problem across all media. At Packt, we take the protection of our copyright and licenses very seriously. If you come across any illegal copies of our works, in any form, on the Internet, please provide us with the location address or website name immediately so that we can pursue a remedy.

Please contact us at copyright@packtpub.com with a link to the suspected pirated material.

We appreciate your help in protecting our authors, and our ability to bring you valuable content.

Questions

You can contact us at questions@packtpub.com if you are having a problem with any aspect of the book, and we will do our best to address it.

1
Introduction to OpenStack and its Deployment Using Packages

In this chapter, we will cover the following:

- Configuring host prerequisites
- Installing MariaDB database
- Installing RabbitMQ
- Installing Keystone – Identity service
- Generating and configuring tokens PKIs
- Installing Glance – images service
- Installing Nova – Compute service
- Installing Neutron networking service
- Configuring Neutron network node
- Configuring compute node for Neutron
- Installing Horizon – web user interface dashboard

Introduction

OpenStack is a cloud operating system software that allows running and managing **Infrastructure as a Service (IaaS)** clouds on the standard commodity hardware. OpenStack is not an operating system of its own, which manages bare metal hardware machines, is a stack of open source software projects. The projects run on top of Linux operating system. The projects usually consist of several components that run as Linux services on top of the operating system.

OpenStack lets users to rapidly deploy instances of virtual machines or Linux containers on the fly, which run different kinds of workloads that serve public online services or deployed privately on company's premise. In some cases, workloads can run both on private environment, and on a public cloud, creating a hybrid model cloud.

OpenStack has a modular architecture. Projects are constructed of functional components. Each project has several components that are responsible for project's sole functionality. An API component exposes its capabilities, functionalities, and objects it manages via standard HTTP Restful API, so it can be consumed as a service by other services and users.

The components are responsible for managing and maintaining services, and the actual implementation of the services leverage exciting technologies such as backend drivers.

Basically, OpenStack is an upper layer management system that leverages existing underlying technologies and presents a standard API layer for services to interconnect and interact.

The computing industry and information technology, in particular, made a major progress in the past 20 year moving toward distributed systems that use common standards. OpenStack is another step forward, introducing a new standard for technologies that were progressing separately in the past two decades, to interconnect in an industry standard manner.

OpenStack projects and components

OpenStack environment consists of projects that provide their functionality as services. Each project is designed to provide a specific function. The core projects are the required services in most OpenStack environments, and in most use cases, an OpenStack environment cannot run without them. Additional projects are optional and provide value and add or fulfill certain functionalities for the cloud.

Core services

Core services provided by OpenStack projects are as follows:

- **Nova** compute service, which launches virtual machines.
- **Glance** serves operating system template images to Nova.
- **Keystone** authenticates and authorizes commands and requests.
- **Neutron** is the project that provides networking for the instances as a service. Older releases used Nova-network service to provide networking connectivity to the instance, which is a part of the Nova project, but efforts are made to deprecate Nova-network in favor of Neutron.

Optional services

Optional services provide additional functionality but are not considered as necessary in every OpenStack environment:

- **Horizon** is the web user interface dashboard
- **Cinder** project provides block storage services
- **Swift** provides object storage services
- **Ceilometer** provides monitoring and telemetry services for billing and chargeback
- **Heat** is OpenStack's orchestration layer
- **Trove** provides database services for instances
- **Zaqar** provides messaging as a service capability for instances
- **Sahara** is a project that delivers Hadoop as a service

The complete list of additional projects is growing rapidly, and every new release has several new projects.

All services use a database service, usually MariaDB to store persistent data, and use a message broker for service inner communication, most commonly, RabbitMQ server.

To better understand this design concept, let's take one project to explore this. Nova is a project that manages the compute resources. Basically, Nova is responsible for launching and managing instances for virtual machines. Nova is implemented via several components such as Linux services. Nova-Compute Linux service is responsible for launching the VM instances. It does not implement a virtualization technology hypervisor, rather it uses a virtualization technology as a supportive backend mechanism, **kernel-based virtual machine** (**KVM**) with the libvirt driver in most cases, to launch KVM instances.

Nova API Linux service exposes Nova's capabilities via RESTful API and allows launching new instances, using standard RESTful API calls. To launch new instances, Nova needs a base image to boot from, and Nova makes an API call to Glance, which is the project responsible for serving images.

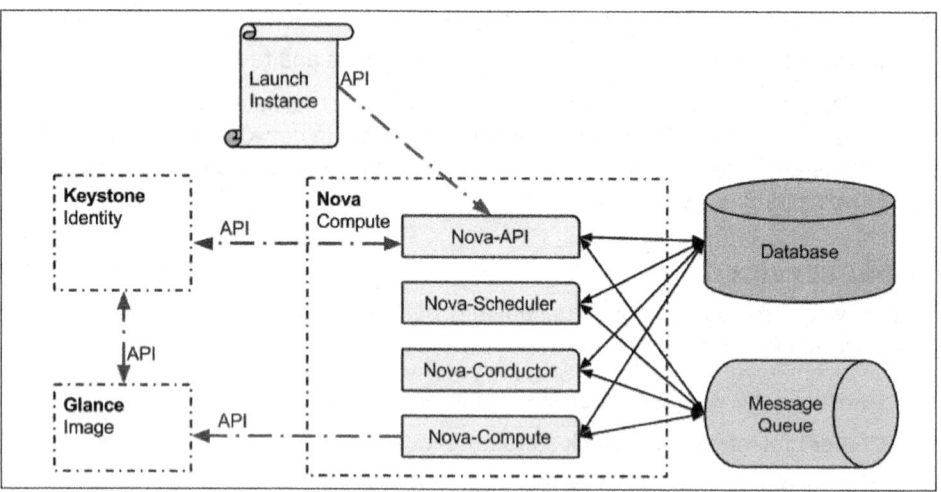

Architectural layouts

OpenStack consists of several core projects—Nova for compute, Glance for images, Cinder for block storage, Keystone for Identity, Neutron for networking, and additional optional services. Each project exposes all its capabilities via RESTful API. The services inner-communicate over RESTful API calls, so when a service requires resources from another service, it makes a RESTful API call to query services' capabilities, list its resources, or call for a certain action.

Every OpenStack project consists of several components. Each component fulfills a certain functionality or performs a certain task. The components are standard POSIX Linux services, which use a message broker server for inner component communication of that project, using RabbitMQ in most cases. The services save their persistent data and objects states in a database.

All OpenStack services use this modular design. Each services has a component that is responsible to receive API calls, and other components are responsible for performing actions, for example, launching a virtual machine or creating a volume, weighing filters and scheduling, or other tasks that are part of project's functionality.

This design makes OpenStack highly modular; the components of each project can be installed on separate hosts while inner communicating via the message broker. There's no single permutation that fits all use cases OpenStack is used for, but there are a few commonly used layouts. Some layouts are easier for management, some focus on scaling compute resources, other layouts focus on scaling object storage, each with its own benefits and drawbacks.

All-In-One layout

In all-in-one layout, all OpenStack's services and components, including the database, message broker, and Nova-Compute service are installed on a single host. All-in-one layout is mostly used for testing OpenStack or while running proof of concept environments to evaluate functionality. While Nova-Compute nodes can be added for additional compute scalability, this layout introduces risks when using a single node as management plane, storage pool, and compute.

Controller-Neutron-computes layout

In **Controller** computes layout, all API services and components responsible for OpenStack management are deployed on a node, named OpenStack controller node. This includes Keystone Identity, Glance for instance images, Cinder block device, Neutron networking, Nova management, Horizon dashboard, message broker, and database services. All networking services are installed on **Neutron Network Node**—L3 Agent, Open vSwitch (L2) Agent, DHCP agent, and metadata service. **Compute Nodes** run **Nova-Compute** services that are responsible for running the instances as shown in the following chart:

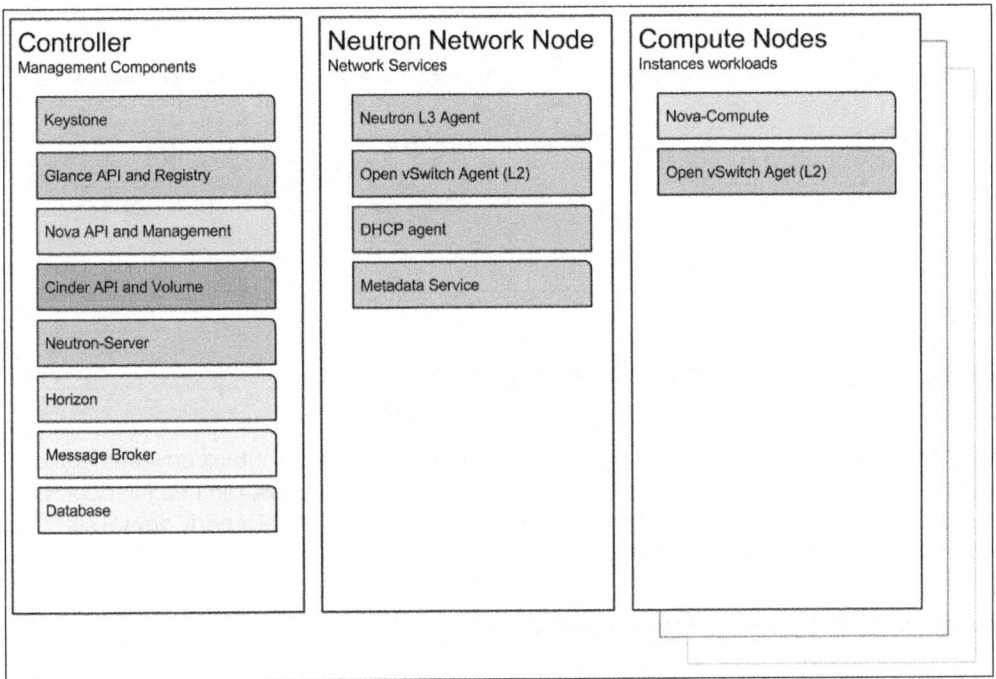

This layout allows the compute resources to scale out to multiple nodes while keeping all management and all API components on a single control plane. The controller is easy to maintain and manage as all API interfaces are on a single node. Neutron network node manages the all layer 2 and layer 3 networks, virtual subnets, and all virtual routers. It is also responsible for routing traffic to external networks, which are not managed by Neutron.

Custom-distributed layout

Typically, large-scale environments run under heavy loads, along with running large amount of instances and handling large amount of simultaneous API calls. To handle such high loads, it is possible to deploy the services in a distributed layout, where every service is installed on its own dedicated node, and every node can individually scale out to additional nodes according to the load of each component. In the following diagram, all services are distributed based on core functionality. All Nova management services are installed on dedicated nodes:

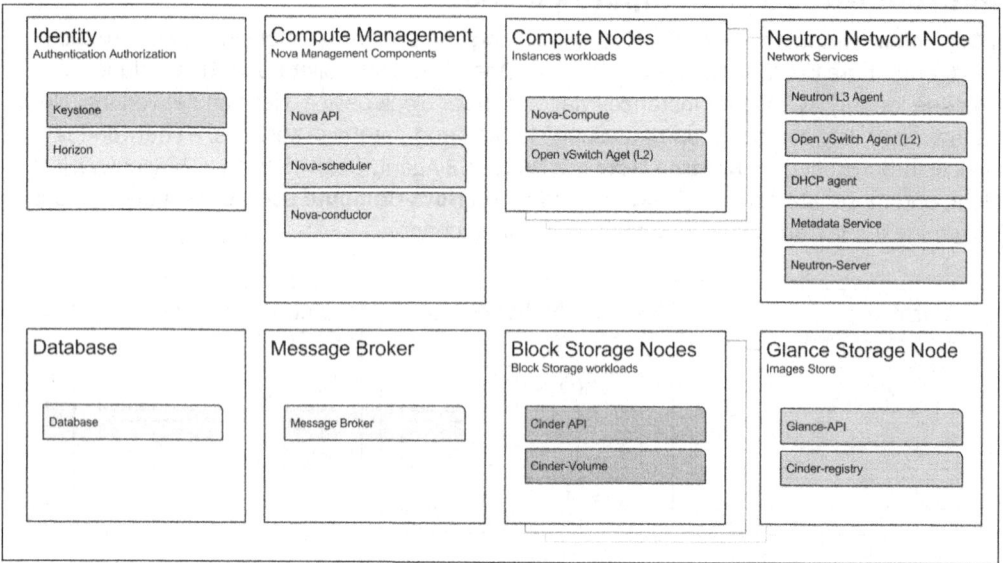

Choosing a deployment method

Project Tuskar aims to become the standard way to deploy and OpenStack environments. While the project started to gain momentum in recent release cycles, the need to deploy OpenStack in a standard predictable manner existed from OpenStacks early days. This need brought various deployment tools to use.

Manual deployment from packages

OpenStack project's source code is available on GitHub, while the different distributions compile the source code and ship it as packaged, RPMs for Red Hat bases operating systems, and .deb files for Ubuntu-based systems. One way to deploy OpenStack is to install distribution packages based on a chosen deployed layout and manually configure all services and components needed for fully operational OpenStack environment. This manual process is fairly complex and requires being familiar with all basic configurations needed for OpenStack to function.

This chapter focuses on packages' deployment and manual configuration of the services, as this is a good practice to become familiar with all the basic configurations and getting ready for more advanced OpenStack configurations.

Configuration management tools (Puppet, Chef, Ansible)

Configuring OpenStack services manually is a complex task, that requires editing lots of files and configuring lots of depending services, as such, it is a very error-prone process. A common way to automate this process is to use configuration management tools, such as Puppet, Chef, or Ansible, for installing OpenStack packages and automate all the configuration needed for OpenStack to operate. There's a large community, developing open source Puppet modules and Chef cookbooks to deploy OpenStack, which are available on GitHub.

PackStack

PackStack is a utility that uses Puppet modules to deploy OpenStack on multiple preinstalled nodes automatically. It requires neither Puppet skills nor being familiar with OpenStack configuration. Installing OpenStack using PackStack is fairly simple; all it reacquires is to execute a single command `#packstack --gen-answer-file` to generate an `answers` file that desires the deployment layout and to initiate deployment run with `#packstack --answer-file=/path/to/packstack_answers.txt`.

Foreman with Staypuft plugin

The project Staypuft is an OpenStack deployment tool, which is based on Foreman, a robust and mature life cycle management tool. Staypuft includes a user interface designed specifically to deploy OpenStack and uses supporting Puppet modules. It also includes a discovery tool to easily add and deploy new hardware, and it can deploy the controller node with high availability configuration for production use.

Staypuft makes it easy to install OpenStack, with lower learning curve than managing Puppet modules manually, and it is more robust than using Packstack. *Chapter 2, Deploying OpenStack Using Staypuft OpenStack Installer*, will describe how to install a new OpenStack environment using Staypuft.

Deploying OpenStack from packages

This chapter covers the manual installation of OpenStack from RDO distribution packages and the manual configuration of all basic OpenStack services. As mentioned earlier, manually installing OpenStack is not the optimal way to set up an OpenStack environment, as it involves numerous manual steps that are not easily reproducible and very error-prone, but the manual process is a great way to get familiar with all OpenStack internal components.

Introduction to OpenStack and its Deployment Using Packages

The following diagram describes a high-level design of most OpenStack services and outlines the steps needed for configuring an OpenStack service:

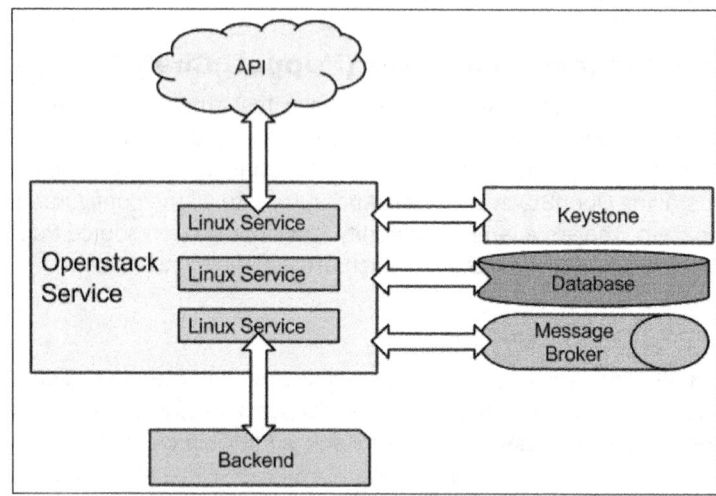

Basic OpenStack service configuration will include configuring the service to use Keystone as authentication strategy, authenticating and authorizing incoming API calls, a database connection in which the service will store metadata about the objects it manages, and the message broker, which the Linux services use to inner communicate.

The most important, and usually the most complex, part is to configure the service to use a backend for its core functionality, for example, Nova, which launches virtual machines, can use libvirtd as a backend services provider that actually launches KVM virtual machines on the local Linux node. Another good example is Keystone that can be configured to use **Lightweight Directory Access Protocol** (**LDAP**) server as a backend to store user credentials instead of storing user credentials in the SQL database.

Environment setup

Over the course of this chapter, we will install and configure OpenStack using RDO distribution packages of kilo release, on top of CentOS 7.0 Linux operating system. We will deploy controller-Neutron-computes layout with a single controller node, one Neutron network node, and one compute node, additional compute nodes can be easily added to the environment following the same steps to install the compute node.

Environment details

- Operating system: CentOS 7.0 or newer
- OpenStack distribution: RDO kilo release
- Architecture layout: controller-Neutron-computes

Every service that we install and configure while following this chapter will require its own database user account, and a Keystone user account. It is highly recommended for security reasons to choose a unique password for each account. For ease of deployment, it is recommended to maintain a password list as in the following table:

Database accounts	Password
root	password
keystone_db_user	keystone_db_password
glance_db_user	keystone_db_password
...	...
Keystone accounts	**Password**
glance	glance
neutron	neutron
...	...

Physical network topology

This chapter focuses on the controller-Neutron-computes topology layout. Before starting the installation of packages, we need to ensure that network interfaces are correctly wired and configured.

All nodes in our environment use eth0 as a management interface; the controller node exposes OpenStack's APIs via eth0. Neutron network node and compute nodes use eth1 for tenant's network; Neutron uses the tenant's network to route traffic between instances. Neutron network node uses eth2 for routing traffic from instances to the public network, which could be organization's IT network or publicly accessible network, as shown in the following diagram:

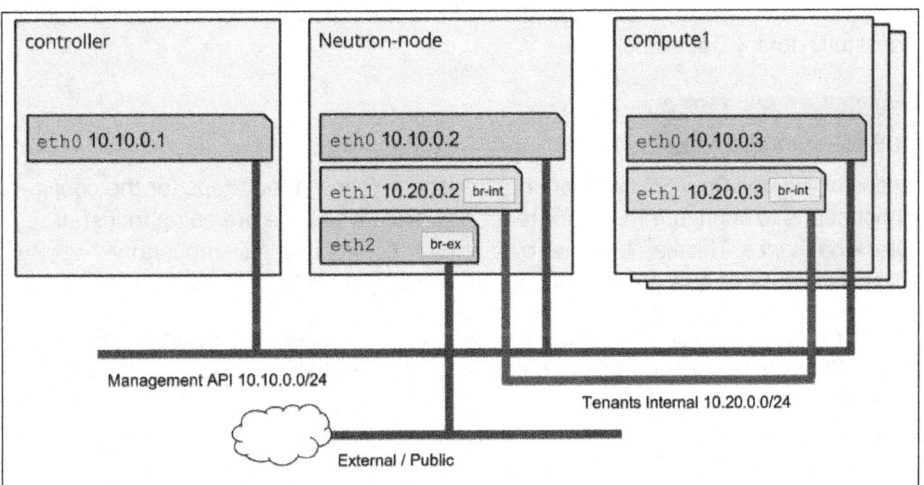

Introduction to OpenStack and its Deployment Using Packages

> Neutron service configuration in this chapter and *Chapter 7, Neutron Networking Service*, Neutron software defined network service will further discuss the creation of bridges needed for Neutron `br-int` and `br-ex`.

All hostnames should be resolvable on to their management network IP addresses.

Role	Host Name	NICs
Controller node	`controller`	`eth0 Management 10.10.0.1/24`
Neutron network node	`neutron`	`eth0 Management 10.10.0.2/24`
		`eth1 Tenant's Internal 10.20.0.2/24`
		`eth2 Public               not set`
Compute node	`compute1`	`eth0 Management     10.10.0.3/24`
		`eth1 Tenant's Internal 10.20.0.3/24`

> Running `NetworkManager` service in a Neutron networking environment is not recommended, and this might cause conflicts with Neutron networking.

Configuring hosts prerequisites

Every host running OpenStack services should have the following prerequisite configurations to successfully deploy OpenStack.

Getting ready

To successfully install OpenStack, every host needs to follow a few steps for the configuration. Every host needs to configure RDO `yum` repository from which we are going to install OpenStack packages. This can be done by manually configuring `yum` repository `/etc/yum.repos.d/OpenStack.repo` or installing them directly from RDO repository.

In addition, every node needs to enable `firewalld` service, enable SELinux and install OpenStack SELinux policies, enable and configure NTP, and also install the OpenStack utils package.

How to do it...

Perform the following steps to install and configure OpenStack prerequisites:

Yum repositories

To install OpenStack RDO distribution, we need to add RDO's `yum` repository on all nodes and `epel`, `yum` repository for additional needed packages:

Run the following commands on all controller, Neutron, and compute nodes.

1. Install `yum-plugin-priorities` packages, which enables repositories management in `yum`:

   `# yum install yum-plugin-priorities -y`

2. Install `rdo-release` package, which configures RDO `repos` in `/etc/yum.repos.d`:

   `# yum install -y https://rdoproject.org/repos/rdo-release.rpm`

3. Install `epel` repository package, which configures `epel` repos in `/etc/yum.repos.d`:

   `# yum install -y epel-release`

Firewall service

The default netfilter `firewalld` service in CentOS 7.0 is firewall. For security reasons, we need to make sure that `firewalld` service is running and enabled, so it is started after reboot:

1. Start `firewalld` service as follows:

   `# systemctl start firewalld.service`

2. Enable `firewalld` service, as follows, so that it's started after host reboot as well:

   `# systemctl enable firewalld.service`

>  Throughout this book, we will open ports needed for OpenStack to operate using the `firewalld-cmd` command.

openstack-utils Package

`openstack-utils` package brings utilities that ease OpenStack configuration and management of OpenStack services. `openstack-utils` includes the following utilities:

- `/usr/bin/openstack-config`: Manipulates OpenStack configuration files
- `/usr/bin/openstack-db`: Creates databases for OpenStack services

Introduction to OpenStack and its Deployment Using Packages

- `/usr/bin/openstack-service`: Control-enabled OpenStack services
- `/usr/bin/openstack-status`: Show status overview of installed OpenStack

Install openstack-utils package:

```
# yum install openstack-utils
```

SELinux

It is highly recommended to ensure that SELinux is enabled and in an enforcing state. the package `openstack-selinux` adds SELinux policy modules for OpenStack services.

1. Ensure that SELinux is enforcing, and run the getenforce command as follows:

   ```
   # getenforce
   ```

   The output should say SELinux is enforcing

2. Install `openstack-selinux` package:

   ```
   # yum install openstack-selinux
   ```

NTP

OpenStack services are deployed over multiple nodes. For services' successful synchronization, all nodes running OpenStack need to have a synchronized system clock, and NTP service can be used for this:

1. Install `ntpd` package as follows:

   ```
   # yum install ntp
   ```

2. Start and enable `ntpd` as follows:

   ```
   # systemctl start ntpd
   # systemctl enable ntpd
   ```

Installing MariaDB database

Most OpenStack projects and their components keep their persistent data and objects' status in a database. MySQL and MariaDB are the most used and tested databases with OpenStack. In our case, and in the most commonly deployed layout, controller-Neutron-compute, the database is installed on the controller node.

Run the following commands on the controller node!

How to do it...

Proceed with the following steps:

1. Install MaridaDB packages as follows:

   `[root@controller ~]# yum install mariadb-galera-server`

   Yum might deploy additional packages after resolving MariaDB's dependencies. A successful installation should output as follows:

   ```
   Installed:
     mariadb-galera-server.x86_64 1:5.5.37-7.el7ost

   Dependency Installed:
     mariadb.x86_64 1:5.5.37-1.el7_0
     mariadb-galera-common.x86_64 1:5.5.37-7.el7ost
     mariadb-libs.x86_64 1:5.5.37-1.el7_0
     perl-DBD-MySQL.x86_64 0:4.023-5.el7
   Complete!
   ```

2. Start MariaDB database service using `systemctl` command as a root:

   `[root@controller ~]# systemctl start mariadb.service`

   If no output is returned, this means the command is completed successfully.

3. Enable it, so it starts automatically after reboot:

   `[root@controller ~]# systemctl enable mariadb.service`

   MariaDB maintains its own user accounts and passwords; `root` is the default administrative user name account that MariaDB uses. We should change the default password for the root account as keeping the default password is a major security treat.

4. Change the database root password as follows, where `new_password` is the password we want to set:

   `[root@controller ~]# mysqladmin -u root password new_password`

   Keep this in the passwords' list; we will need to create databases for the services we will deploy in the following parts of the chapter.

There's more...

Almost all components require access to the database; hence, we should keep port 3306 open for new connections on the controller node:

`[root@controller ~]# firewall-cmd --add-port=3306/tcp --permanent`

Introduction to OpenStack and its Deployment Using Packages

Installing RabbitMQ

OpenStack uses a message broker for components to inner communicate. Red Hat-based operating systems (for example, RHEL, CentOS, and Fedora) can run RabbitMQ or QPID message brokers. Both provide roughly similar performance, but as RabbitMQ is more widely used message broker with OpenStack, we are going use it as a message broker for our OpenStack environment.

How to do it...

1. Install RabbitMQ from the yum repository:

    Run the following commands on the controller node!

    ```
    [root@controller ~]# yum install rabbitmq-server -y
    ```

    RabbitMQ is written in erlang and will probably bring some erlang dependency packages along.

2. To start the RabbitMQ Linux services, start a service named `rabbitmq`-server:

    ```
    [root@controller ~]# systemctl start rabbitmq-server.service
    ```

3. Now enable it, to make sure that it starts on a system reboot:

    ```
    [root@controller ~]# systemctl enable rabbitmq-server.service
    ```

There's more...

RabbitMQ maintains its own user accounts and passwords. By default, the user name `guest` is created with the default password `guest`. As it is a major security concern to keep default password, we should change this password. We can use the command `rabbitmqctl` to change `guest`'s account password:

```
[root@controller ~]# rabbitmqctl change_password guest guest_password
Changing password for user "guest" ...
...done.
```

We need to allow other services to be able to access the message broker over the firewall using `firewall-cmd` command:

```
[root@controller ~]# firewall-cmd --add-port=5672/tcp --permanent
success
```

Installing Keystone – Identity service

Keystone project provides Identity as a service for all OpenStack services and components. It is recommended to authenticate users and authorize access of OpenStack components. For Example, if a user would like to launch a new instance, Keystone is responsible for making sure that the user account, which issued the instance launch command, is a known authenticated user account and the account has permissions to launch the instance.

Keystone also provides a services catalog, which OpenStack serves, users and other services can query Keystone for the services of a particular OpenStack environment. For each service, Keystone returns an endpoint, which is a network-accessible URL from where users and services can access a certain service.

In this chapter, we are going to configure Keystone to use MariaDB as the backend data store provides, which is the most common configuration. Keystone can also use user account details on an LDAP server or Microsoft Active Directory, which will be covered in *Chapter 4, Keystone Identity Service*.

Getting Ready

Before installing and configuring Keystone, we need to prepare a database for Keystone to use, configure it's user's permissions, and open needed firewall ports, so other nodes would be able to communicate with it. Keystone is usually installed on the controller node as part of OpenStack's control plane.

Run the following commands on the controller node!

Create Keystone database

1. To create a database for Keystone, use MySQL command to access the MariaDB instance, This will ask you to type the password you selected for the MariaDB root user:

   ```
   [root@controller ~]# mysql -u root -p
   ```

2. Create a database named `keystone`:

   ```
   MariaDB [(none)]> CREATE DATABASE keystone;
   ```

3. Create a user account named `keystone` with the selected password instead of `'my_keystone_db_password'`:

   ```
   MariaDB [(none)]> GRANT ALL ON keystone.* TO 'keystone'@'%' IDENTIFIED BY 'my_keystone_db_password';
   ```

4. Grant access for `keystone` user account to the `keystone` database:

   ```
   MariaDB [(none)]> GRANT ALL ON keystone.* TO 'keystone'@'localhost' IDENTIFIED BY 'my_keystone_db_password';
   ```

Introduction to OpenStack and its Deployment Using Packages

5. Flush database privileges to ensure that they are effective immediately:

   `MariaDB [(none)]> FLUSH PRIVILEGES;`

6. At this point, you can exit the MySQL client:

   `MariaDB [(none)]> quit`

Open Keystone service firewall ports

Keystone service uses port *5000* for public access and port *35357* for administration.

```
[root@controller ~]# firewall-cmd --add-port=5000/tcp --permanent
[root@controller ~]# firewall-cmd --add-port=35357/tcp --permanent
```

How to do it...

Proceed with the following steps:

Install service packages

By now, all OpenStack's prerequisites, including a database service and a message broker, should be installed and configured, and this is the first OpenStack service we install. First, we need to install, configure, enable, and start the package.

Install `keystone` package using `yum` command as follows:

```
[root@controller ~]# yum install -y openstack-keystone
```

This will also install Python supporting packages and additional packages for more advanced backend configurations.

Configure database connection

Keystone's database connection string is set in `/etc/keystone/keystone.conf`; we can use the `#openstack-config` command to configure the connection string.

1. Run the `openstack-config` command with your chosen keystone database user details and database IP address:

   ```
   [root@controller ~]# openstack-config --set
   /etc/keystone/keystone.conf    sql connection
   mysql://keystone:'my_keystone_db_password'@10.10.0.1/keystone
   ```

2. After the database is configured, we can create the Keystone database tables using `db_sync` command:

   ```
   [root@controller ~]# su keystone -s /bin/sh -c "keystone-manage db_sync"
   ```

Chapter 1

 To make sure that the Keystone database is populated successfully, verify the Keystone database exists using MySql command #`mysql -u root -p -e 'show databases;'` which provides database's root account password.

Keystone service basic configuration

Before starting the Keystone service, we need to make some initial service configurations for it to start properly.

Configure administrative token

Keystone can use a token by which it will identify the administrative user:

1. Set a custom token or use `openssl` command to generate a random token:

   `[root@controller ~]# export SERVICE_TOKEN=$(openssl rand -hex 10)`

2. Store the token in a file for use in the next steps:

   `[root@controller ~]# echo $SERVICE_TOKEN > ~/keystone_admin_token`

   We need to configure Keystone to use the token we created, we can manually edit the Keystone configuration file `/etc/keystone/keystone.conf` and manually remove comment mark # next to `admin_token` or we can use the command `openstack-config` to set the needed property.

    `openstack-config` command is provided by # `yum install openstack-utils`.

3. Use `openstack-config` command to configure `service_token` parameter as follows:

   `[root@controller ~]# openstack-config --set /etc/keystone/keystone.conf DEFAULT admin_token $SERVICE_TOKEN`

Generating and configuring tokens PKIs

Keystone uses cryptographically signed tokens with a private key and is matched against x509 certificate with a public key. *Chapter 4, Keystone Identity Service* discusses more advanced configurations. In this chapter, we use `keystone-manage pki_setup` command to generate PKI key pairs and to configure Keystone to use it.

Introduction to OpenStack and its Deployment Using Packages

How to do it...

Proceed with the following steps:

1. Generate PKI keys using `keystone-manage pki_setup` command:

   `[root@controller ~]# keystone-manage pki_setup --keystone-user keystone --keystone-group keystone`

   > In `keystone-manage pki_setup`, we use Keystone Linux user and group accounts, which were created when `openstack-keystone` package was installed.

2. Change ownership of the generated PKI files:

   `[root@controller ~]# chown -R keystone:keystone /var/log/keystone /etc/keystone/ssl/`

3. Configure Keystone service to use the generated PKI files:

   `[root@controller ~]# openstack-config --set /etc/keystone/keystone.conf signing token_format PKI`

   `[root@controller ~]# openstack-config --set /etc/keystone/keystone.conf signing certfile /etc/keystone/ssl/certs/signing_cert.pem`

   `[root@controller ~]# openstack-config --set /etc/keystone/keystone.conf signing keyfile /etc/keystone/ssl/private/signing_key.pem`

   `[root@controller ~]# openstack-config --set /etc/keystone/keystone.conf signing ca_certs /etc/keystone/ssl/certs/ca.pem`

   `[root@controller ~]# openstack-config --set /etc/keystone/keystone.conf signing key_size 1024`

   `[root@controller ~]# openstack-config --set /etc/keystone/keystone.conf signing valid_days 3650`

   `[root@controller ~]# openstack-config --set /etc/keystone/keystone.conf signing ca_password None`

Starting and enabling service

At this point, Keystone is configured and readily run as follows:

`[root@controller ~]# systemctl start openstack-keystone`

Enable Keystone to start after system reboot:

`[root@controller ~]# systemctl enable openstack-keystone`

Configuring Keystone endpoints

We need to configure a Keystone service endpoint for other services to operate properly:

1. Set the `SERVICE_TOKEN` environment parameter using the `keystone_admin_token` we generated on basic Keystone configuration step:

   ```
   [root@controller ~]# export SERVICE_TOKEN=`cat ~/keystone_admin_token`
   ```

2. Set the `SERVICE_ENDPOINT` environment parameter with Keystone's endpoint URL using your controller's IP address:

   ```
   [root@controller ~]# export SERVICE_ENDPOINT="http://10.10.0.1:35357/v2.0"
   ```

3. Create a Keystone service entry:

   ```
   [root@el7-icehouse-controller ~]# keystone service-create --name=keystone --type=identity --description="Keystone Identity service"
   ```

   An output of a successful execution should look similar to the following, with a different unique ID:

   ```
   +-------------+----------------------------------+
   |  Property   |              Value               |
   +-------------+----------------------------------+
   | description |     Keystone Identity service    |
   |   enabled   |              True                |
   |     id      | 1fa0e426e1ba464d95d16c6df0899047 |
   |    name     |            keystone              |
   |    type     |            identity              |
   +-------------+----------------------------------+
   ```

   The `endpoint-create` command allows us to set a different IP addresses that are accessible from public and from internal sources. At this point, we may use our controller's management NIC IP to access Keystone endpoint.

4. Create Keystone service endpoint using keystone endpoint-create command:

   ```
   [root@controller ~]# keystone endpoint-create
   --service keystone
   --publicurl 'http://10.10.0.1:5000/v2.0'
   --adminurl 'http://10.10.0.1:35357/v2.0'
   --internalurl 'http://10.10.0.1:5000/v2.0'
   ```

5. Create services tenant:

   ```
   [root@controller ~(keystone_admin)]# keystone tenant-create --name services --description "Services Tenant"
   ```

Introduction to OpenStack and its Deployment Using Packages

Keystone administrator account

1. Create an administrative account within Keystone:

   ```
   [root@controller ~]# keystone user-create --name admin --pass password
   ```

2. Create the `admin` role:

   ```
   [root@controller ~]# keystone role-create --name admin
   ```

3. Create an `admin` tenant:

   ```
   [root@controller ~]# keystone tenant-create --name admin
   ```

4. Add an `admin` roles to the admin user with the `admin` tenant:

   ```
   [root@el7-icehouse-controller ~]# keystone user-role-add --user admin --role admin --tenant admin
   ```

5. Create `keystonerc_admin` file with the following content:

   ```
   [root@controller ~]# cat ~/keystonerc_admin
   export OS_USERNAME=admin
   export OS_TENANT_NAME=admin
   export OS_PASSWORD=password
   export OS_AUTH_URL=http://10.10.0.1:35357/v2.0/
   export PS1='[\u@\h \W(keystone_admin)]\$ '
   ```

6. To load the environment variables, run source command:

   ```
   [root@controller ~]# source keystonerc_admin
   ```

Keystone user account

We may also create an unprivileged user account that has no administration permissions on our newly created OpenStack environment:

1. Create the user account in Keystone:

   ```
   [root@controller ~(keystone_admin)]# keystone user-create --name USER --pass password
   ```

2. Create a new tenant:

   ```
   [root@el7-icehouse-controller ~(keystone_admin)]# keystone tenant-create --name TENANT
   ```

3. Assign the user account to the newly created tenant:

   ```
   [root@el7-icehouse-controller ~(keystone_admin)]# keystone user-role-add --user USER --role _member_ --tenant TENANT
   ```

4. Create keystonerc_user file with the following content:

```
[root@controller ~(keystone_admin)]# cat ~/keystonerc_user
export OS_USERNAME=USER
export OS_TENANT_NAME=TENANT
export OS_PASSWORD=password
export OS_AUTH_URL=http://10.10.0.1:5000/v2.0/
export PS1='[\u@\h \W(keystone_user)]\$ '
```

There's more...

If installation and configuration of Keystone service was successful, Keystone should be operational, and we execute a keystone command to verify that it is operational.

Verify successful installation

Use the command `#tenant-list` to list the existing tenants:

`[root@controller ~(keystone_admin)]# keystone tenant-list`

The output of successful tenant creation should look like this:

```
+----------------------------------+----------+---------+
|                id                |   name   | enabled |
+----------------------------------+----------+---------+
| a5b7bf37d1b646cb8ec0eb35481204c4 |  admin   |  True   |
| fafb926db0674ad9a34552dc05ac3a18 | services |  True   |
+----------------------------------+----------+---------+
```

Installing Glance – images service

Glance images service provides services that allow us to store and retrieve operating system disk images to launch instances from. In our example, environment Glance service is installed on the controller node. Glance service consists of two services: Glance API, which is responsible for all API interactions, and `glance-registry`, which manages image database registry. Each has a configuration file under `/etc/glance/`.

Getting ready

Before configuring Glance, we need to create a database for it and grant the needed database credentials. We need to create user account for Glance in the Keystone user registry for Glance to be able to authenticate against Keystone. Finally, we will need to open appropriate firewall ports.

Introduction to OpenStack and its Deployment Using Packages

Create database

Use MySQL command with root a account to create the Glance database:

`[root@controller ~(keystone_admin)]# mysql -u root -p`

1. Create Glance database:

   `MariaDB [(none)]> CREATE DATABASE glance_db;`

2. Create Glance database user account and grant access permissions, where `my_glance_db_password` is your password:

   `MariaDB [(none)]> GRANT ALL ON glance_db.* TO 'glance_db_user'@'%' IDENTIFIED BY 'my_glance_db_password';`

   `MariaDB [(none)]> GRANT ALL ON glance.* TO 'glance_db'@'localhost' IDENTIFIED BY 'my_glance_db_password';`

3. Flush all changes:

   `MariaDB [(none)]> FLUSH PRIVILEGES;`

4. At this point, we can quit the MariaDB client:

   `MariaDB [(none)]> quit`

5. Create Glance tables:

   `[root@controller glance(keystone_admin)]# glance-manage db_sync`

Create Glance service credentials and endpoint in Keystone

Gain Keystone admin privileges to create Glance service account in Keystone:

`[root@controller ~]# source keystonerc_admin`

1. Create a Keystone user account for Glance:

   `[root@controller ~(keystone_admin)]# keystone user-create --name glance --pass glance_password`

2. Add an `admin` role to the `glance` user and services `tenants`:

   `[root@controller ~(keystone_admin)]# keystone user-role-add --user glance --role admin --tenant services`

3. Create a `glance` service:

   `[root@controller ~(keystone_admin)]# keystone service-create --name glance --type image --description "Glance Image Service"`

4. Create an endpoint for `glance` service:

   ```
   [root@controller ~(keystone_admin)]# keystone endpoint-create
   --service glance --publicurl "http://10.10.0.1:9292" --adminurl
   "http://10.10.0.1:9292" --internalurl "http://10.10.0.1:9292"
   ```

Open service firewall ports

1. Set Glance to use port 9292, edit /etc/glance/glance-api.conf with following lines:

   ```
   bind_host = 10.10.0.1
   bind_port = 9292
   ```

2. Add a firewall rule:

   ```
   [root@controller ~(keystone_admin)]# firewall-cmd --permanent
   --add-port=9292/tcp
   ```

Install service packages

Install Glance service packages using `yum` command:

```
[root@controller ~]# yum install -y openstack-glance
```

Service configuration

At this point, all prerequisites for Glance should be ready and we can go ahead and configure Glance. We need to set its database connection, configure Glance to use RabbitMQ, and configure Glances authentication strategy to use Keystone.

How to do it...

Follow these steps to configure Glance image service:

Configure database connection

1. Set the connection string for `glance-api`:

   ```
   [root@controller ~(keystone_admin)]# openstack-config --set
   /etc/glance/glance-api.conf    DEFAULT sql_connection
   mysql://glance_db_user:glance_db_password@10.10.0.1/glance_db
   ```

2. Set connection string for `glance-registry`:

   ```
   [root@el7-icehouse-controller ~(keystone_admin)]#
   openstack-config --set /etc/glance/glance-registry.conf
   DEFAULT sql_connection mysql://glance_db_user:glance_db_
   password@10.10.0.1/glance_db
   ```

Introduction to OpenStack and its Deployment Using Packages

3. Configure the message broker using `openstack-config` command:

   ```
   # openstack-config --set /etc/glance/glance-api.conf DEFAULT \
     rpc_backend rabbit
   # openstack-config --set /etc/glance/glance-api.conf DEFAULT \
     rabbit_host 10.10.0.1
   # openstack-config --set /etc/glance/glance-api.conf DEFAULT \
     rabbit_userid guest
   # openstack-config --set /etc/glance/glance-api.conf DEFAULT \
     rabbit_password guest_password
   ```

Configure Glance service

1. Configure Glance to use Keystone as an authentication method:

   ```
   [root@controller ~(keystone_admin)]# openstack-config --set /etc/glance/glance-api.conf paste_deploy flavor keystone

   [root@controller ~(keystone_admin)]# openstack-config --set /etc/glance/glance-api.conf keystone_authtoken auth_host 10.10.0.1

   [root@controller ~(keystone_admin)]# openstack-config --set /etc/glance/glance-api.conf keystone_authtoken auth_port 35357

   [root@controller ~(keystone_admin)]# openstack-config --set /etc/glance/glance-api.conf keystone_authtoken auth_protocol http

   [root@controller ~(keystone_admin)]# openstack-config --set /etc/glance/glance-api.conf keystone_authtoken admin_tenant_name services

   [root@controller ~(keystone_admin)]# openstack-config --set /etc/glance/glance-api.conf keystone_authtoken admin_user glance

   [root@controller ~(keystone_admin)]# openstack-config --set /etc/glance/glance-api.conf keystone_authtoken admin_password glance_password
   ```

2. Now configure `glance-registry` to use Keystone for authentication:

   ```
   [root@controller ~(keystone_admin)]# openstack-config --set /etc/glance/glance-registry.conf paste_deploy flavor keystone

   [root@controller ~(keystone_admin)]# openstack-config --set /etc/glance/glance-registry.conf keystone_authtoken auth_host 192.168.200.258

   [root@controller ~(keystone_admin)]# openstack-config --set /etc/glance/glance-registry.conf keystone_authtoken auth_port 35357
   ```

Chapter 1

```
[root@controller ~(keystone_admin)]# openstack-config --set
/etc/glance/glance-registry.conf   keystone_authtoken
auth_protocol http
[root@controller ~(keystone_admin)]# openstack-config --set
/etc/glance/glance-registry.conf   keystone_authtoken
admin_tenant_name services
[root@controller ~(keystone_admin)]# openstack-config --set
/etc/glance/glance-registry.conf   keystone_authtoken admin_user
glance
[root@controller ~(keystone_admin)]# openstack-config --set
/etc/glance/glance-registry.conf   keystone_authtoken
admin_password password
```

> By default, Glance will store images as files in a local directory /var/lib/glance/images/, so this configuration is not needed at this point.

3. Start and enable the service:

   ```
   [root@controller ~]# systemctl start openstack-glance-api
   [root@controller ~]# systemctl start openstack-glance-registry
   ```

There's more...

If the installation and configuration was successful, we can upload our fist image to Glance registry. CirrOS Linux image is a good candidate as it is extremely small in size and functional enough to test most OpenStack's functionalities.

Verify successful installation

If glance was successfully installed and configured, we may upload our fist image.

1. First, download a CirrOS image to the controller node:

   ```
   [root@controller glance(keystone_admin)]# wget
   http://download.cirros-cloud.net/0.3.4/cirros-0.3.4-x86_64-disk.img
   ```

   Then, upload the image to Glance registry using glance image-create
   command:

   ```
   [root@controller glance(keystone_admin)]# glance image-create
     --name="cirros-0.3.2-x86_64" --disk-format=qcow2
   --container-format=bare --is-public=true --file
   cirros-0.3.2-x86_64-disk.img
   ```

25

Introduction to OpenStack and its Deployment Using Packages

2. List all glance images using glance image-list command:

   ```
   [root@controller glance(keystone_admin)]# glance image-list
   If the upload of the image was successful, the Cirros image will
   appear in the list.
   ```

Installing Nova – Compute service

Nova-Compute service implements the compute service, which is the main part of an IaaS cloud. Nova is responsible for launching and managing instance of virtual machines. The compute service scales horizontally on standard hardware.

Getting ready

In our environment, we deploy a Controller/Computes layout. In the first step, we need to configure management services on the controller node and only then to add compute nodes to the environment. On the controller node, first we need to prepare the database, create a Keystone account, then open the needed firewall ports.

Run the following steps on the controller node!

Create database

1. Access the database instance using MySQL command:

   ```
   [root@controller ~]# mysql -u root -p
   ```

2. Create Nova database:

   ```
   MariaDB [(none)]> CREATE DATABASE nova_db;
   ```

3. Create Nova credentials and allow access:

   ```
   MariaDB [(none)]> GRANT ALL PRIVILEGES ON nova_db.* TO
   'nova_db_user'@'localhost' IDENTIFIED BY 'nova_db_password';
   MariaDB [(none)]> GRANT ALL PRIVILEGES ON nova_db.* TO
   'nova_db_user'@'%' IDENTIFIED BY 'nova_db_password';
   ```

4. Create Nova database tables:

   ```
   [root@controller ~]# su -s /bin/sh -c "nova-manage db sync"
   nova
   ```

Create Keystone service credentials and endpoint

1. Create Nova service account in Keystone:

   ```
   [root@controller ~]# keystone user-create --name=nova
   --pass=nova_password
   ```

Chapter 1

```
[root@controller ~]# keystone user-role-add --user=nova
--tenant=services --role=admin
```

2. Create an endpoint for Nova

```
[root@controller ~]# keystone endpoint-create --service=nova
--publicurl=http://10.10.0.1:8774/v2/%\(tenant_id\) |
--internalurl=http://10.10.0.1:8774/v2/%\(tenant_id\s
--adminurl=http://10.10.0.1:8774/v2/%\(tenant_id\)s
```

Open service firewall ports

1. Add firewall rules:

    ```
    [root@controller ~]# firewall-cmd --permanent
    --add-port=8774/tcp
    ```

    ```
    [root@controller ~]# firewall-cmd --permanent
    --add-port=6080/tcp
    ```

    ```
    [root@controller ~]# firewall-cmd --permanent
    --add-port=6081/tcp
    ```

    ```
    [root@controller ~]# firewall-cmd --permanent
    --add-port=5900-5999/tcp
    ```

2. Reload firewall rules to take effect:

    ```
    [root@controller ~]# firewall-cmd --reload
    ```

Install service packages

Install service packages using `yum` command:

```
[root@controller ~]# yum install -y openstack-nova-api
openstack-nova-cert openstack-nova-conductor  openstack-nova-console
openstack-nova-novncproxy penstack-nova-scheduler python-novaclient
```

How to do it...

Follow these steps to configure Nova-Compute service:

Configure database connection

Using `openstack-config` command, we need to set the connection to the database:

```
[root@controller ~]# openstack-config --set /etc/nova/nova.conf
database connection
mysql://nova_db_user:nova_db_password@controller/nova_db
```

```
[root@controller ~]# su -s /bin/sh -c "nova-manage db sync" nova
```

Configure message broker

Set connection to RabbitMQ message broker:

```
[root@controller ~]# openstack-config --set /etc/nova/nova.conf DEFAULT rpc_backend rabbit

[root@controller ~]# openstack-config --set /etc/nova/nova.conf DEFAULT rabbit_host 10.10.0.1
```

Configure service

1. Set local IP address of the controller:

   ```
   # openstack-config --set /etc/nova/nova.conf DEFAULT my_ip 10.10.0.1
   # openstack-config --set /etc/nova/nova.conf DEFAULT vncserver_listen 10.10.0.1
   # openstack-config --set /etc/nova/nova.conf DEFAULT vncserver_proxyclient_address 10.10.0.1
   ```

2. Configure Keystone as an authentication method:

   ```
   # openstack-config --set /etc/nova/nova.conf DEFAULT auth_strategy keystone
   # openstack-config --set /etc/nova/nova.conf keystone_authtoken auth_uri http://10.10.0.1:5000
   # openstack-config --set /etc/nova/nova.conf keystone_authtoken auth_host 10.10.0.1
   # openstack-config --set /etc/nova/nova.conf keystone_authtoken auth_protocol http
   # openstack-config --set /etc/nova/nova.conf keystone_authtoken auth_port 35357
   # openstack-config --set /etc/nova/nova.conf keystone_authtoken admin_user nova
   # openstack-config --set /etc/nova/nova.conf keystone_authtoken admin_tenant_name services
   # openstack-config --set /etc/nova/nova.conf keystone_authtoken admin_password nova_password
   ```

Start and enable Service

Using systemctl command, we can start and enable the service so that it starts after reboot:

```
[root@controller ~]# systemctl start openstack-nova-api
[root@controller ~]# systemctl start openstack-nova-cert
[root@controller ~]# systemctl start openstack-nova-consoleauth
[root@controller ~]# systemctl start openstack-nova-scheduler
[root@controller ~]# systemctl start openstack-nova-conductor
[root@controller ~]# systemctl start openstack-nova-novncproxy
```

```
[root@controller ~]# systemctl enable openstack-nova-api
[root@controller ~]# systemctl enable openstack-nova-cert
[root@controller ~]# systemctl enable openstack-nova-consoleauth
[root@controller ~]# systemctl enable openstack-nova-scheduler
[root@controller ~]# systemctl enable openstack-nova-conductor
[root@controller ~]# systemctl enable openstack-nova-novncproxy
```

Verify successful installation

On successful Nova installation and configuration, you should be able to execute this:

```
[root@el7-icehouse-controller ~(keystone_admin)]# nova image-list
+-------------------+----------------------+--------+--------+
| ID                | Name                 | Status | Server |
+-------------------+----------------------+--------+--------+
| eb9c6911-...      | cirros-0.3.2-x86_64  | ACTIVE |        |
+-------------------+----------------------+--------+--------+
```

After the controller node is successfully installed and configured, we may add additional compute nodes to the OpenStack environment.

Configure compute nodes

Now we can proceed and configure the compute services on the compute node.

Run the following steps on the compute node!

Install service packages

Using `yum` command, install Nova-Compute package:

```
# yum install openstack-nova-compute
```

Configure database connection

Configure the Nova database connection:

```
[root@compute1 ~]# openstack-config --set /etc/nova/nova.conf database connection mysql://nova_db_user:nova_db_password@controller/nova_db
```

Configure message broker

Configure Nova to access the message broker:

```
[root@compute1 ~]# openstack-config --set /etc/nova/nova.conf DEFAULT rpc_backend rabbit
[root@compute1 ~]# openstack-config --set /etc/nova/nova.conf DEFAULT rabbit_host 10.10.0.1
```

Introduction to OpenStack and its Deployment Using Packages

Configure service

1. Edit /etc/nova/nova.conf for the compute node to use Keystone authentication:

   ```
   [root@compute1 ~]# openstack-config --set /etc/nova/nova.conf DEFAULT auth_strategy keystone
   [root@compute1 ~]# openstack-config --set /etc/nova/nova.conf keystone_authtoken auth_uri http://controller:5000
   [root@compute1 ~]# openstack-config --set /etc/nova/nova.conf keystone_authtoken auth_host controller
   [root@compute1 ~]# openstack-config --set /etc/nova/nova.conf keystone_authtoken auth_protocol http
   [root@compute1 ~]# openstack-config --set /etc/nova/nova.conf keystone_authtoken auth_port 35357
   [root@compute1 ~]# openstack-config --set /etc/nova/nova.conf keystone_authtoken admin_user nova
   [root@compute1 ~]# openstack-config --set /etc/nova/nova.conf keystone_authtoken admin_tenant_name service
   [root@compute1 ~]# openstack-config --set /etc/nova/nova.conf keystone_authtoken admin_password nova_password
   ```

2. Configure the remote console for instances terminal access:

   ```
   [root@compute1 ~]# openstack-config --set /etc/nova/nova.conf DEFAULT my_ip 192.168.200.159
   [root@compute1 ~]# openstack-config --set /etc/nova/nova.conf DEFAULT vnc_enabled True
   [root@compute1 ~]# openstack-config --set /etc/nova/nova.conf DE
   \FAULT vncserver_listen 0.0.0.0
   [root@compute1 ~]# openstack-config --set /etc/nova/nova.conf DEFAULT vncserver_proxyclient_address 192.168.200.159
   [root@compute1 ~]# openstack-config --set /etc/nova/nova.conf \
       DEFAULT novncproxy_base_url http://controller:6080/vnc_auto.html
   ```

3. Configure which glance service to use to retrieve images:

   ```
   [root@compute1 ~]# openstack-config --set /etc/nova/nova.conf DEFAULT glance_host controller
   ```

> If you are installing the compute node on a virtual machine, configure Nova to the user QEMU emulation instated of the default KVM backend. To configure QEMU, run the following command:
>
> ```
> [root@compute1 ~]# openstack-config --set /etc/nova/nova.conf libvirt virt_type qemu
> ```

Chapter 1

Start and enable Service

Using `systemctl` command, start and enable the service:

```
[root@compute1 ~]# systemctl start libvirtd
[root@compute1 ~]# systemctl start openstack-nova-compute
[root@compute1 ~]# systemctl enable libvirtd
[root@compute1 ~]# systemctl enable openstack-nova-compute
```

Installing Neutron – networking service

Neutron networking service is responsible for the creation and management of layer 2 networks, layer 3 subnets, routers, and services, such as firewalls, VPNs, and DNS. Neutron service is constructed of Neutron-server service, which serves the Neutron API and interacts with the Neutron components since we deploy controller-Neutron-compute layout that we need to install and configure neutron-server and **Modular Layer 2** (**ML2**) plugin on the controller node. Then, we will configure layer 3, DHCP, and metadata services on the Neutron network node. We will configure the compute node to use Neutron networking services.

Getting ready

Before configuring Neutron services, we need to create a Database that will hold Neutron's objects, a Keystone endpoint for Neutron, open the needed firewall ports, and install all needed Neutron packages on the controller, Neutron network node, and on compute nodes.

Run the following commands on the controller node!

Create database

1. Access the database instance using MySQL command with the root user account:

    ```
    [root@controller ~]# mysql -u root -p
    ```

2. Create a new database for Neutron called `neutron`:

    ```
    MariaDB [(none)]> CREATE DATABASE neutron;
    ```

3. Create a database user account named `neutron_db_user` with the password `neutron_db_password` and grant access to the newly created database:

    ```
    MariaDB [(none)]> GRANT ALL PRIVILEGES ON neutron.* TO 'neutron_user_db'@'localhost' IDENTIFIED BY 'neutron_db_password';
    MariaDB [(none)]> GRANT ALL PRIVILEGES ON neutron.* TO 'neutron_user_db'@'%' IDENTIFIED BY 'neutron_db_password';
    ```

Create Keystone service credentials and endpoint

Keep in mind that for using Keystone command, we need to source Keystone environment parameters with admin credentials: `# source ~/keystonerc_admin`.

```
[root@controller ~(keystone_admin)]# keystone user-create --name neutron --pass password
```

```
[root@controller ~(keystone_admin)]# keystone user-role-add --user neutron --tenant services --role admin
```

```
[root@controller ~(keystone_admin)]# keystone service-create --name neutron --type network --description "OpenStack Networking"
```

Create a new endpoint for Neutron in Keystone services catalog:

```
[root@controller ~(keystone_admin)]# keystone endpoint-create \
  --service neutron \
  --publicurl http://controller:9696 \
  --adminurl http://controller:9696 \
  --internalurl http://controller:9696
```

Open service firewall ports

Add firewall rule to open TCP port 9696:

```
[root@controller ~]# firewall-cmd --permanent --add-port=9696/tcp
```

```
[root@controller ~]# firewall-cmd --reload
```

Install service packages

Install Neutron server and ML2 plugin packages on the controller:

```
[root@controller ~]# yum install -y openstack-neutron openstack-neutron-ml2
```

How to do it...

We start by configuring Neutron server service on the controller node. We will configure Neutron to access the database and message broker. Then, we will configure Neutron to use Keystone, as it's an authentication strategy. We will use ML2 driver backend and configure Neutron to use it. Finally, we will configure Nova service to use Neutron and ML2 plugin as networking services.

Configure database connection

Use OpenStack configure command to configure the connection string to the database:

```
[root@controller ~]# openstack-config --set /etc/neutron/neutron.conf database connection mysql://neutron_db_user:neutron_db_password@controller/neutron_db
```

Chapter 1

Configure message broker

Configure Neutron to use RabbitMQ message broker:

> Remember to change 10.10.0.1 to your controller management IP.

```
[root@controller ~]# openstack-config --set /etc/neutron/neutron.conf DEFAULT rpc_backend rabbit
[root@controller ~]# openstack-config --set /etc/neutron/neutron.conf DEFAULT rabbit_host 10.10.0.1
```

Configure Neutron service

1. Configure Neutron to use Keystone as an authentication strategy:

    ```
    [root@controller ~]# openstack-config --set /etc/neutron/neutron.conf DEFAULT \
       auth_strategy keystone

    [root@controller ~]# openstack-config --set /etc/neutron/neutron.conf keystone_authtoken \
       auth_uri http://controller:5000

    [root@controller ~]# openstack-config --set /etc/neutron/neutron.conf keystone_authtoken \
       auth_host controller

    [root@controller ~]# openstack-config --set /etc/neutron/neutron.conf keystone_authtoken \
       auth_protocol http

    [root@controller ~]# openstack-config --set /etc/neutron/neutron.conf keystone_authtoken \
       auth_port 35357

    [root@controller ~]# openstack-config --set /etc/neutron/neutron.conf keystone_authtoken \
       admin_tenant_name services

    [root@controller ~]# openstack-config --set /etc/neutron/neutron.conf keystone_authtoken \
       admin_user neutron

    [root@controller ~]# openstack-config --set /etc/neutron/neutron.conf keystone_authtoken \
       admin_password password
    ```

2. Configure Neutron to synchronize networking topology changes with Nova:

    ```
    [root@controller ~]# openstack-config --set /etc/neutron/neutron.conf DEFAULT \
       notify_nova_on_port_status_changes True
    ```

```
[root@controller ~]# openstack-config --set
/etc/neutron/neutron.conf DEFAULT \
   notify_nova_on_port_data_changes True
[root@controller ~]# openstack-config --set
/etc/neutron/neutron.conf DEFAULT \
   nova_url http://controller:8774/v2
[root@controller ~]# openstack-config --set
/etc/neutron/neutron.conf DEFAULT \
   nova_admin_username nova
[root@controller ~]# openstack-config --set
/etc/neutron/neutron.conf DEFAULT \
   nova_admin_tenant_id $(keystone tenant-list | awk '/ services / { print $2 }')
[root@controller ~]# openstack-config --set
/etc/neutron/neutron.conf DEFAULT \
   nova_admin_password passowrd
[root@controller ~]# openstack-config --set
/etc/neutron/neutron.conf DEFAULT \
   nova_admin_auth_url http://controller:35357/v2.0
```

3. Now configure Neutron to use ML2 Neutron plugin:

```
[root@controller ~]# openstack-config --set
/etc/neutron/neutron.conf DEFAULT \
   core_plugin ml2
[root@controller ~]# openstack-config --set
/etc/neutron/neutron.conf DEFAULT \
   service_plugins router
```

4. Configure ML2 plugin to use Open vSwitch agent with GRE segregation for virtual networks for instances:

```
[root@controller ~]# openstack-config --set
/etc/neutron/plugins/ml2/ml2_conf.ini ml2 \
   type_drivers gre
[root@controller ~]# openstack-config --set
/etc/neutron/plugins/ml2/ml2_conf.ini ml2 \
   tenant_network_types gre
[root@controller ~]# openstack-config --set
/etc/neutron/plugins/ml2/ml2_conf.ini ml2 \
   mechanism_drivers openvswitch
[root@controller ~]# openstack-config --set
/etc/neutron/plugins/ml2/ml2_conf.ini ml2_type_gre \
   tunnel_id_ranges 1:1000
```

```
[root@controller ~]# openstack-config --set
/etc/neutron/plugins/ml2/ml2_conf.ini securitygroup \
   firewall_driver neutron.agent.linux.iptables_firewall.
OVSHybridIptablesFirewallDriver
[root@controller ~]# openstack-config --set
/etc/neutron/plugins/ml2/ml2_conf.ini securitygroup \
   enable_security_group True
```

5. Once Neutron and ML2 are configured, we need to configure Nova to use Neutron as its networking provider:

   ```
   [root@controller ~]# openstack-config --set /etc/nova/nova.conf
   DEFAULT network_api_class nova.network.neutronv2.api.API

   [root@controller ~]# openstack-config --set /etc/nova/nova.conf
   DEFAULT neutron_url http://controller:9696

   [root@controller ~]# openstack-config --set /etc/nova/nova.conf
   DEFAULT neutron_auth_strategy keystone

   [root@controller ~]# openstack-config --set /etc/nova/nova.conf
   DEFAULT neutron_admin_tenant_name service

   [root@controller ~]# openstack-config --set /etc/nova/nova.conf
   DEFAULT neutron_admin_username neutron

   [root@controller ~]# openstack-config --set /etc/nova/nova.conf
   DEFAULT neutron_admin_password NEUTRON_PASS

   [root@controller ~]# openstack-config --set /etc/nova/nova.conf
   DEFAULT neutron_admin_auth_url http://controller:35357/v2.0

   [root@controller ~]# openstack-config --set /etc/nova/nova.conf
   DEFAULT linuxnet_interface_driver
   nova.network.linux_net.LinuxOVSInterfaceDriver

   [root@controller ~]# openstack-config --set /etc/nova/nova.conf
   DEFAULT firewall_driver nova.virt.firewall.NoopFirewallDriver

   [root@controller ~]# openstack-config --set /etc/nova/nova.conf
   DEFAULT security_group_api neutron
   ```

6. Since we are using ML2 Neutron plugin, we need to add a symbolic link associated with ML2 and Neutron plugin as follows:

   ```
   [root@controller ~]# ln -s plugins/ml2/ml2_conf.ini
   /etc/neutron/plugin.ini
   ```

7. Prepare Nova to use Neutron metadata service:

   ```
   [root@controller ~]# openstack-config --set /etc/nova/nova.conf
   DEFAULT service_neutron_metadata_proxy true
   [root@controller ~]# openstack-config --set /etc/nova/nova.conf
   DEFAULT neutron_metadata_proxy_shared_secret SHARED_SECRET
   ```

Introduction to OpenStack and its Deployment Using Packages

Start and enable service

1. If Nova services are running, we need to restart them

   ```
   [root@controller ~]# systemctl restart openstack-nova-api
   [root@controller ~]# systemctl restart openstack-nova-scheduler
   [root@controller ~]# systemctl restart openstack-nova-conductor
   ```

2. At this point, we can start and enable Neutron-server service:

   ```
   [root@controller ~]# systemctl start neutron-server
   [root@controller ~]# systemctl enable neutron-server
   ```

   This concludes configuring Neutron server on the controller node, now we can configure Neutron network node.

Configuring Neutron network node

After we have configured Neutron-server on the controller node, we can proceed and configure the network server that is responsible for routing and connecting the OpenStack environment to the public network.

How to do it...

Neutron network node runs the networking services layer 2 management agent, DHCP service, L3 management agent, and metadata services agent. We will install and configure Neutron network node services to use the ML2 plugin.

Run the following commands on Neutron network node!

1. Enable IP forwarding and reverse path filtering, edit `/etc/sysctl.conf` to contain the following:

   ```
   net.ipv4.ip_forward=1
   net.ipv4.conf.all.rp_filter=0
   net.ipv4.conf.default.rp_filter=0
   ```

   and apply the new settings:

   ```
   [root@nnn ~]# sysctl -p
   ```

2. Then install the needed packages:

   ```
   [root@nnn ~]# yum install openstack-neutron openstack-neutron-ml2 openstack-neutron-openvswitch
   ```

Configure message broker

Configure Neutron to use RabbitMQ message broker of the controller:

> Remember to change 10.10.0.1 to your controller management IP.

```
[root@nnn ~]# openstack-config --set /etc/neutron/neutron.conf DEFAULT rpc_backend rabbit
[root@nnn ~]# openstack-config --set /etc/neutron/neutron.conf DEFAULT rabbit_host 10.10.0.1
```

Configure Neutron service

1. Configure Neutron to use Keystone as an authentication strategy:

   ```
   [root@nnn ~]# openstack-config --set /etc/neutron/neutron.conf DEFAULT \ auth_strategy keystone
   [root@nnn ~]# openstack-config --set /etc/neutron/neutron.conf keystone_authtoken auth_uri http://controller:5000
   [root@nnn ~]# openstack-config --set /etc/neutron/neutron.conf keystone_authtoken auth_host controller
   [root@nnn ~]# openstack-config --set /etc/neutron/neutron.conf keystone_authtoken auth_protocol http
   [root@nnn ~]# openstack-config --set /etc/neutron/neutron.conf keystone_authtoken auth_port 35357
   [root@nnn ~]# openstack-config --set /etc/neutron/neutron.conf keystone_authtoken admin_tenant_name services
   [root@nnn ~]# openstack-config --set /etc/neutron/neutron.conf keystone_authtoken admin_user neutron
   [root@nnn ~]# openstack-config --set /etc/neutron/neutron.conf keystone_authtoken admin_password password
   ```

2. Configure Neutron to use the ML2 Neutron plugin:

   ```
   [root@nnn ~]# openstack-config --set /etc/neutron/neutron.conf DEFAULT core_plugin ml2
   [root@nnn ~]# openstack-config --set /etc/neutron/neutron.conf DEFAULT service_plugins router
   ```

3. Configure Layer 3 agent that provides routing services for instances:

   ```
   [root@nnn ~]# openstack-config --set /etc/neutron/l3_agent.ini DEFAULT interface_driver neutron.agent.linux.interface.OVSInterfaceDriver
   [root@nnn ~]# openstack-config --set /etc/neutron/l3_agent.ini DEFAULT use_namespaces True
   ```

4. Configure the DHCP agent, which provides DHCP services for instances:

   ```
   [root@nnn ~]# openstack-config --set
   /etc/neutron/dhcp_agent.ini DEFAULT interface_driver
   neutron.agent.linux.interface.OVSInterfaceDriver

   [root@nnn ~]# openstack-config --set
   /etc/neutron/dhcp_agent.ini DEFAULT dhcp_driver
   neutron.agent.linux.dhcp.Dnsmasq

   [root@nnn ~]# openstack-config --set
   /etc/neutron/dhcp_agent.ini DEFAULT use_namespaces True
   ```

5. Configure instances Metadata service:

   ```
   [root@nnn ~]# openstack-config --set
   /etc/neutron/metadata_agent.ini DEFAULT \
     auth_url http://controller:5000/v2.0

   [root@nnn ~]# openstack-config --set
   /etc/neutron/metadata_agent.ini DEFAULT \
     auth_region regionOne

   [root@nnn ~]# openstack-config --set
   /etc/neutron/metadata_agent.ini DEFAULT \
     admin_tenant_name services

   [root@nnn ~]# openstack-config --set
   /etc/neutron/metadata_agent.ini DEFAULT \
     admin_user neutron

   [root@nnn ~]# openstack-config --set
   /etc/neutron/metadata_agent.ini DEFAULT \
     admin_password password

   [root@nnn ~]# openstack-config --set
   /etc/neutron/metadata_agent.ini DEFAULT \
     nova_metadata_ip controller

   [root@nnn ~]# openstack-config --set
   /etc/neutron/metadata_agent.ini DEFAULT \
     metadata_proxy_shared_secret SHARED_SECRET
   ```

6. Configure the ML2 plugin to use GRE tunneling segregation:

   ```
   [root@nnn ~]# openstack-config --set
   /etc/neutron/plugins/ml2/ml2_conf.ini ml2 \
     type_drivers gre

   [root@nnn ~]# openstack-config --set
   /etc/neutron/plugins/ml2/ml2_conf.ini ml2 \
     tenant_network_types gre
   ```

```
[root@nnn ~]# openstack-config --set
/etc/neutron/plugins/ml2/ml2_conf.ini ml2 \
  mechanism_drivers openvswitch
[root@nnn ~]# openstack-config --set
/etc/neutron/plugins/ml2/ml2_conf.ini ml2_type_gre \
  tunnel_id_ranges 1:1000
[root@nnn ~]# openstack-config --set
/etc/neutron/plugins/ml2/ml2_conf.ini ovs \
  local_ip 10.20.0.2
[root@nnn ~]# openstack-config --set
/etc/neutron/plugins/ml2/ml2_conf.ini ovs \
  tunnel_type gre
[root@nnn ~]# openstack-config --set
/etc/neutron/plugins/ml2/ml2_conf.ini ovs \
  enable_tunneling True
[root@nnn ~]# openstack-config --set
/etc/neutron/plugins/ml2/ml2_conf.ini securitygroup \
  firewall_driver neutron.agent.linux.
iptables_firewall.OVSHybridIptablesFirewallDriver
[root@nnn ~]# openstack-config --set
/etc/neutron/plugins/ml2/ml2_conf.ini securitygroup \
  enable_security_group True
```

7. Create bridges for Neutron layer 2 and Neutron layer 3 agents. First, start the Open vSwitch service:

   ```
   [root@nnn ~]# systemctl start openvswitch
   [root@nnn ~]# systemctl enable openvswitch
   ```

8. Create a bridge for instances' inner-commutation:

   ```
   [root@nnn ~]# ovs-vsctl add-br br-int
   ```

9. Create a bridge that the instance will use for communication with public networks:

   ```
   [root@nnn ~]# ovs-vsctl add-br br-ex
   ```

10. Bind the external bridge with the NIC used for external communication:

    ```
    [root@nnn ~]# ovs-vsctl add-port br-ex eth2
    ```

11. Create symbolic link for ML2 Neutron plugin:

    ```
    [root@nnn ~]# ln -s plugins/ml2/ml2_conf.ini /etc/neutron/plugin.ini
    ```

Introduction to OpenStack and its Deployment Using Packages

Start and enable service

1. At this point, we can start and enable L2 Open vSwitch agent, L3 agent, HDCP agent, and metadata agent services:

   ```
   [root@nnn ~]# systemctl start neutron-openvswitch-agent
   [root@nnn ~]# systemctl start neutron-l3-agent
   [root@nnn ~]# systemctl start neutron-dhcp-agent
   [root@nnn ~]# systemctl start neutron-metadata-agent
   [root@nnn ~]# systemctl enable neutron-openvswitch-agent
   [root@nnn ~]# systemctl enable neutron-l3-agent
   [root@nnn ~]# systemctl enable neutron-dhcp-agent
   [root@nnn ~]# systemctl enable neutron-metadata-agent
   ```

2. This concludes configuring Neutron network node. Now we can configure the Nova-Compute nodes to use Neutron networking.

Configuring compute node for Neutron

After we have configured the Neutron network node, we can go ahead and configure our compute nodes to use Neutron networking service.

How to do it...

When the controller and Neutron network node are ready, we can configure Nova-Compute node to use Neutron for networking. We will configure Neutron access to the message broker. Then, we will configure Neutron to use ML2 plugin with GRE tunneling segmentation.

Run the following commands on `compute1`!

1. Disable reverse path filtering, Edit /etc/sysctl.conf to contain the following:

   ```
   net.ipv4.conf.all.rp_filter=0
   net.ipv4.conf.default.rp_filter=0
   ```

   and apply the new configuration:

   ```
   [root@compute1 ~]# sysctl -p
   ```

2. Install the Neutron ML2 and Open vSwitch packages:

   ```
   [root@compute1 ~]# yum install -y openstack-neutron-ml2 openstack-neutron-openvswitch
   ```

Configure message broker

Configure Neutron to use RabbitMQ message broker of the controller:

> Remember to change 10.10.0.1 to your controller management IP.

```
[root@compute1 ~]# openstack-config --set /etc/neutron/neutron.conf DEFAULT rpc_backend rabbit
[root@compute1 ~]# openstack-config --set /etc/neutron/neutron.conf DEFAULT rabbit_host 10.10.0.1
```

Configure Neutron service

1. Configure Neutron to use Keystone as an authentication strategy:

    ```
    [root@compute1 ~]# openstack-config --set /etc/neutron/neutron.conf DEFAULT
       auth_strategy keystone

    [root@compute1 ~]# openstack-config --set /etc/neutron/neutron.conf keystone_authtoken \
       auth_uri http://controller:5000

    [root@compute1 ~]# openstack-config --set /etc/neutron/neutron.conf keystone_authtoken \
       auth_host controller

    [root@compute1 ~]# openstack-config --set /etc/neutron/neutron.conf keystone_authtoken \
       auth_protocol http

    [root@compute1 ~]# openstack-config --set /etc/neutron/neutron.conf keystone_authtoken \
       auth_port 35357

    [root@compute1 ~]# openstack-config --set /etc/neutron/neutron.conf keystone_authtoken \
       admin_tenant_name services

    [root@compute1 ~]# openstack-config --set /etc/neutron/neutron.conf keystone_authtoken \
       admin_user neutron

    [root@compute1 ~]# openstack-config --set /etc/neutron/neutron.conf keystone_authtoken \
       admin_password password
    ```

2. Now configure Neutron to use ML2 Neutron plugin:

   ```
   [root@compute1 ~]# openstack-config --set
   /etc/neutron/neutron.conf DEFAULT core_plugin ml2
   [root@compute1 ~]# openstack-config --set
   /etc/neutron/neutron.conf DEFAULT service_plugins router
   ```

3. Configure the ML2 Plugin to use GRE tunneling segregation:

   ```
   [root@compute1 ~]# openstack-config --set
   /etc/neutron/plugins/ml2/ml2_conf.ini ml2 \
      type_drivers gre
   [root@compute1 ~]# openstack-config --set
   /etc/neutron/plugins/ml2/ml2_conf.ini ml2 \
      tenant_network_types gre
   [root@compute1 ~]# openstack-config --set
   /etc/neutron/plugins/ml2/ml2_conf.ini ml2 \
      mechanism_drivers openvswitch
   [root@compute1 ~]# openstack-config --set
   /etc/neutron/plugins/ml2/ml2_conf.ini ml2_type_gre \
      tunnel_id_ranges 1:1000
   [root@compute1 ~]# openstack-config --set
   /etc/neutron/plugins/ml2/ml2_conf.ini ovs \
      local_ip 10.20.0.3
   [root@compute1 ~]# openstack-config --set
   /etc/neutron/plugins/ml2/ml2_conf.ini ovs \
      tunnel_type gre
   [root@compute1 ~]# openstack-config --set
   /etc/neutron/plugins/ml2/ml2_conf.ini ovs \
      enable_tunneling True
   [root@compute1 ~]# openstack-config --set
   /etc/neutron/plugins/ml2/ml2_conf.ini securitygroup \
      firewall_driver neutron.agent.linux.iptables_firewall.OVSHybridIptablesFirewallDriver
   [root@compute1 ~]# openstack-config --set
   /etc/neutron/plugins/ml2/ml2_conf.ini securitygroup \
      enable_security_group True
   ```

4. Create bridges for Neutron layer 2 and Neutron layer 3 agents. First, start the enable vSwitch service:

   ```
   [root@compute1 ~]# systemctl start openvswitch
   [root@compute1 ~]# systemctl enable openvswitch
   ```

———————————————————————————————————— Chapter 1

5. After starting Open vSwitch service, we can create the needed bridge:

    ```
    [root@compute1 ~]# ovs-vsctl add-br br-int
    ```

6. Configure Nova to use Neutron Networking:

    ```
    [root@compute1 ~]# openstack-config --set /etc/nova/nova.conf DEFAULT network_api_class nova.network.neutronv2.api.API

    [root@compute1 ~]# openstack-config --set /etc/nova/nova.conf DEFAULT neutron_url http://controller:9696

    [root@compute1 ~]# openstack-config --set /etc/nova/nova.conf DEFAULT neutron_auth_strategy keystone

    [root@compute1 ~]# openstack-config --set /etc/nova/nova.conf DEFAULT neutron_admin_tenant_name service

    [root@compute1 ~]# openstack-config --set /etc/nova/nova.conf DEFAULT neutron_admin_username neutron

    [root@compute1 ~]# openstack-config --set /etc/nova/nova.conf DEFAULT neutron_admin_password NEUTRON_PASS

    [root@compute1 ~]# openstack-config --set /etc/nova/nova.conf DEFAULT neutron_admin_auth_url http://controller:35357/v2.0

    [root@compute1 ~]# openstack-config --set /etc/nova/nova.conf DEFAULT linuxnet_interface_driver nova.network.linux_net.LinuxOVSInterfaceDriver

    [root@compute1 ~]# openstack-config --set /etc/nova/nova.conf DEFAULT firewall_driver nova.virt.firewall.NoopFirewallDriver

    [root@compute1 ~]# openstack-config --set /etc/nova/nova.conf DEFAULT security_group_api neutron
    ```

7. Create a symbolic link for ML2 Neutron plugin:

    ```
    [root@compute1 ~]# ln -s plugins/ml2/ml2_conf.ini /etc/neutron/plugin.ini
    ```

8. Restart the Nova-Compute service:

    ```
    [root@compute1 ~]# systemctl restart openstack-nova-compute
    ```

9. Start and enable Neutron Open vSwitch agent service:

    ```
    [root@compute1 ~]# systemctl start neutron-openvswitch-agent
    [root@compute1 ~]# systemctl enable neutron-openvswitch-agent
    ```

Introduction to OpenStack and its Deployment Using Packages

Creating Neutron networks

At this point, we should have the controller, Neutron network node, and `compute1` configured for using Neutron networking. We can go ahead and create Neutron virtual networks needed for instances to be able to communicate with external public networks. We are going to create two layer 2 networks, one for the instances, and another to connect external networks.

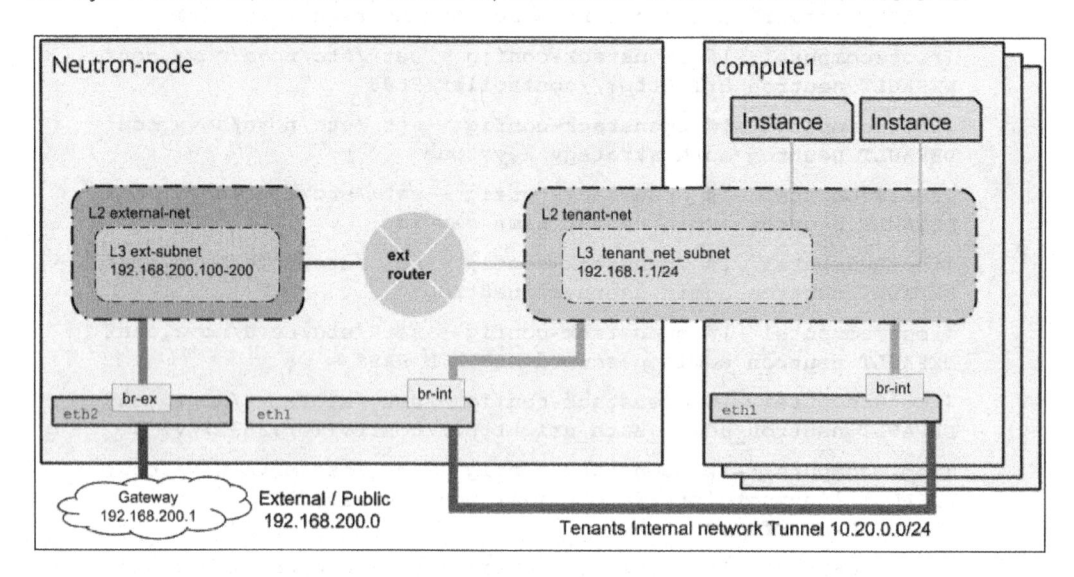

Run the following commands on the controller node!

By default, networks are own and managed by the Admin user, under Admin tenant and shared for other tenants' use.

1. Source Admin tenant credentials:

    ```
    [root@controller ~]# source keystonerc_admin
    ```

2. Create an external shared network:

    ```
    [root@controller ~(keystone_admin)]# neutron net-create external-net --shared --router:external=True
    ```

    In this example, we allocate a range of IPs from our existing external physical network, 192.168.200.0/24 for instances to use when communicating with the Internet or with external hosts in the IT environment.

3. Create a subnet in the newly created network:

    ```
    [root@controller ~(keystone_admin)]# neutron subnet-create external-net --name ext-subnet --allocation-pool start=192.168.200.100,end=192.168.200.200 --disable-dhcp --gateway 192.168.200.1 192.168.200.0/24
    ```

Chapter 1

The IP range is ought to be routable by the external public network and not overlap with the existing configured networks. *Chapter 7, Neutron Networking Service*, will further discuss Neutron networks planning.

4. Create a tenant network, which is an isolated network for instances to inner-communicate:

   ```
   [root@controller ~(keystone_admin)]# neutron net-create tenant_net
   ```

   ```
   [root@controller ~(keystone_admin)]# neutron subnet-create tenant_net --name tenant_net_subnet --gateway 192.168.1.1 192.168.1.0/24
   ```

   ```
   [root@controller ~(keystone_admin)]# neutron router-create ext-router
   ```

   ```
   [root@controller ~(keystone_admin)]# neutron router-interface-add ext-router tenant-subnet
   ```

   ```
   [root@controller ~(keystone_admin)]# neutron router-gateway-set ext-router external-net
   ```

Installing Horizon – web user interface dashboard

Horizon dashboard service is the web user interface for users to consume OpenStack services and for administrator to manage and operate OpenStack.

Getting ready

Install packages needed for Horizon as follows:

```
[root@controller ~]# yum install mod_wsgi openstack-dashboard
Use firewall-cmd command to open port 80:
[root@controller ~]# firewall-cmd --permanent --add-port=80/tcp
[root@controller ~]# firewall-cmd --reload
Configure SELinux:
# setsebool -P httpd_can_network_connect on
```

45

Introduction to OpenStack and its Deployment Using Packages

How to do it...

Perform the following steps to configure and enable the Horizon dashboard service:

1. Edit /etc/openstack-dashboard/local_settings:

   ALLOWED_HOSTS = ['localhost', '*']

   OPENSTACK_HOST = "controller"

2. Start and enable service. At this point, we can start and enable Neutron-server service:

   ```
   [root@controller ~]# systemctl start httpd
   [root@controller ~]# systemctl enable httpd
   ```

How it works...

Horizon is a Django-based web application, running on Apache HTTPD service, it interacts with all services' APIs to gather information from OpenStack's services and to create new resources.

There's more...

We can verify whether Horizon dashboard service was installed successfully after we completed configuring the service.

Verify successful installation

You can now access the dashboard via web browser at http://controller/dashboard using the admin user account and password chosen during the admin account creation.

2
Deploying OpenStack Using Staypuft OpenStack Installer

In this chapter, we will cover the following:

- Setting up the environment
- Installing Staypuft packages
- Discovering hosts for provisioning
- Creating a new OpenStack deployment
- Configuring a network
- Allocating hosts to roles
- Configuring host networking
- Deploying OpenStack

Introduction

Installing OpenStack manually, as outlined in *Chapter 1, Introduction to OpenStack and its Deployment Using Packages*, allows the maximum level of customization, but it introduces a level of difficulty to deploy OpenStack consistently across multiple nodes, as it requires performing countless manual steps repeatedly. Project Staypuft simplifies OpenStack production installations; Staypuft is a wizard-based installer that automates the OpenStack configuration and deployment process. Staypuft is a plugin built on top of Foreman, an open source life cycle management tool, and it leverages Foreman's capabilities. Staypuft can automatically discover and orchestrate the provisioning of new bare-metal controllers and computes. It can deploy highly available controllers with all required HAProxy and pacemaker configurations.

Deploying OpenStack Using Staypuft OpenStack Installer

Setting up the environment

Before deploying Staypuft server and preparing it for a new OpenStack deployment, we need to prepare the environment with necessary prerequisites for the deployment.

Getting ready

In this chapter, we will use Staypuft to deploy controller/Neutron/Computes layout, we will need to prepare networks for the environment and prepare the host that will serve as the Staypuft host.

Networks layout

We will need to make sure that all machines are connected to a dedicated network that will be used for provisioning. The Staypuft host and Neutron node need to have access to a public network. All compute nodes and Neutron network node need to be connected to the tenant network. See the following diagram:

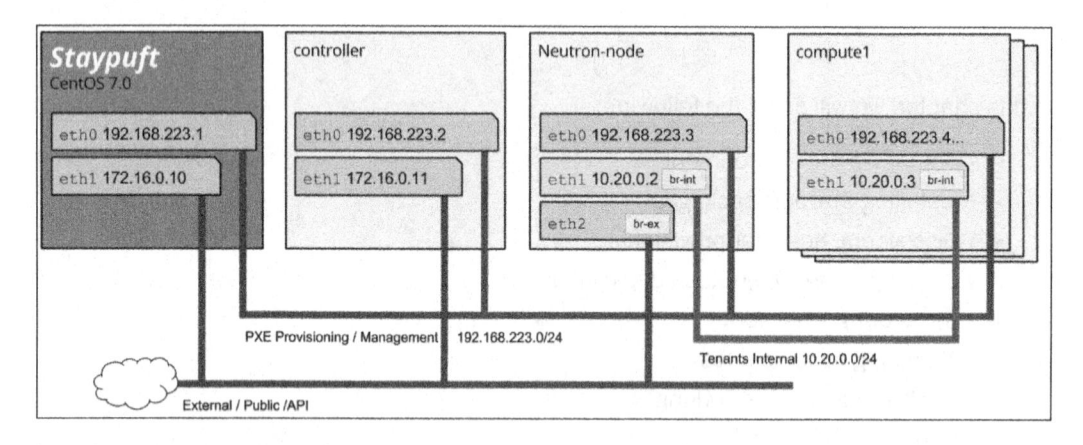

```
Staypuft            controller          Neutron-node         compute1
CentOS 7.0

eth0 192.168.223.1  eth0 192.168.223.2  eth0 192.168.223.3   eth0 192.168.223.4...
eth1 172.16.0.10    eth1 172.16.0.11    eth1 10.20.0.2 br-int eth1 10.20.0.3 br-int
                                        eth2        br-ex

                    PXE Provisioning / Management  192.168.223.0/24
                                                              Tenants Internal 10.20.0.0/24
                    External / Public /API
```

Provisioning PXE network

Staypuft automatically stands up a PXE environment with Cobbler, TFTP, DHCP, and DNS on the Staypuft host. Staypuft uses the provisioning network to deploy the base operating system of the hosts that serve as controllers, Neutron, and compute nodes and later deploys and manages the nodes via Puppet.

> Make sure that the PXE provisioning network does not run any DHCP/PXE services to avoid conflicts with services managed by Staypuft.

The Tenant network

Traffic generated by the instances is transmitted over the Tenant network. Staypuft creates br-int bridges for Tenant's network traffic on Neutron and compute nodes.

External public network

The external public network is used to access the public Internet network. The Staypuft machine is used as a gateway to access public Internet network to retrieve OpenStack RPM packages and deploy them on Controller/Neutron/Compute nodes. The Controller node provides access to OpenStack API and Horizon web dashboard over the public network. Neutron Network node runs L3 agent and, when needed, routes traffic coming from instances over the Tenant's network to the external public network. In this chapter, we assume that the Tenant and external public networks are both running external DHCP services.

Staypuft host

The Staypuft machine should be installed with CentOS 7.0 operating system. It should have at least 4GB of memory, should be configured with fully qualified domain name (FQDN) that matches the domain name of the network to be provisioned, and does not conflict with any existing domain names. The Staypuft host should have at least two network interfaces. We will use the first NIC eth0 as the provisioning NIC on our isolated PXE network and the second NIC eth1 to access the Internet to retrieve RPM packages.

How to do it...

We need to configure the Staypuft host to serve as a gateway, forward traffic coming from the management network to the public network, and allow the controller and compute nodes to access public YUM repositories. We will configure YUM repository to download and install all needed packages and enable the Network Time Protocol (ntpd) service.

Configure Staypuft to serve as an Internet gateway

Proceed with the following steps:

1. Edit the kernel parameter's configuration file /etc/sysctl.conf and allow IP forwarding. Set the following parameter:

   `net.ipv4.ip_forward = 1`

2. Execute the sysctl command to append the new configuration:

   `[root@staypuft.example.com ~]# sysctl -p`

3. Set an iptables masquerade to forward traffic coming from the management network eth0 to the public network eth1:

   `[root@staypuft.example.com ~]# iptables -t nat -A POSTROUTING -o eth1 -j MASQUERADE`

Deploying OpenStack Using Staypuft OpenStack Installer

```
[root@staypuft.example.com ~]# iptables -I FORWARD 1 -s
192.168.223.0/24 -j ACCEPT
[root@staypuft.example.com ~]# iptables -I FORWARD 1 -d
192.168.223.0/24 -j ACCEPT
[root@staypuft.example.com ~]# service iptables save
```

Setting YUM repositories

Proceed with the following steps:

1. Create a new YUM repository configuration file for Foreman having filename /etc/yum.repos.d/foreman.repo and the following content:

   ```
   [foreman]
   name=Foreman
   baseurl=http://yum.theforeman.org/releases/1.6/el7/x86_64/
   enabled=1
   gpgcheck=0
   ```

2. Create a new YUM repository configuration file for Foreman_Plugins, having filename /etc/yum.repos.d/foreman-plugins.repo and the following content:

   ```
   [foreman_plugins]
   name=Foreman_Plugins
   baseurl=http://yum.theforeman.org/plugins/1.6/el7/x86_64/
   enabled=1
   gpgcheck=0
   ```

3. Enable Network Time Protocol. Start and enable the NTP service:

   ```
   [root@staypuft.example.com ~]# systemctl start ntpd
   [root@staypuft.example.com ~]# systemctl enable ntpd
   ```

There's more...

During the installation, you will be asked to provide a path to CentOS 7.0 repository.

In the next section, we will start the Staypuft installer, which installs Staypuft on the host. The installer also opens all needed firewall ports on the host and sets all needed configuration.

Installing Staypuft packages

At this point, we have all the needed prerequisites configured and we should be ready to proceed installing Staypuft packages and running the Installer pre configuration script.

Getting ready

It is recommended to run on the latest update of the operating system. We can use `yum` to update the system:

`[root@staypuft.example.com ~]# yum update`

Use the `yum install` command to install the `staypuft` installer package, which brings all dependence packages.

`[root@staypuft.example.com ~]# yum install foreman-installer-staypuft`

How to do it...

The Staypuft installer takes care of installing Foreman and the Staypuft plugin on top of it. Then, it configures the host and Foreman, including all necessary networks, firewall, SELinux, and repository configurations, so the Staypuft host is ready to deploy new OpenStack deployments after the setup process.

1. Execute the `staypuft-installer` command to install and setup Staypuft:

    `[root@staypuft.example.com ~]# staypuft-installer`

2. Select option `2. eth0` to be used as the provisioning NIC. This NIC will be used to serve PXE and DHCP; make sure that there are not conflicting services on this network.

```
[root@staypuft ~]# staypuft-installer
Please select NIC on which you want provisioning enabled:
1. eth0
2. eth1
? 1
```

Deploying OpenStack Using Staypuft OpenStack Installer

3. Configure networking settings to match your environment. The installer automatically sets all settings according to the runtime environment. If any of the address needs to be changed, enter the corresponding number `280095`, change the parameter, choose `1`, and click on *ENTER* to continue.

```
Networking setup:
         Network interface: 'eth0'
                IP address: '192.168.223.2'
              Network mask: '255.255.255.0'
           Network address: '192.168.223.0'
              Host Gateway: '172.16.0.1'
          DHCP range start: '192.168.223.3'
            DHCP range end: '192.168.223.254'
              DHCP Gateway: '192.168.223.2'
             DNS forwarder: '172.16.0.1'
                    Domain: 'example.com'
               Foreman URL: 'https://staypuft.example.com'
             NTP sync host: '0.rhel.pool.ntp.org'
                  Timezone: 'US/Eastern'
Configure networking on this machine: ✓
Configure firewall on this machine: ✓

The installer can configure the networking and firewall rules on this machine wi
th the above configuration. Default values are populated from the this machine's
 existing networking configuration.

If you DO NOT want to configure networking please set 'Configure networking on t
his machine' to No before proceeding. Do this by selecting option 'Do not config
ure networking' from the list below.

How would you like to proceed?:
1. Proceed with the above values
2. Change Network interface
3. Change IP address
4. Change Network mask
5. Change Network address
6. Change Host Gateway
7. Change DHCP range start
8. Change DHCP range end
9. Change DHCP Gateway
10. Change DNS forwarder
11. Change Domain
12. Change Foreman URL
13. Change NTP sync host
14. Change Timezone
15. Do not configure networking
16. Do not configure firewall
17. Cancel Installation
```

Chapter 2

> Make sure that the DHCP gateway and DNS forwarder represent the values in your existing network and the name of the domain matches the FQDN of the machine that runs Staypuft.

4. Configure client authentication. You may set the machine's public SSH key, change the root's password, enter number 3 to change root password, choose a new password, choose 1, and click on *ENTER* to process.

```
Configure client authentication
        SSH public key: ''
        Root password: '*******************************************'

Please set a default root password for newly provisioned machines. If you choose
 not to set a password, it will be generated randomly. The password must be a mi
nimum of 8 characters. You can also set a public ssh key which will be deployed
to newly provisioned machines.

How would you like to proceed?:
1. Proceed with the above values
2. Change SSH public key
3. Change Root password
4. Toggle Root password visibility
3
new value for root password
********
enter new root password again to confirm
********
Configure client authentication
        SSH public key: ''
        Root password: '********'

Please set a default root password for newly provisioned machines. If you choose
 not to set a password, it will be generated randomly. The password must be a mi
nimum of 8 characters. You can also set a public ssh key which will be deployed
to newly provisioned machines.

How would you like to proceed?:
1. Proceed with the above values
2. Change SSH public key
3. Change Root password
4. Toggle Root password visibility
1
```

Deploying OpenStack Using Staypuft OpenStack Installer

5. Set the installation media path, type 1, and set the path to a local repository of CentOS 7.0, or the online CentOS path, `http://mirror.centos.org/centos/7/os/x86_64`. Then type 2 and click on *ENTER* to proceed.

```
Now you should configure installation media which will be used for provisioning.
Note that if you don't configure it properly, host provisioning won't work until
 you configure installation media manually.

Enter RHEL repo path:
1. Set RHEL repo path (http or https URL): http://
2. Proceed with configuration
3. Skip this step (provisioning won't work)
1
Path: http://mirror.centos.org/centos/7/os/x86_64

Enter RHEL repo path:
1. Set RHEL repo path (http or https URL): http://mirror.centos.org/centos/7/os/x86_64
2. Proceed with configuration
3. Skip this step (provisioning won't work)
```

> If you do not enter the correct path, you may change it from the Staypuft web user interface on a later stage.

6. Once the installation process is complete, the output with user credentials to the Staypuft host will appear. Make a note of Staypuft's URL and user credentials, as they will be needed in the next step.

```
Starting to seed provisioning data
Use 'base_RedHat_7' hostgroup for provisioning
  Success!
    * Foreman is running at https://staypuft.example.com
        Initial credentials are admin / iyeguv6oE6QeLpEr
    * Foreman Proxy is running at https://staypuft.example.com:8443
    * Puppetmaster is running at port 8140
    The full log is at /var/log/rhel-osp-installer/rhel-osp-installer.log
[root@staypuft ~]#
```

How it works...

The Staypuft installer is a collection of Puppet modules that installs everything required for a full working Foreman setup with the Staypuft plugin. It uses RPM packaging and adds necessary configuration for the complete installation.

―――――――――――――――――――――――――――――――――― Chapter 2

Components include the Foreman web user interface, Smart Proxy, Passenger (for the Puppet master and Foreman itself), TFTP, DNS, and DHCP servers and the Staypuft web user interface plugin. It is configurable, and the Puppet modules can be read or run in `no-op` mode to see what changes it will make.

- By default, the Staypuft installer will configure the following:
- Apache HTTP with SSL (using a Puppet-signed certificate)
- Foreman running under `mod_passenger`
- Smart Proxy configured for Puppet, TFTP, and SSL
- Puppet master running under `mod_passenger`
- Puppet agent configured
- TFTP server
- ISC DHCP server
- BIND DNS server
- Cobbler PXE server

There's more...

The Staypuft installer is based on `foreman-installer`, allowing to leverage Foreman's native capabilities, such as automating the installation process and using more advanced options.

See also...

The Foreman documentation page for `foreman-installer` lists all installer options at http://theforeman.org/manuals/1.6/index.html#3.2ForemanInstaller.

Deploying OpenStack using Staypuft

Now Staypuft is set up and ready to deploy OpenStack. Further, we will prepare hosts to be deployed as Controller, Compute nodes, and Neutron Network Node. Then, we will set up a new deployment using the Staypuft web user interface, trigger Staypuft to orchestrate a deployment of the base operating system, then deploy OpenStack packages, and configure all OpenStack services.

Discovering hosts for provisioning

Before creating a new OpenStack deployment, we need to add hosts to Staypuft to be provisioned as OpenStack nodes. Staypuft uses the host's auto discovery via the PXE provisioning network.

Deploying OpenStack Using Staypuft OpenStack Installer

Getting ready

We will need to access the Staypuft user interface and then make sure that the hosts we plan to deploy as Controller, Compute, and Neutron are ready for the deployment.

Accessing the Staypuft web user interface

Access the Staypuft web user interface. On completion of the previous section, `staypuft-installer` provided a URL, and the password for the admin account that was generated for the environment. Open your web browser and navigate to the URL that was provided by `staypuft-installer`. Log in with the **Username** admin and **Password** that was provided. In this example, we used the name `http://Staypuft.example.com`.

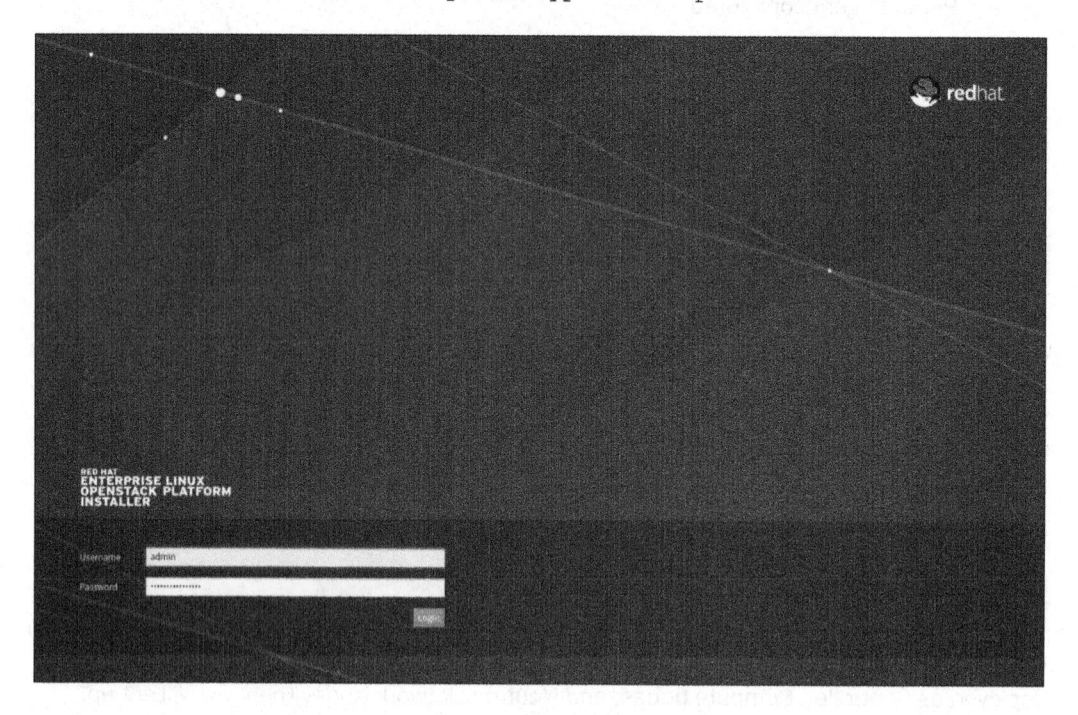

In case you didn't make a note of the password that was generated, you can locate the file `/etc/foreman/staypuft-installer.answers.yaml` under `admin_password`.

To change the default generated password for the Admin user account, navigate on the upper right-hand side menu to **Administer | Users**, click on **Admin**, select a new password, and click on **Submit**.

Chapter 2

To change the installation media path that was set up during the staypuft-installer process, navigate to the upper menu, to **Hosts | Installation Media**. Click on an installation media name, and **Options** menu will open. Set a new path and click on **Submit**.

How to do it...

Proceed with the following steps:

1. Make sure that the hosts are connected to the provisioning network as described in the networking setup section in **SettingUp Environmnet**.
2. Boot the hosts using the PXE network boot option. This host will boot into the following image and will automatically register the host with Staypuft.

```
[    0]




 _____                                 
|  ___|__  _ __ ___ _ __ ___   __ _ _ __  
| |_ / _ \| '__/ _ \ '_ ` _ \ / _` | '_ \ 
|  _| (_) | | |  __/ | | | | | (_| | | | |
|_|  \___/|_|  \___|_| |_| |_|\__,_|_| |_|
 ____  _                                  
|  _ \(_)___  ___ _____   _____ _ __ _   _ 
| | | | / __|/ __/ _ \ \ / / _ \ '__| | | |
| |_| | \__ \ (_| (_) \ V /  __/ |  | |_| |
|____/|_|___/_____/ \_/ \___|_|   \__, |
                                     |___/ 




[    0] This is Foreman Discovery 0.5.9999-P, tty1 is reserved for logs.
[    0] Some interesting facts about this system:
```

Deploying OpenStack Using Staypuft OpenStack Installer

> If the **Foreman Discovery** screen is not shown, verify that the hosts are set to boot from the PXE network, and they are on the PXE provisioning network according to the network diagram.

3. Confirm whether all hosts were registered by navigating to **Hosts | Discovered Hosts** in Staypuft web UI upper menu. Verify whether all the hosts to be deployed are registered.

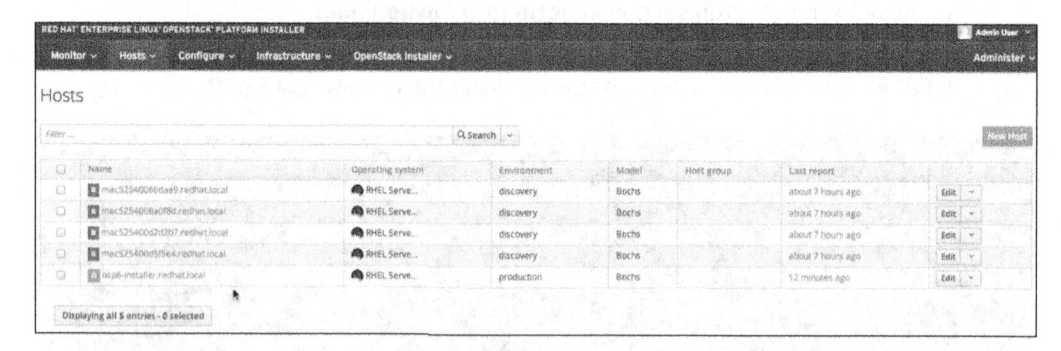

> To remove a host for the discovered hosts, click on host's name and click on **Delete** on the upper right-hand side.

Creating a new OpenStack deployment

At this point, we are ready to create a new OpenStack deployment and provision the Controller, Neutron, and Compute nodes. We will create a new deployment, configure general deployment settings, create and assign subnets and service networks. Then, we will configure Neutron, Glance, and Cinder services. When the deployment configuration is ready, we will assign hosts for each OpenStack role and deploy the environment.

How to do it...

Proceed with the following steps:

1. Create a new deployment by navigating in the upper menu to **OpenStack Installer | New Deployment**.

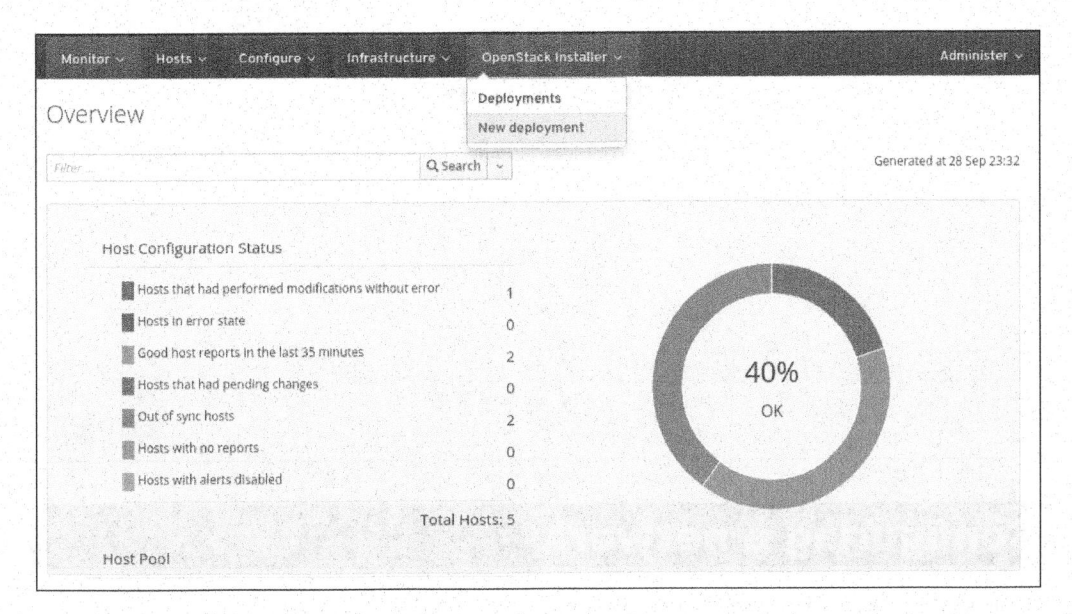

2. Choose a new name for the deployment in the **Name** text and fill the description text.

3. Select **Controller/Compute** layout in the **High Availability** section. If you would like to deploy highly available controllers layout, keep in mind that this layout requires at least three nodes for the **Controller** role.

4. Choose **RabbitMQ** as the message provider. Staypuft can deploy RabbitMQ and QPID. Since RabbitMQ is more widely used in the OpenStack community, its testing coverage with OpenStack is better.

5. Choose **Generate random password for each service** in the **Service Password** section for Staypuft to automatically generate an individual password for each deployed OpenStack Service. This provides a better level of security for OpenStack Services.

Deploying OpenStack Using Staypuft OpenStack Installer

6. Click on **Next** to proceed to the next step.

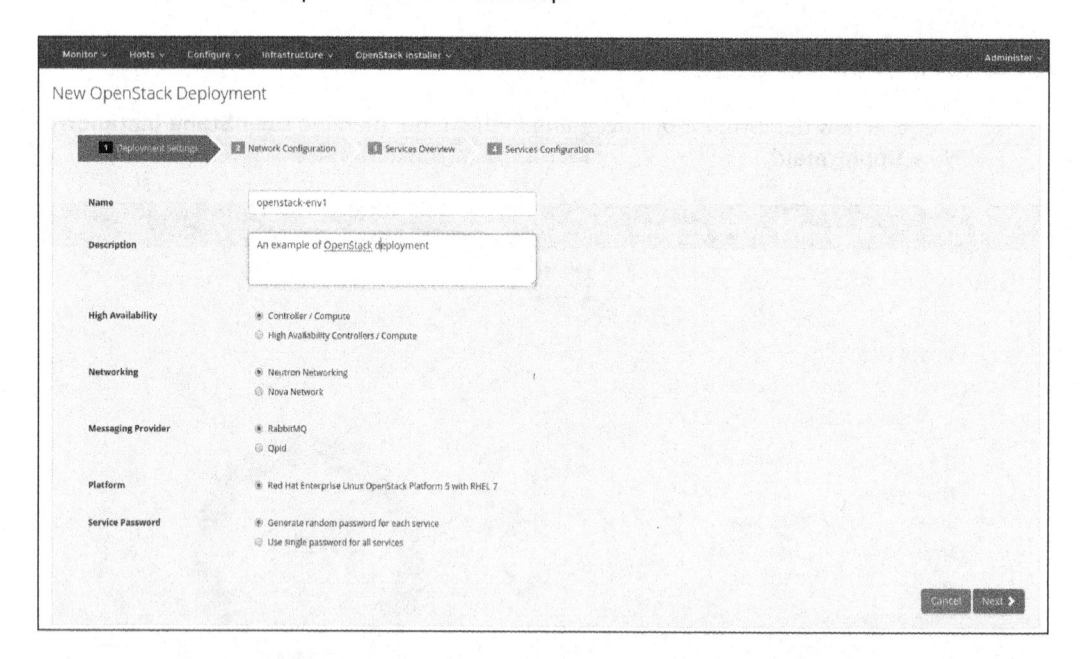

Configuring a network

In this step, we will create the subnets we plan to use for OpenStack services and assign network roles to the corresponding subnets. At a later stage, we will assign the newly created subnets to physical network interfaces, which will be used for these network roles.

How to do it...

Proceed with the following steps:

1. On the network configuration screen, which appeared in addition to the existing 'default' subnet, click on the **New Subnet** button and create an additional subnet for the tenant's traffic. This subnet will be used for instances' internal communication.

    Network name: Tenant network

    Network address: 10.20.0.0

    Network mask: 255.255.255.0

    IPAM: none

    Boot mode: DHCP

Chapter 2

This configuration uses an existing DHCP service on the subnet to assign IP address to network interfaces attached.

2. Drag and drop the **Tenant** network role from the default subnet to the newly created Tenant subnet, as can be seen in the following image:

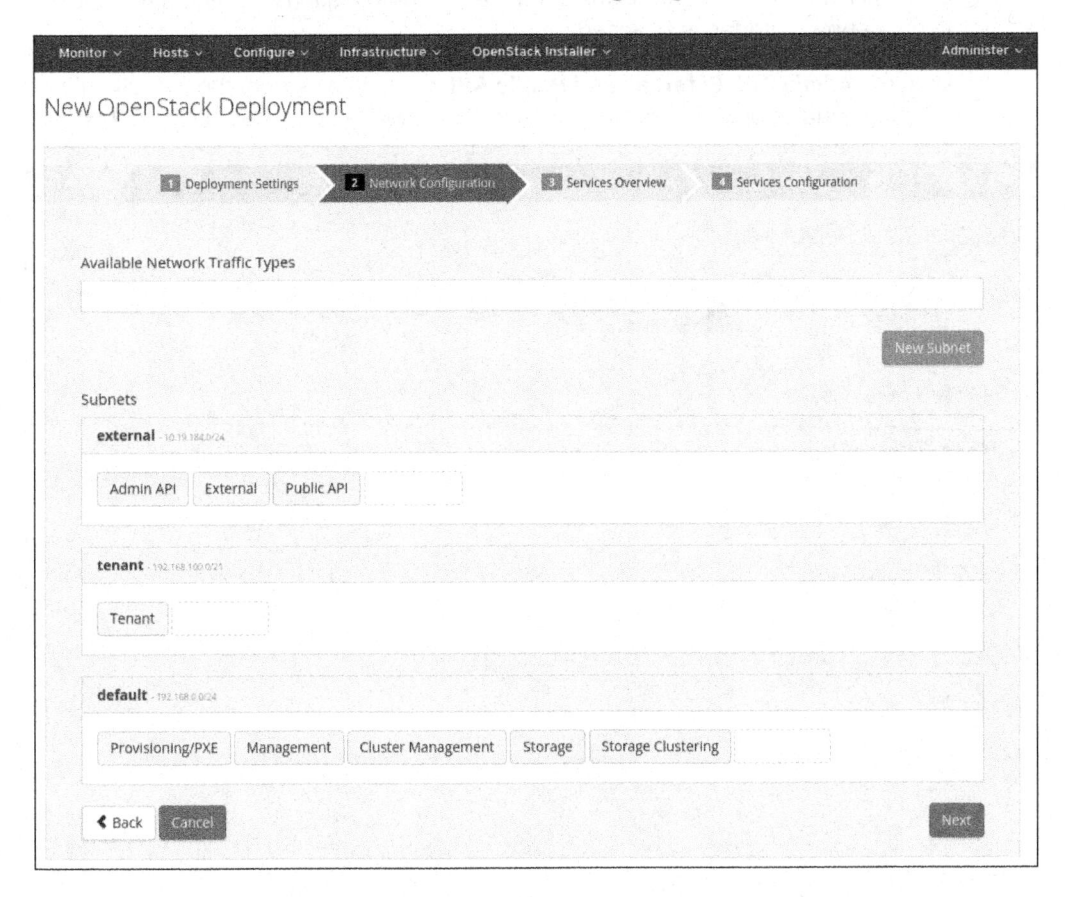

3. Create an additional subnet for external public network. Neutron network node will route traffic from the Tenant to this network. The controller will allow access to OpenStack's API via the external network. Click on **New Subnet** and use your existing network parameters. In this chapter, we will use the following:

   Network name: external network

   Network address: 172.16.0.0

   Network mask: 255.255.255.0

   Gateway address: 172.16.0.254

Deploying OpenStack Using Staypuft OpenStack Installer

Primary DNS server: 8.8.8.8

IPAM: none

Boot mode: DHCP

This configuration uses an existing DHCP service on the subnet to assign IP address to the network interfaces attached.

4. Drag the **Admin API**, **External**, and **Public API** network roles from the default subnet to the external subnet created in step 3 as on the following screen. Click on **Next**.

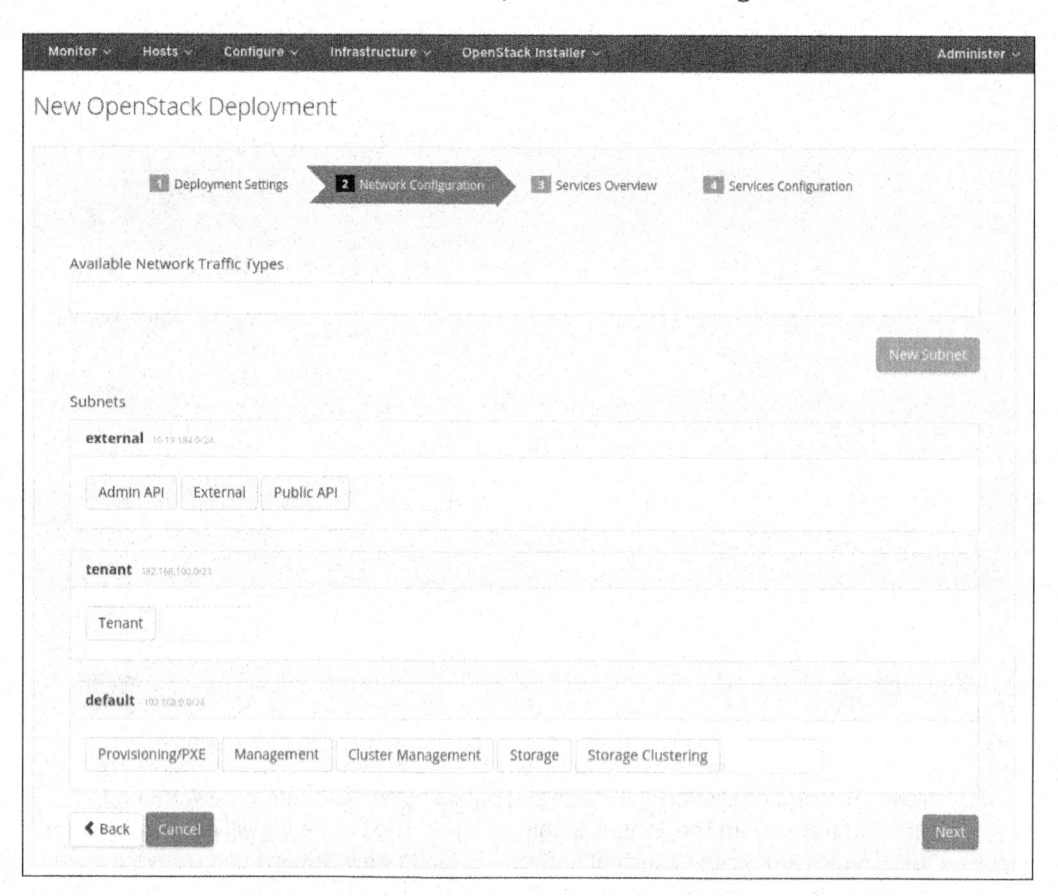

Chapter 2

Services configuration

Now we can set the backends for the Neutron, Glance, and Cinder services, and set their configuration options.

How to do it...

Proceed with the following steps:

1. Review the deployed OpenStack services in each of the roles, then click on **Next**.

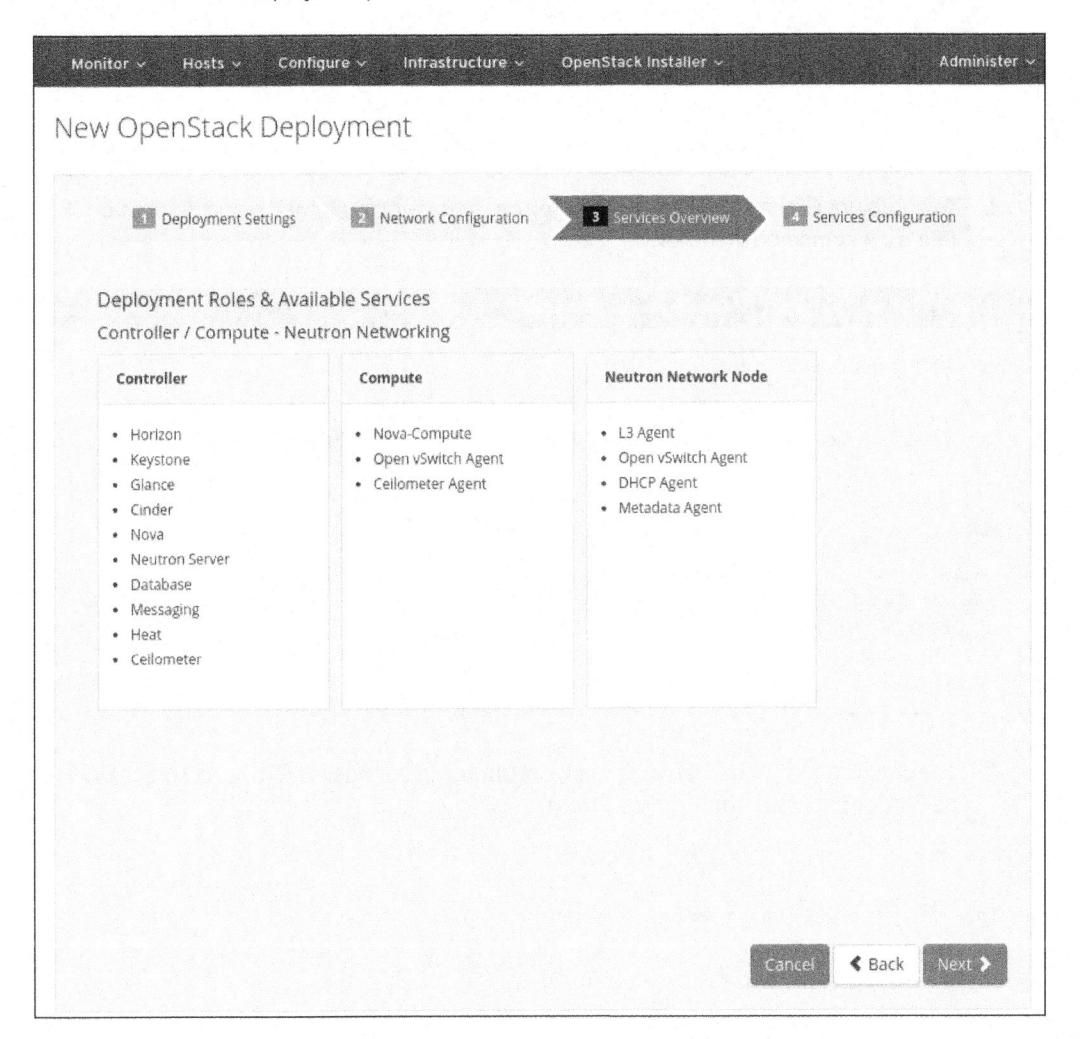

Deploying OpenStack Using Staypuft OpenStack Installer

2. Configure Neutron service by selecting the VXLAN network type for Tenants.

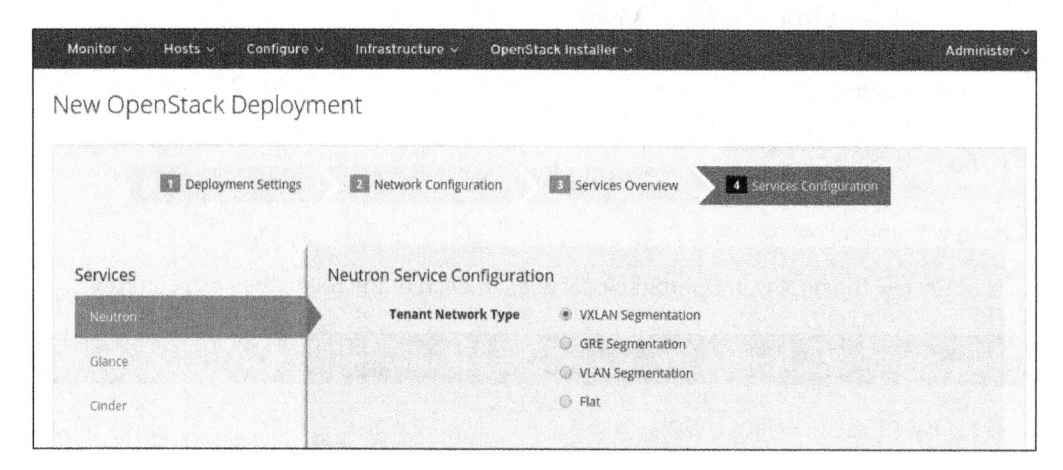

3. To configure Glance service, select **Glance** on the services menu and select **Local File** as a glance backend driver.

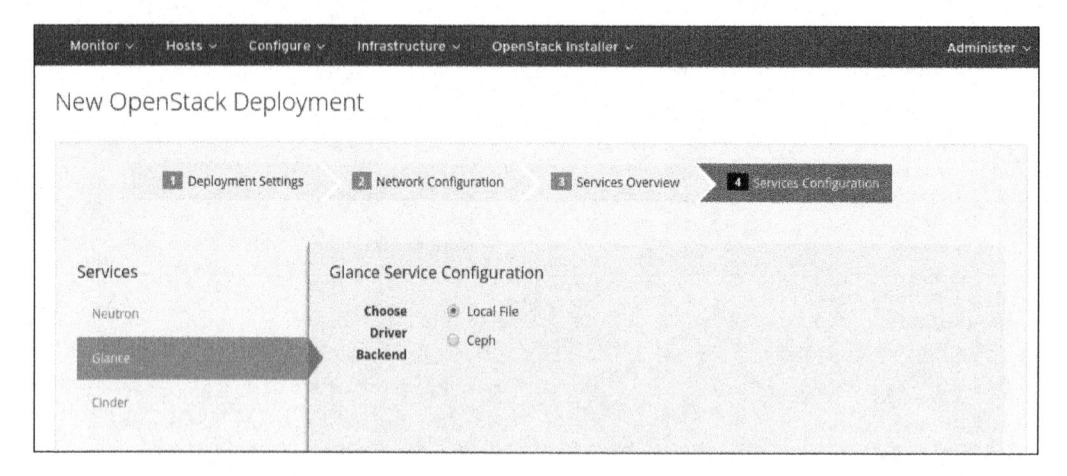

4. To configure the Cinder Service, click on **Cinder** in services menu, and select **LVM** as Cinder backend, then click on **Next**.

Chapter 2

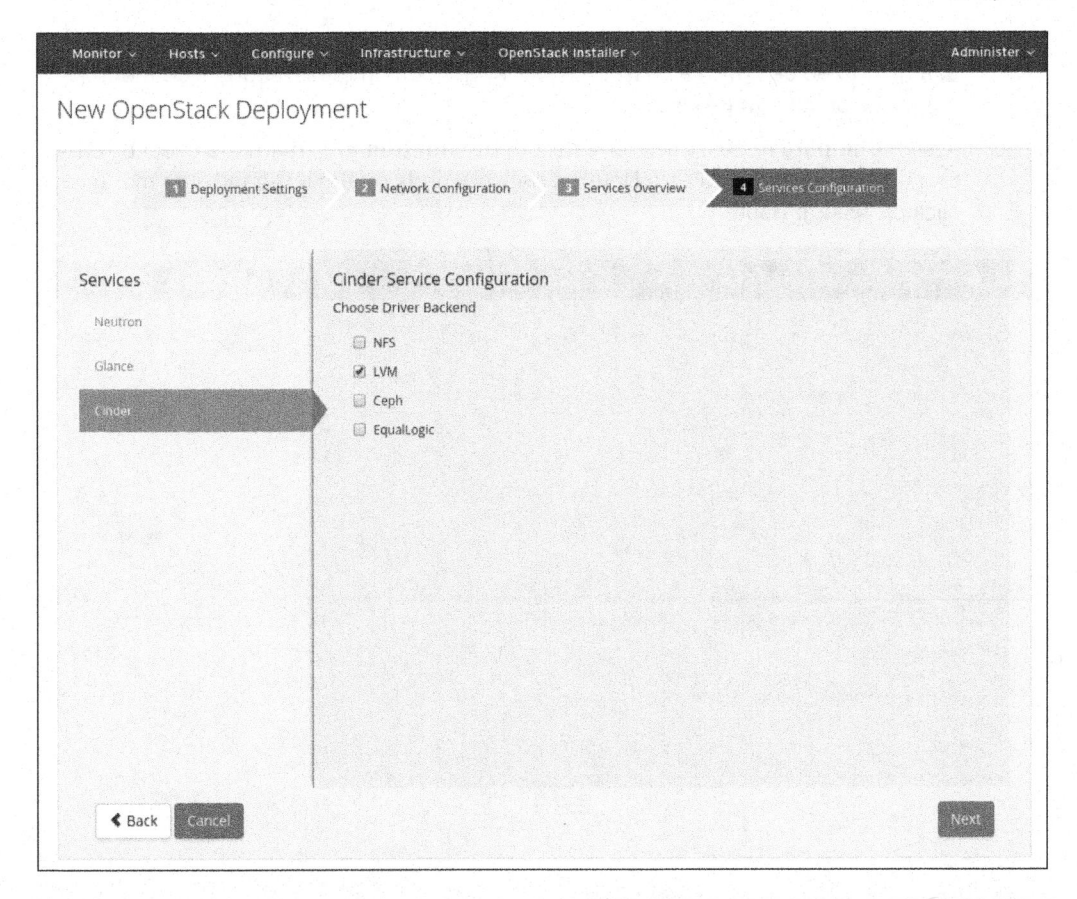

Allocating hosts to roles

After we have set the services' configuration options, we need to assign hosts to the deployments roles. Staypuft will provision the hosts and will install and configure the OpenStack services based on the roles' association.

Assign hosts to the Controller, Neutron, and Compute roles.

How to do it...

Proceed with the following steps:

1. Assign **Controller** node: Click on **+**, next to the **Controller** role, mark the checkbox next to a host to be deployed as a controller node on the left-hand side menu, and click on **Assign Hosts**.

Deploying OpenStack Using Staypuft OpenStack Installer

2. Assign **Neutron** node: Click on **+**, next to the **Neutron** role, mark the checkbox next to a host to be deployed as a Neutron network node on the left-hand side menu, and click on **Assign Hosts**.

3. Assign **Compute** nodes: Click on **+** next to the **Neutron** role, mark the checkbox next to a host to be deployed as a Neutron network node on the left-hand side menu, and click on **Assign Hosts**.

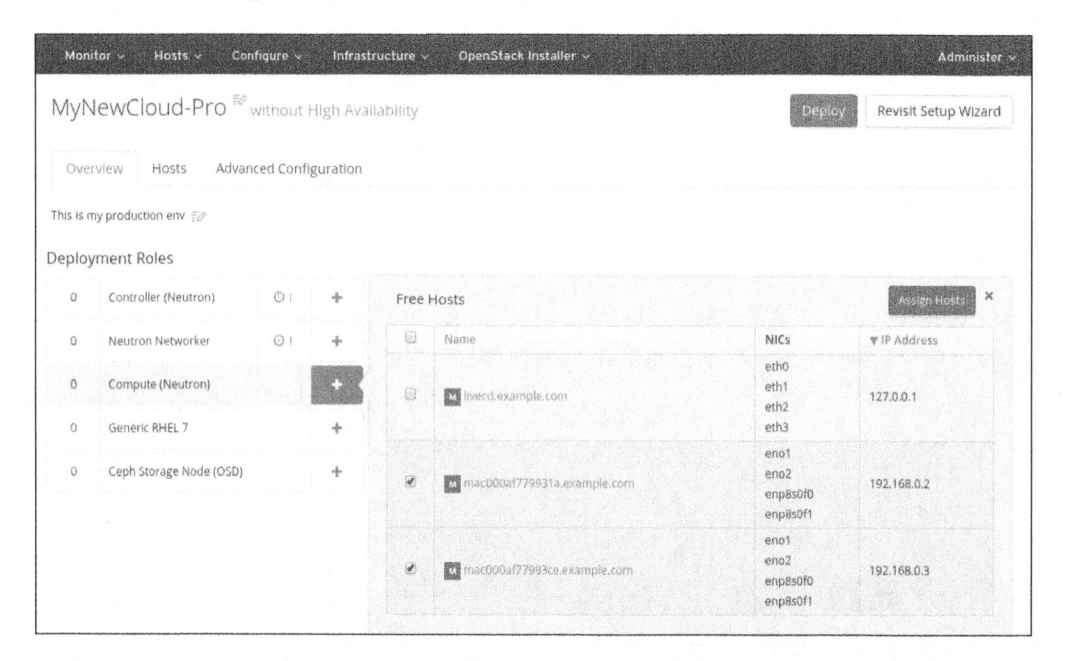

Configuring host networking

After assigning hosts to their roles, we can configure the hosts' network interfaces. We will assign network interfaces to their appropriate subnets.

How to do it...

Proceed with the following steps:

1. Select the **Hosts** tab and click on **Assigned**.

2. Mark the checkbox next to the **Controller** node. Click on **Configure Networks**, and a pop up will appear. Drag the external network to the appropriate network interface and click on **Done**.

3. Mark the checkbox next to the **Neutron** node; click on **Configure Networks**; drag the external network to the appropriate network interface; then, drag the Tenant network to an appropriate network interface; and click on **Done**.

4. Mark the checkbox next to the **Compute** nodes, click on **Configure Networks**; drag the Tenant network to appropriate network interface; and click on **Done**.

Name	Deployment Role	CPUs (cores)	Memory (GB)	NICs	IP Address
mac000af77993ce.example.com	Compute (Neutron)			eno1 eno2 enp8s0f0 enp8s0f1	192.168.0.3
mac000af779931a.example.com	Compute (Neutron)			eno1 eno2 enp8s0f0 enp8s0f1	192.168.0.2
mac000af779932a.example.com	Controller (Neutron)			eno1 eno2 enp8s0f0 enp8s0f1	192.168.0.5
mac000af7799318.example.com	Neutron Networker			eno1 eno2 enp8s0f0 enp8s0f1	192.168.0.4

5. After selecting the nodes, drag and drop the networks to their corresponding network interfaces.

Configure Networks

Configured Networks

- **external** — External + Public API
- **tenant** — Tenant

Network Interfaces

enp8s0f0
- **default** — Provisioning/PXE + Management + Cluster Management + Admin API + Storage + Storage Clustering

eno1
- **tenant** — Tenant

eno2
- **external** — External + Public API

enp8s0f1

[Cancel] [Done]

Deploying OpenStack

At this point, the deployment configuration is ready, and we can proceed to deploy our OpenStack Cloud.

Chapter 2

How to do it...

Proceed with the following steps:

Go to **Overview**, and when ready, click on **Deploy** on the upper right-hand side coroner. A popup will appear with the deployment overview, click on **Deploy** to begin the deployment.

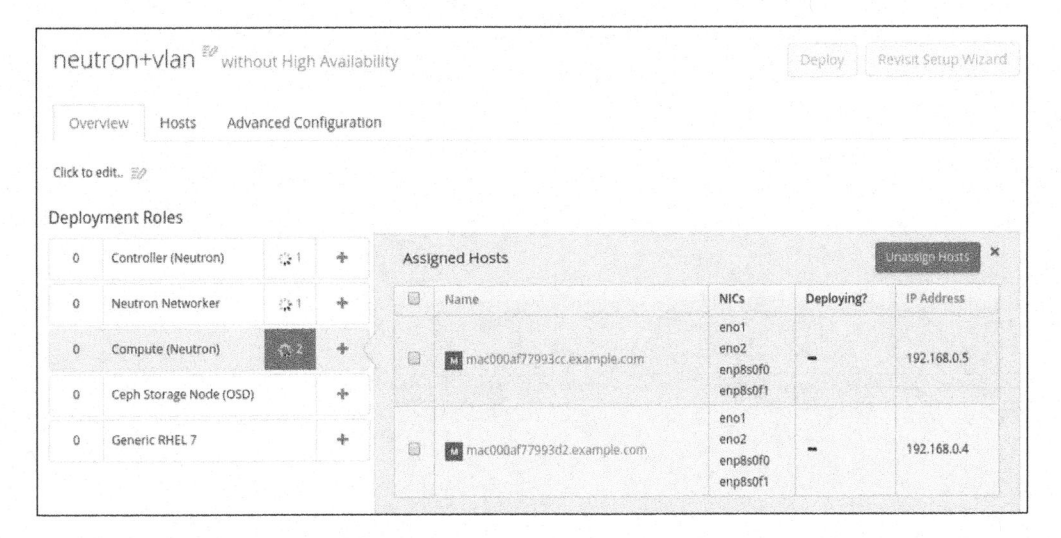

Verifying successful installation

When the deployment is successfully completed, a confirmation message will appear on the screen. To verify a successful deployment, click on, and navigate to the **Horizon URL**.

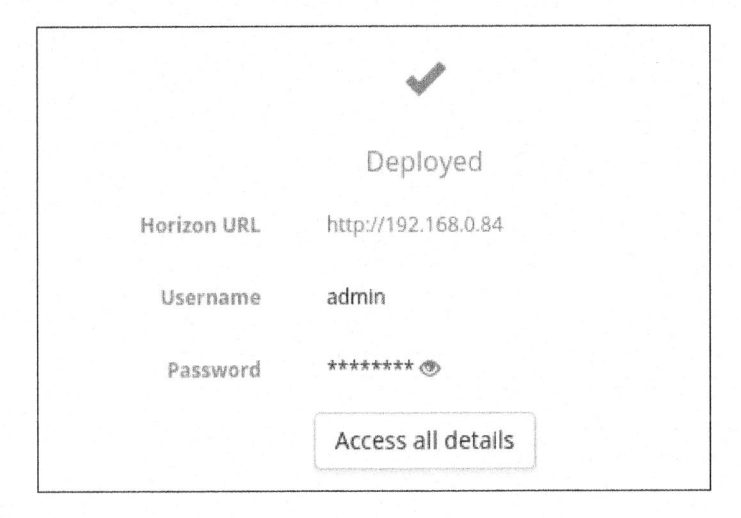

3
Deploying Highly Available OpenStack

In this chapter, we will cover the following:

- Installing Pacemaker
- Installing HAProxy
- Configuring Galera cluster for MariaDB
- Installing RabbitMQ with mirrored queues
- Configuring highly available OpenStack services

Introduction

Many organizations choose OpenStack for its distributed architecture and ability to deliver the **Infrastructure as a Service** (**IaaS**) platform for mission-critical applications. In such environments, it is crucial to configure all OpenStack services in a highly available configuration to provide as much possible uptime for the control plane services of the cloud. Deploying a highly available control plane for OpenStack can be achieved in various configurations. Each of these configurations would serve a certain set of demands and introduce a growing set of prerequisites.

This chapter expands the OpenStack services configuration described in *Chapter 1, Introduction to OpenStack and its Deployment Using Packages*, and discusses how to configure each of the OpenStack services, database, and message broker in a highly available configuration. Pacemaker is used to create active-active clusters to guarantee services' resilience to possible faults. Pacemaker is also used to create a virtual IP addresses for each of the services. HAProxy serves as a load balancer for incoming calls to service APIs.

Deploying Highly Available OpenStack

[> This chapter discusses neither the high availably of virtual machine instances nor Nova-Compute service of the hypervisor.]

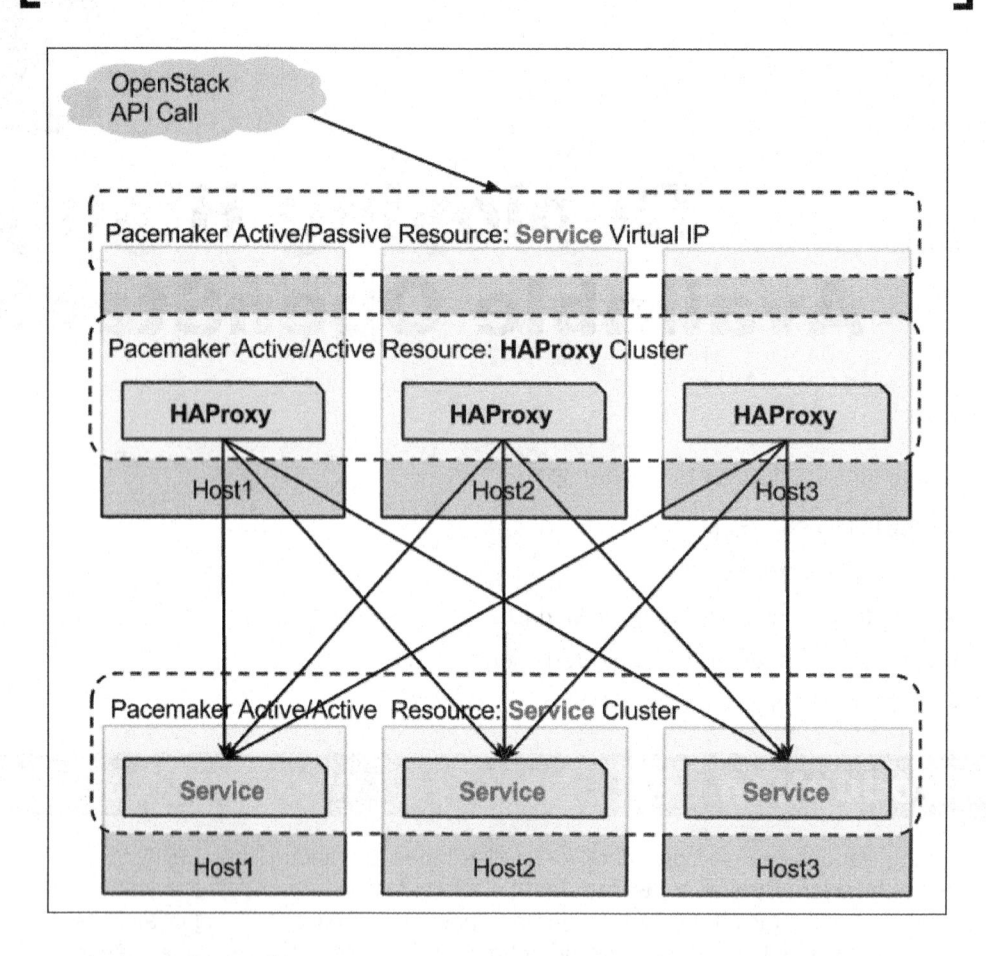

Most of the OpenStack services are stateless. OpenStack services store persistently in a SQL database, which is potentially a single point of failure we should make highly available. In this chapter, we will deploy a highly available database using MariaDB and Galera, which implements multimaster replication. To ensure availability of the message bus, we will configure RabbitMQ with mirrored queues.

This chapter discusses configuring each service separately on three controllers' layout that runs OpenStack controller services, including Neutron, database, and RabbitMQ message bus. All can be configured on several controller nodes, or each service could be implemented on its separate set of hosts.

Installing Pacemaker

All OpenStack services consist of system Linux services. The first step of ensuring services' availability is to configure Pacemaker clusters for each service, so Pacemaker monitors the services. In case of failure, Pacemaker restarts the failed service. In addition, we will use Pacemaker to create a virtual IP address for each of OpenStack's services to ensure services are accessible using the same IP address when failures occurs and the actual service has relocated to another host.

In this section, we will install Pacemaker and prepare it to configure highly available OpenStack services.

Getting ready

To ensure maximum availability, we will install and configure three hosts to serve as controller nodes. Prepare three controller hosts with identical hardware and network layouts. We will base our configuration for most of the OpenStack services on the configuration used in a single controller layout, and we will deploy Neutron network services on all three controller nodes.

How to do it...

Run the following steps on three highly available controller nodes:

1. Install `pacemaker` packages:

   ```
   [root@controller1 ~]# yum install -y pcs pacemaker corosync fence-agents-all resource-agents
   ```

2. Enable and start the `pcsd` service:

   ```
   [root@controller1 ~]# systemctl enable pcsd
   [root@controller1 ~]# systemctl start pcsd
   ```

3. Set a password for `hacluster` user; the password should be identical on all the nodes:

   ```
   [root@controller1 ~]# echo 'password' | passwd --stdin hacluster
   ```

   > We will use the `hacluster` password through the HAProxy configuration.

Deploying Highly Available OpenStack

4. Authenticate all controller nodes running using `-p` option to give the password on the command line, and provide the same password you have set in the previous step:

   ```
   [root@controller1 ~] # pcs cluster auth controller1 controller2 controller3 -u hacluster -p password --force
   ```

   > At this point, you may run `pcs` commands from a single controller node instead of running commands on each node separately.

There's more...

You may find the complete Pacemaker documentation, which includes installation documentation, complete configuration reference, and examples on Cluster Labs website at http://clusterlabs.org/doc/.

Installing HAProxy

Addressing high availability for OpenStack includes avoiding high load of a single host and ensuring incoming TCP connections to all API endpoints are balanced across the controller hosts. We will use HAProxy, an open source load balancer, which is particularly suited for HTTP load balancing as it supports session persistence and layer 7 processing.

Getting ready

In this section, we will install HAProxy on all controller hosts, configure Pacemaker cluster for HAproxy services, and prepare for OpenStack services configuration.

How to do it...

Run the following steps on all controller nodes:

1. Install HAProxy package:

   ```
   # yum install -y haproxy
   ```

2. Enable nonlocal binding Kernel parameter:

   ```
   # echo net.ipv4.ip_nonlocal_bind=1 >> /etc/sysctl.d/haproxy.conf
   # echo 1 > /proc/sys/net/ipv4/ip_nonlocal_bind
   ```

Chapter 3

3. Configure HAProxy load balancer settings for the GaleraDB, RabbitMQ, and Keystone service, as shown in the following diagram:

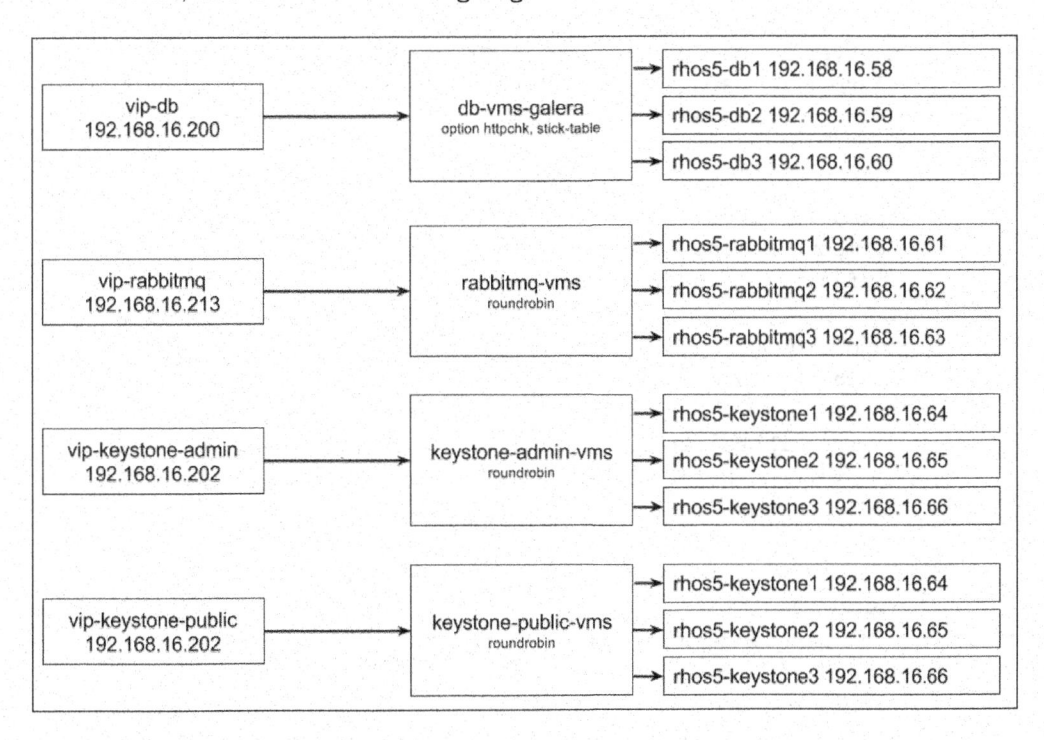

```
vip-db                    db-vms-galera           → rhos5-db1 192.168.16.58
192.168.16.200    →    option httpchk, stick-table  → rhos5-db2 192.168.16.59
                                                  → rhos5-db3 192.168.16.60

                                                  → rhos5-rabbitmq1 192.168.16.61
vip-rabbitmq             rabbitmq-vms             → rhos5-rabbitmq2 192.168.16.62
192.168.16.213    →    roundrobin                 → rhos5-rabbitmq3 192.168.16.63

                                                  → rhos5-keystone1 192.168.16.64
vip-keystone-admin       keystone-admin-vms       → rhos5-keystone2 192.168.16.65
192.168.16.202    →    roundrobin                 → rhos5-keystone3 192.168.16.66

                                                  → rhos5-keystone1 192.168.16.64
vip-keystone-public      keystone-public-vms      → rhos5-keystone2 192.168.16.65
192.168.16.202    →    roundrobin                 → rhos5-keystone3 192.168.16.66
```

4. Edit `/etc/haproxy/haproxy.cfg` with the following configuration:

```
global
    daemon
defaults
    mode tcp
    maxconn 10000
    timeout connect 2s
    timeout client 10s
    timeout server 10s

frontend vip-db
    bind 192.168.16.200:3306
    timeout client 90s
    default_backend db-vms-galera

backend db-vms-galera
    option httpchk
```

```
            stick-table type ip size 2
            stick on dst
            timeout server 90s
            server rhos5-db1 192.168.16.58:3306 check inter 1s port 9200
            server rhos5-db2 192.168.16.59:3306 check inter 1s port 9200
            server rhos5-db3 192.168.16.60:3306 check inter 1s port 9200

        frontend vip-rabbitmq
            bind 192.168.16.213:5672
            timeout client 900m
            default_backend rabbitmq-vms

        backend rabbitmq-vms
            balance roundrobin
            timeout server 900m
            server rhos5-rabbitmq1 192.168.16.61:5672 check inter 1s
            server rhos5-rabbitmq2 192.168.16.62:5672 check inter 1s
            server rhos5-rabbitmq3 192.168.16.63:5672 check inter 1s

        frontend vip-keystone-admin
            bind 192.168.16.202:35357
            default_backend keystone-admin-vms
        backend keystone-admin-vms
            balance roundrobin
            server rhos5-keystone1 192.168.16.64:35357 check inter 1s
            server rhos5-keystone2 192.168.16.65:35357 check inter 1s
            server rhos5-keystone3 192.168.16.66:35357 check inter 1s

        frontend vip-keystone-public
            bind 192.168.16.202:5000
            default_backend keystone-public-vms
        backend keystone-public-vms
            balance roundrobin
            server rhos5-keystone1 192.168.16.64:5000 check inter 1s
            server rhos5-keystone2 192.168.16.65:5000 check inter 1s
            server rhos5-keystone3 192.168.16.66:5000 check inter 1s
```

> This configuration file is an example for configuring HAProxy with load balancer for the MariaDB, RabbitMQ, and Keystone service.

5. We need to authenticate on all nodes before we are allowed to change the configuration to configure all nodes from one point. Use the previously configured `hacluster` user and password to do this.

   # pcs cluster auth controller1 controller2 controller3 -u hacluster -p password --force

6. Create a Pacemaker cluster for HAPRoxy service as follows:

   Note that you can run `pcs` commands now from a single controller node.

   # pcs cluster setup --name ha-controller controller1 controller2 controller3
   # pcs cluster enable --all
   # pcs cluster start --all

7. Finally, using `pcs resource create` command, create a cloned `systemd` resource that will run a highly available active-active HAProxy service on all controller hosts:

   pcs resource create lb-haproxy systemd:haproxy op monitor start-delay=10s --clone

8. Create the virtual IP address for each of the services:

   # pcs resource create vip-db IPaddr2 ip=192.168.16.200
   # pcs resource create vip-rabbitmq IPaddr2 ip=192.168.16.213
   # pcs resource create vip-keystone IPaddr2 ip=192.168.16.202

9. You may use `pcs status` command to verify whether all resources are successfully running:

   # pcs status

Configuring Galera cluster for MariaDB

Galera is a multimaster cluster for MariaDB, which is based on synchronous replication between all cluster nodes. Effectively, Galera treats a cluster of MariaDB nodes as one single master node that reads and writes to all nodes. Galera replication happens at transaction commit time, by broadcasting the transaction write set to the cluster for application. Client connects directly to the DBMS and experiences close to the native DBMS behavior. **write set replication** (**wsrep**) API defines the interface between Galera replication and the DBMS:

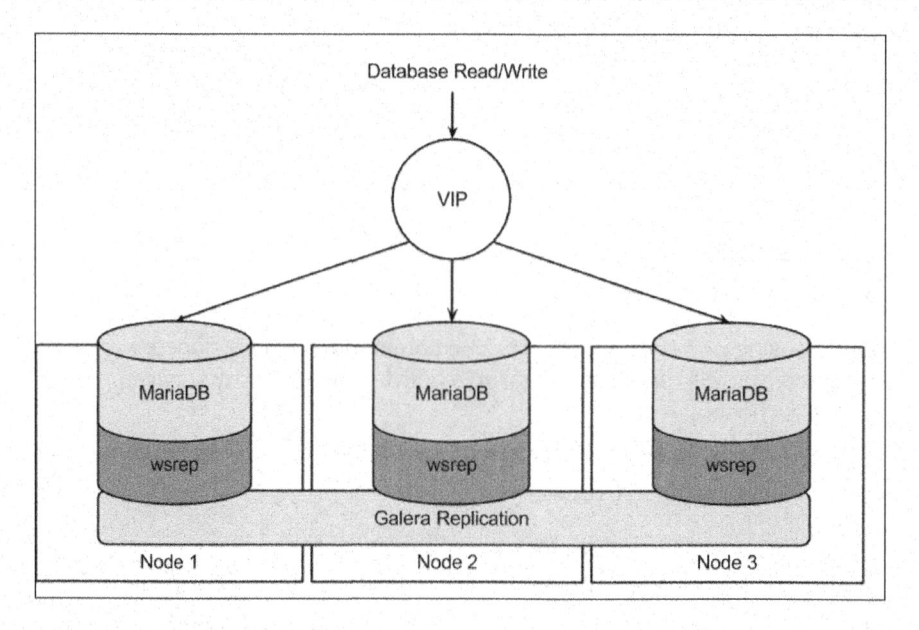

Getting ready

In this section, we will install Galera cluster packages for MariaDB on our three controller nodes, then we will configure Pacemaker to monitor all Galera services.

Pacemaker can be stopped on all cluster nodes, as shown, if it is running from the previous steps:

```
# pcs cluster stop --all
```

How to do it...

Perform the following steps on all controller nodes:

1. Install `galera` packages for MariaDB:

    ```
    # yum install -y mariadb-galera-server xinetd resource-agents
    ```

Chapter 3

2. Edit `/etc/sysconfig/clustercheck` and add the following lines:

   ```
   MYSQL_USERNAME="clustercheck"
   MYSQL_PASSWORD="password"
   MYSQL_HOST="localhost"
   MYSQL_PORT="3306"
   ```

3. Edit Galera configuration file `/etc/my.cnf.d/galera.cnf` with the following lines:

   > Make sure to enter host's IP address at the `bind-address` parameter.

   ```
   [mysqld]
   skip-name-resolve=1
   binlog_format=ROW
   default-storage-engine=innodb
   innodb_autoinc_lock_mode=2
   innodb_locks_unsafe_for_binlog=1
   query_cache_size=0
   query_cache_type=0
   bind-address=[host-IP-address]
   wsrep_provider=/usr/lib64/galera/libgalera_smm.so
   wsrep_cluster_name="galera_cluster"
   wsrep_slave_threads=1
   wsrep_certify_nonPK=1
   wsrep_max_ws_rows=131072
   wsrep_max_ws_size=1073741824
   wsrep_debug=0
   wsrep_convert_LOCK_to_trx=0
   wsrep_retry_autocommit=1
   wsrep_auto_increment_control=1
   wsrep_drupal_282555_workaround=0
   wsrep_causal_reads=0
   wsrep_notify_cmd=
   wsrep_sst_method=rsync
   ```

   > You can learn more on each of the Galera's default options on the documentation page at `http://galeracluster.com/documentation-webpages/configuration.html`.

4. Add the following lines to the `xinetd` configuration file `/etc/xinetd.d/galera-monitor`:

```
service galera-monitor
{
        port            = 9200
        disable         = no
        socket_type     = stream
        protocol        = tcp
        wait            = no
        user            = root
        group           = root
        groups          = yes
        server          = /usr/bin/clustercheck
        type            = UNLISTED
        per_source      = UNLIMITED
        log_on_success  =
        log_on_failure  = HOST
        flags           = REUSE
}
```

5. Start and enable the `xinetd` service:

```
# systemctl enable xinetd
# systemctl start xinetd
# systemctl enable pcsd
# systemctl start pcsd
```

6. Authenticate on all nodes. Use the previously configured `hacluster` user and password to do this as follows:

```
# pcs cluster auth controller1 controller2 controller3 -u hacluster -p password --force
```

> Now commands can be run from a single controller node.

7. Create a Pacemaker cluster for the Galera service:

```
# pcs cluster setup --name controller-db controller1 controller2 controller3
# pcs cluster enable --all
# pcs cluster start --all
```

Chapter 3

8. Add the Galera service resource to the Galera Pacemaker cluster:

   ```
   # pcs resource create galera galera enable_creation=true
   wsrep_cluster_address="gcomm://controller1,controller2,controll
   er3" meta master-max=3 ordered=true op promote timeout=300s on-
   fail=block --master
   ```

9. Create a user for `clustercheck xinetd` service:

   ```
   mysql -e "CREATE USER 'clustercheck'@'localhost' IDENTIFIED BY
   'password';"
   ```

See also

You can find the complete Galera documentation, which includes installation documentation and complete configuration reference and examples in Galera cluster website at `http://galeracluster.com/documentation-webpages/`.

Installing RabbitMQ with mirrored queues

RabbitMQ is used as a message bus for services to inner-communicate. The queues are located on a single node that makes the RabbitMQ service a single point of failure. To avoid RabbitMQ being a single point of failure, we will configure RabbitMQ to use mirrored queues across multiple nodes. Each mirrored queue consists of one master and one or more slaves, with the oldest slave being promoted to the new master, if the old master disappears for any reason. Messages published to the queue are replicated to all slaves.

Getting ready

In this section, we will install RabbitMQ packages on our three controller nodes and configure RabbitMQ to mirror its queues across all controller nodes, then we will configure Pacemaker to monitor all RabbitMQ services.

How to do it...

Perform the following steps on all controller nodes:

1. Install RabbitMQ packages on all controller nodes:

   ```
   # yum -y install rabbitmq-server
   ```

2. Start and enable `rabbitmq-server` service:

   ```
   # systemctl start rabbitmq-server
   # systemctl stop rabbitmq-server
   ```

Deploying Highly Available OpenStack

3. RabbitMQ cluster nodes use a cookie to determine whether they are allowed to communicate with each other; for nodes to be able to communicate, they must have the same cookie. Copy `erlang.cookie` from `controller1` to `controller2` and `controller3`:

    ```
    [root@controller1 ~]# scp /var/lib/rabbitmq/.erlang.cookie
    root@controller2:/var/lib/rabbitmq/
    [root@controller1 ~]## scp /var/lib/rabbitmq/.erlang.cookie
    root@controller3:/var/lib/rabbitmq/
    ```

4. Start and enable Pacemaker on all nodes:

    ```
    # systemctl enable pcsd
    # systemctl start pcsd
    ```

    > Since we already authenticated all nodes of the cluster in the previous section, we can now run following commands on `controller1`.

5. Create a new Pacemaker cluster for RabbitMQ service as follows:

    ```
    [root@controller1 ~]# pcs cluster setup --name rabbitmq controller1 controller2 controller3
    [root@controller1 ~]# pcs cluster enable --all
    [root@controller1 ~]# pcs cluster start --all
    ```

6. To the Pacemaker cluster, add a `systemd` resource for RabbitMQ service:

    ```
    [root@controller1 ~]# pcs resource create rabbitmq-server systemd:rabbitmq-server op monitor start-delay=20s --clone
    ```

7. Since all RabbitMQ nodes must join the cluster one at a time, stop RabbitMQ on `controller2` and `controller3`:

    ```
    [root@controller2 ~]# rabbitmqctl stop_app
    [root@controller3 ~]# rabbitmqctl stop_app
    ```

8. Join `controller2` to the cluster and start RabbitMQ on it:

    ```
    [root@controller2 ~]# rabbitmqctl join_cluster rabbit@controller1
    [root@controller2 ~]# rabbitmqctl start_app
    ```

9. Now join `controller3` to the cluster as well, and start RabbitMQ on it:

    ```
    [root@controller3 ~]# rabbitmqctl join_cluster
    ```

Chapter 3

```
rabbit@controller1
[root@controller3 ~]# rabbitmqctl start_app
```

10. At this point, the cluster should be configured, and we need to set RabbitMQ's HA policy to mirror the queues to all RabbitMQ cluster nodes as follows:

```
[root@controller1 ~]# rabbitmqctl set_policy HA '^(?!amq\.).*'
'{"ha-mode": "all"}'
```

There's more...

The RabbitMQ cluster should be configured with all the queues cloned to all controller nodes. To verify the cluster's state, you can use the `rabbitmqctl cluster_status` and `rabbitmqctl list_policies` commands from each of controller nodes as follows:

```
[root@controller1 ~]# rabbitmqctl cluster_status
[root@controller1 ~]# rabbitmqctl list_policies
```

To verify Pacemaker's cluster status, you may use `pcs` status command as follows:

```
[root@controller1 ~]# pcs status
```

See also

For a complete documentation on how RabbitMQ implements the mirrored queues feature any additional configuration options, you can refer to project's documentation pages at https://www.rabbitmq.com/clustering.html and https://www.rabbitmq.com/ha.html.

Configuring highly available OpenStack services

Most OpenStack services are stateless web services that keep persistent data on a SQL database and use a message bus for inner-service communication. We will use Pacemaker and HAProxy to run OpenStack services in an active-active highly available configuration, so traffic for each of the services is load balanced across all controller nodes and cloud can be easily scaled out to more controller nodes if needed. We will configure Pacemaker clusters for each of the services that will run on all controller nodes. We will also use Pacemaker to create a virtual IP addresses for each of OpenStack's services, so rather than addressing a specific node, services will be addressed by their corresponding virtual IP address. We will use HAProxy to load balance incoming requests to the services across all controller nodes.

Deploying Highly Available OpenStack

Get ready

In this section, we will use the virtual IP address we created for the services with Pacemaker and HAProxy in previous sections. We will also configure OpenStack services to use the highly available Galera-clustered database, and RabbitMQ with mirrored queues.

This is an example for the Keystone service.

How to do it...

Perform the following steps on all controller nodes:

1. Install the Keystone service on all controller nodes:

   ```
   yum install -y openstack-keystone openstack-utils
   openstack-selinux
   ```

2. Generate a Keystone service token on `controller1` and copy it to `controller2` and `controller3` using `scp`:

   ```
   [root@controller1 ~]# export SERVICE_TOKEN=$(openssl rand -hex 10)
   [root@controller1 ~]# echo $SERVICE_TOKEN > ~/keystone_admin_token
   [root@controller1 ~]# scp ~/keystone_admin_token root@controller2:~/keystone_admin_token
   [root@controller1 ~]# scp ~/keystone_admin_token root@controller3:~/keystone_admin_token
   ```

3. Export the Keystone service token on `controller2` and `controller3` as well:

   On `controller2` and `controller3`

   ```
   [root@controller2 ~]# export SERVICE_TOKEN=$(cat ~/keystone_admin_token)
   [root@controller3 ~]# export SERVICE_TOKEN=$(cat ~/keystone_admin_token)
   ```

   > Perform the following commands on all controller nodes.

4. Configure the `keystone` service on all controller nodes to use `vip-rabbit`:

   ```
   # openstack-config --set /etc/keystone/keystone.conf DEFAULT admin_token $SERVICE_TOKEN
   # openstack-config --set /etc/keystone/keystone.conf DEFAULT rabbit_host vip-rabbitmq
   ```

5. Configure the `keystone` service endpoints to point to Keystone virtual IP:

   ```
   # openstack-config --set /etc/keystone/keystone.conf DEFAULT admin_endpoint 'http://vip-keystone:%(admin_port)s/'
   # openstack-config --set /etc/keystone/keystone.conf DEFAULT public_endpoint 'http://vip-keystone:%(public_port)s/'
   ```

6. Configure `keystone` to connect to the SQL databases; use the Galera cluster virtual IP:

   ```
   # openstack-config --set /etc/keystone/keystone.conf database connection mysql://keystone:keystonetest@vip-mysql/keystone
   # openstack-config --set /etc/keystone/keystone.conf database max_retries -1
   ```

7. On `controller1`, create Keystone KPI and sync the database:

   ```
   [root@controller1 ~]# keystone-manage pki_setup --keystone-user keystone --keystone-group keystone
   [root@controller1 ~]# chown -R keystone:keystone /var/log/keystone    /etc/keystone/ssl/
   [root@controller1 ~] su keystone -s /bin/sh -c "keystone-manage db_sync"
   ```

8. Using `scp`, copy Keystone SSL certificates from `controller1` to `controller2` and `controller3`:

   ```
   [root@controller1 ~]# rsync -av /etc/keystone/ssl/ controller2:/etc/keystone/ssl/
   [root@controller1 ~]# rsync -av /etc/keystone/ssl/ controller3:/etc/keystone/ssl/
   ```

9. Make sure that Keystone user is the owner of newly copied files `controller2` and `controller3`:

   ```
   [root@controller2 ~]# chown -R keystone:keystone /etc/keystone/ssl/
   [root@controller3 ~]# chown -R keystone:keystone /etc/keystone/ssl/
   ```

10. Create a `systemd` resource for the Keystone service, use `--clone` to ensure it runs with active-active configuration:

    ```
    [root@controller1 ~]# pcs resource create keystone
    systemd:openstack-keystone op monitor start-delay=10s --clone
    ```

11. Create endpoint and user accounts for Keystone with the Keystone VIP as given:

    ```
    [root@controller1 ~]# export SERVICE_ENDPOINT="http://vip-keystone:35357/v2.0"
    ```

    ```
    [root@controller1 ~]# keystone service-create --name=keystone
    --type=identity --description="Keystone Identity Service"
    ```

    ```
    [root@controller1 ~]# keystone endpoint-create --service keystone
    --publicurl 'http://vip-keystone:5000/v2.0' --adminurl 'http://
    vip-keystone:35357/v2.0' --internalurl 'http://vip-keystone:5000/
    v2.0'
    ```

    ```
    [root@controller1 ~]# keystone user-create --name admin --pass
    keystonetest
    [root@controller1 ~]# keystone role-create --name admin
    [root@controller1 ~]# keystone tenant-create --name admin
    [root@controller1 ~]# keystone user-role-add --user admin --role
    admin --tenant admin
    ```

12. Create all controller nodes on a `keystonerc_admin` file with OpenStack admin credentials using the Keystone VIP:

    ```
    cat > ~/keystonerc_admin << EOF
    export OS_USERNAME=admin
    export OS_TENANT_NAME=admin
    export OS_PASSWORD=password
    export OS_AUTH_URL=http://vip-keystone:35357/v2.0/
    export PS1='[\u@\h \W(keystone_admin)]\$ '
    EOF
    ```

13. Source the `keystonerc_admin` credentials file to be able to run the authenticated OpenStack commands:

    ```
    [root@controller1 ~]# source ~/keystonerc_admin
    ```

14. At this point, you should be able to execute the Keystone commands and create the `Services` tenant:

    ```
    [root@controller1 ~]# keystone tenant-create --name services
    --description "Services Tenant"
    ```

See also

A complete highly available OpenStack deployment includes Keystone, Nova, Glance, and Horizon. See appendix on Packt's website for complete configurations for all of the services' URLs.

4
Keystone Identity Service

In this chapter, we will cover the following:

- Configuring Keystone with the MariaDB backend
- Generating and configuring tokens PKIs
- Configuring Keystone with Microsoft Active Directory and LDAP
- Configuring Keystone caching with Memcached
- Securing Keystone with SSL

Introduction

Keystone is an OpenStack project that provides Identity as a service to OpenStack services and components. Keystone is responsible for authenticating users and services, and authorizing access to OpenStack components.

Keystone also provides a service catalog that users and other services can query to discover the services OpenStack provides. For each service, Keystone Catalog returns an endpoint that is a network-accessible URL from where users and services can access a certain service.

Keystone, by default, runs under a built-in Eventlet Python service, but it can be configured to run under the Apache httpd service that provides better security and scalability.

Keystone Identity Service

Keystone services are as follows:

- **keystone-all** service implements both the API and middleware that invokes Identity services from a backend Identity provider, which could be the native OpenStack database server, an LDAP server, or Microsoft Active Directory. Keystone service exposes endpoints of all services that are network-accessible URL addresses through which the various OpenStack services are accessible.

- Keystone configuration file are as follows:

    /etc/keystone/keystone.conf ini formatted configuration file is the main Keystone configuration file, which contains the following sections:

    - [DEFAULT]: General configuration
    - [assignment]: Assignment system driver configuration
    - [auth]: Authentication plugin configuration
    - [cache]: Caching layer configuration
    - [catalog]: Service catalog driver configuration
    - [credential]: Credential system driver configuration
    - [endpoint_filter]: Endpoint filtering extension configuration
    - [endpoint_policy]: Endpoint policy extension configuration
    - [federation]: Federation driver configuration
    - [identity]: Identity system driver configuration
    - [identity_mapping]: Identity mapping system driver configuration
    - [kvs]: KVS storage backend configuration
    - [ldap]: LDAP configuration options
    - [memcache]: Memcache configuration options
    - [oauth1]: OAuth 1.0a system driver configuration
    - [os_inherit]: Inherited role assignment extension
    - [paste_deploy]: Pointer to the PasteDeploy configuration file
    - [policy]: Policy system driver configuration for RBAC
    - [revoke]: Revocation system driver configuration
    - [saml]: SAML configuration options
    - [signing]: Cryptographic signatures for PKI based tokens
    - [ssl]: SSL configuration
    - [token]: Token driver & token provider configuration
    - [trust]: Trust extension configuration

- /etc/keystone/keystone.<domain_name>.conf starting with the Juno release, Keystone allows you to configure an Identity driver for specific domains.

Configuring Keystone with the MariaDB backend

Keystone is responsible for user authentication and authorizing access to the OpenStack components if the authenticated user has the appropriate permissions. In this section, we will configure Keystone to use MariaDB database as a local user accounts directory, so Keystone stores user accounts information on the database.

Getting ready

Before you configure Keystone, we need to prepare the database for Keystone to use, configure its user permissions, and open the needed firewall ports so that other nodes would be able to communicate with it. Keystone is usually installed on the controller node as part of OpenStack's control plane.

Create Keystone database

To create a database for Keystone, use the MySQL command to access the MariaDB instance. This will ask you to type the password that you selected for MariaDB root user:

```
[root@controller ~]# mysql -u root -p
```

Create a database named `keystone`:

```
MariaDB [(none)]> CREATE DATABASE keystone;
```

Create a user account named `keystone` with the selected password instead of `my_password`:

```
MariaDB [(none)]> GRANT ALL ON keystone.* TO 'keystone'@'%'
IDENTIFIED BY 'my_keystone_db_password';
```

Grant access for `keystone` user account to the `keystone` database:

```
MariaDB [(none)]> GRANT ALL ON keystone.* TO 'keystone'@'localhost'
IDENTIFIED BY 'my_keystone_db_password';
```

Flush database privileges to ensure that they are effective immediately:

```
MariaDB [(none)]> FLUSH PRIVILEGES;
```

At this point, you can exit the MariaDB client:

```
MariaDB [(none)]> quit
```

Keystone Identity Service

Open Keystone service Firewall ports

Keystone service uses port *5000* for public access and port *35357* for administration, which is indicated as follows:

```
[root@controller ~]# firewall-cmd --add-port=5000/tcp --permanent
[root@controller ~]# firewall-cmd --add-port=35357/tcp --permanent
```

How to do it...

Proceed with the following steps:

Install service packages

By now, all OpenStack's prerequisites, including a database service and a message broker, should be installed and configured. This is the first OpenStack service we install. First, we need to install the package, then to configure, enable, and start it.

1. Install the `rdo-release` package, which configures RDO repos in `/etc/yum.repos.d`:

   ```
   [root@controller ~]# yum install -y https://rdoproject.org/repos/rdo-release.rpm
   ```

2. Install Keystone package using the `yum` command:

   ```
   [root@controller ~]# yum install -y openstack-keystone
   ```

   > Installing Keystone will also install Python-supporting packages and additional packages for more advanced backend configurations.

Configure database connection

Keystone's database connection string is set in `/etc/keystone/keystone.conf`, we can use `#openstack-config` command to configure the connection string.

1. Run the `openstack-config` command on the controller node with your chosen Keystone database user details and database IP address:

   ```
   [root@controller ~]# openstack-config --set
   /etc/keystone/keystone.conf     sql connection
    mysql://keystone:'my_keystone_db_password'@10.10.0.1/keystone
   ```

2. After the database is configured, we can create the Keystone database tables using the `db_sync` command:

   `[root@controller ~]# su keystone -s /bin/sh -c "keystone-manage db_sync"`

Keystone service basic configuration

Before starting the Keystone service, we need to make some initial service configuration for it to start properly.

Configure administrative token

Run the following steps to configure the administrative token:

1. Keystone can use a token by which it will identify the administrative user. We can set a custom token or use the `openssl` command to generate a random token:

   `[root@controller ~]# export SERVICE_TOKEN=$(openssl rand -hex 10)`

2. We can store the token in a file for use in further steps:

   `[root@controller ~]# echo $SERVICE_TOKEN > ~/keystone_admin_token`

   We need to configure Keystone to use the token we created. We can manually edit the Keystone configuration file `/etc/keystone/keystone.conf` and manually remove the comment mark # next to `admin_token` or we can use the command `openstack-config` to set the needed property.

   > The `openstack-config` command is provided by `# yum install openstack-utils`.

3. Use `openstack-config` command to configure the `service_token` parameter:

   `[root@controller ~]# openstack-config --set /etc/keystone/keystone.conf DEFAULT admin_token $SERVICE_TOKEN`

Generating and configuring tokens PKIs

Keystone uses cryptographically signed tokens with a private key and are matched against x509 certificate with public key. *Chatper 5, Glance Image Service* discusses advanced configurations. In this recipe, we will use `keystone-manage pki_setup` command to generate PKI key pairs and configure Keystone to use it.

How to do it...

Proceed with the following steps:

1. Generate PKI keys using the `keystone-manage pki_setup` command:

   ```
   [root@controller ~]# keystone-manage pki_setup --keystone-user keystone --keystone-group keystone
   ```

   > In `keystone-manage pki_setup`, we use Keystone Linux user and group accounts, which were created when `openstack-keystone` packaged was installed.

2. Change the ownership of the generated PKI files:

   ```
   [root@controller ~]# chown -R keystone:keystone /var/log/keystone /etc/keystone/ssl/
   ```

3. Configure Keystone service to use the generated PKI files:

   ```
   [root@controller ~]# openstack-config --set /etc/keystone/keystone.conf signing token_format PKI
   [root@controller ~]# openstack-config --set /etc/keystone/keystone.conf signing certfile /etc/keystone/ssl/certs/signing_cert.pem
   [root@controller ~]# openstack-config --set /etc/keystone/keystone.conf signing keyfile /etc/keystone/ssl/private/signing_key.pem
   [root@controller ~]# openstack-config --set /etc/keystone/keystone.conf signing ca_certs /etc/keystone/ssl/certs/ca.pem
   [root@controller ~]# openstack-config --set /etc/keystone/keystone.conf signing key_size 1024
   [root@controller ~]# openstack-config --set /etc/keystone/keystone.conf signing valid_days 3650
   [root@controller ~]# openstack-config --set /etc/keystone/keystone.conf signing ca_password None
   ```

Start and enable service

1. At this point, Keystone is configured and readily run:

   ```
   [root@controller ~]# systemctl start openstack-keystone
   ```

2. Enable Keystone to start after the system's reboot:

   ```
   [root@controller ~]# systemctl enable openstack-keystone
   ```

Configuring Keystone endpoints

We need to configure a Keystone service endpoint for other services to operate properly as follows:

1. Set the SERVICE_TOKEN environment parameter using the keystone_admin_token we generated on basic Keystone configuration step:

   ```
   [root@controller ~]# export SERVICE_TOKEN=`cat ~/keystone_admin_token`
   ```

2. Set the SERVICE_ENDPOINT environment parameter with Keystone's endpoint URL using your controller's IP address:

   ```
   [root@controller ~]# export SERVICE_ENDPOINT="http://10.10.0.1:35357/v2.0"
   ```

3. Create a Keystone service entry:

   ```
   [root@el7-icehouse-controller ~]# keystone service-create --name=keystone --type=identity --description="Keystone Identity service"
   ```

   An output of a successful execution should look similar to the following, with a different unique ID:

   ```
   +-------------+----------------------------------+
   |   Property  |              Value               |
   +-------------+----------------------------------+
   | description |     Keystone Identity service    |
   |   enabled   |               True               |
   |      id     | 1fa0e426e1ba464d95d16c6df0899047 |
   |     name    |             keystone             |
   |     type    |             identity             |
   +-------------+----------------------------------+
   ```

   endpoint-create command allows setting different IP address that are accessible from public, and from Internal sources, at this point we will use our controller's management NIC IP to access Keystone endpoint.

4. Create Keystone service endpoint using the keystone endpoint-create command:

   ```
   [root@controller ~]# keystone endpoint-create
   --service keystone
   --publicurl 'http://10.10.0.1:5000/v2.0'
   ```

Keystone Identity Service

```
--adminurl 'http://10.10.0.1:35357/v2.0'
--internalurl 'http://10.10.0.1:5000/v2.0'
```

5. Create `services` tenant:

   ```
   [root@controller ~(keystone_admin)]# keystone tenant-create
   --name services --description "Services Tenant"
   ```

Keystone administrator account

1. Create an administrative account within Keystone :

   ```
   [root@controller ~]# keystone user-create --name admin --pass password
   ```

2. Create the `admin` role:

   ```
   [root@controller ~]# keystone role-create --name admin
   ```

3. Create an `admin` tenant:

   ```
   [root@controller ~]# keystone tenant-create --name admin
   ```

4. Add the `admin` user, an `admin` roles, and the `admin` tenant:

   ```
   [root@el7-icehouse-controller ~]# keystone user-role-add
   --user admin --role admin --tenant admin
   ```

5. Create `keystonerc_admin` file, with the following content:

   ```
   [root@controller ~]# cat ~/keystonerc_admin
   export OS_USERNAME=admin
   export OS_TENANT_NAME=admin
   export OS_PASSWORD=password
   export OS_AUTH_URL=http://10.10.0.1:35357/v2.0/
   export PS1='[\u@\h \W(keystone_admin)]\$ '
   ```

6. To load the environment variables, run the `source` command:

   ```
   [root@controller ~]# source keystonerc_admin
   ```

Keystone user account

While providing users with access to OpenStack tenants, the provided user accounts should not be administrative accounts. We recommend you to create an unprivileged user account that has no administration permissions on our OpenStack environment.

Follow these steps to create an unprivileged user account:

1. Create the user account in Keystone:

   ```
   [root@controller ~(keystone_admin)]# keystone user-create
   --name USER --pass password
   ```

2. Create a new tenant:

   ```
   [root@el7-icehouse-controller ~(keystone_admin)]# keystone tenant-create --name TENANT
   ```

3. Assign the user account to the newly created tenant:

   ```
   [root@el7-icehouse-controller ~(keystone_admin)]# keystone user-role-add --user USER --role _member_ --tenant TENANT
   ```

4. Create `keystonerc_user` file with the following content:

   ```
   [root@controller ~(keystone_admin)]# cat ~/keystonerc_user
   export OS_USERNAME=USER
   export OS_TENANT_NAME=TENANT
   export OS_PASSWORD=password
   export OS_AUTH_URL=http://10.10.0.1:5000/v2.0/
   export PS1='[\u@\h \W(keystone_user)]\$ '
   ```

There's more...

If installation and configuration of Keystone was successful, Keystone should be operational, and we start `keystone` command to verify that it is operational.

The command `#tenant-list` can be used to see the existing tenants:

```
[root@controller ~(keystone_admin)]# keystone tenant-list
```

The output of successful tenant creation should look as follows:

```
+----------------------------------+----------+---------+
|                id                |   name   | enabled |
+----------------------------------+----------+---------+
| a5b7bf37d1b646cb8ec0eb35481204c4 |  admin   |  True   |
| fafb926db0674ad9a34552dc05ac3a18 | services |  True   |
+----------------------------------+----------+---------+
```

Configuring Keystone with Microsoft Active Directory and LDAP

Typically, most organizations use Microsoft Active Directory as an organization user directory and identity management system, when Active Directory is responsible for authenticating and authorizing users and applications. While deploying OpenStack, Keystone can leverage Microsoft Active Directory as a centralized identity management system, so all the organization's user accounts are stored in a single directory and OpenStack can retrieve existing users' accounts.

Keystone Identity Service

Getting ready

In this section, we will configure Keystone to use an existing Microsoft Active Directory in a *Ready Only LDAP* configuration. In this configuration, Keystone will be able to retrieve user accounts from Microsoft Active Directory without requiring to make any change with Active Directory Schema or user accounts.

In this configuration, Keystone uses Microsoft Active Directory to store user accounts, and MariaDB server to store assignments of roles, domains, and tenants to user's account.

Since Keystone will only use Microsoft Active Directory for all user accounts, all OpenStack service users (Nova, Cinder, Glance, Swift, and so on) won't exist in Keystone Database and all user accounts will need to be created in Active Directory. Before you process with this chapter, create OpenStack service's user accounts using the same passwords used for service's configuration (that is, for Nova user account, use password configured in `/etc/nova/nova.conf` or updated password stored in Nova configuration file).

How to do it...

Follow these steps to configure Keystone to use Microsoft Active Directory in the *Read Only* mode:

1. Use `openstack-config` command to edit in Keystone configuration file, edit Identity section to use LDAP backend:

   ```
   [root@controller ~]# openstack-config --set
   /etc/keystone/keystone.conf   identity driver
   keystone.identity.backends.ldap.Identity
   ```

2. Now edit assignment section to use the MariaDB backend:

   ```
   [root@controller ~]# openstack-config --set
   /etc/keystone/keystone.conf   assignment driver
   keystone.assignment.backends.sql.Assignment
   ```

3. Configure the LDAP section to point to the Active Directory server with an administrator's user account:

   ```
   [root@controller ~]# openstack-config --set
   /etc/keystone/keystone.conf   ldap url
   ldap://192.168.122.86
   [root@controller ~]# openstack-config --set
   /etc/keystone/keystone.conf   ldap user
   cn=Administrator,cn=users,DC=win2012dom,DC=com
   [root@controller ~]# openstack-config --set
   /etc/keystone/keystone.conf   ldap password
   <<ADMIN_PASSWORD>>
   ```

```
[root@controller ~]# openstack-config --set
/etc/keystone/keystone.conf  ldap suffix
DC=win2012dom,DC=com
[root@controller ~]# openstack-config --set
/etc/keystone/keystone.conf  ldap use_dumb_member   False
[root@controller ~]# openstack-config --set
/etc/keystone/keystone.conf  ldap allow_subtree_delete False
```

4. Configure the needed Active Directory classes and attributes:

```
[root@controller ~]# openstack-config --set
/etc/keystone/keystone.conf  ldap
user_tree_dn    CN=Users,DC=win2012dom,DC=com
[root@controller ~]# openstack-config --set
/etc/keystone/keystone.conf  ldap
user_objectclass    person
[root@controller ~]# openstack-config --set
/etc/keystone/keystone.conf  ldap
user_id_attribute    cn
[root@controller ~]# openstack-config --set
/etc/keystone/keystone.conf  ldap
user_name_attribute  sAMAccountName
[root@controller ~]# openstack-config --set
/etc/keystone/keystone.conf  ldap
user_mail_attribute   userPrincipalName
[root@controller ~]# openstack-config --set
/etc/keystone/keystone.conf  ldap
user_enabled_attribute    userAccountControl
[root@controller ~]# openstack-config --set
/etc/keystone/keystone.conf  ldap
user_enabled_mask    2
[root@controller ~]# openstack-config --set
/etc/keystone/keystone.conf  ldap
user_enabled_default    512
```

5. Set explicit configuration to prevent Keystone from creating user and group accounts. This is mostly needed for backward compatibility:

```
[root@controller ~]# openstack-config --set
/etc/keystone/keystone.conf  ldap
user_allow_create    False
[root@controller ~]# openstack-config --set
/etc/keystone/keystone.conf  ldap
user_allow_update    False
[root@controller ~]# openstack-config --set
```

Keystone Identity Service

```
              /etc/keystone/keystone.conf   ldap
              user_allow_delete   False
              [root@controller ~]# openstack-config --set
              /etc/keystone/keystone.conf   ldap
              group_allow_create    False
              [root@controller ~]# openstack-config --set
              /etc/keystone/keystone.conf   ldap
              group_allow_update    False
              [root@controller ~]# openstack-config --set
              /etc/keystone/keystone.conf   ldap
              group_allow_delete    False
```

6. When the keystone configuration file is ready, restart the Keystone service:

   ```
   [root@controller ~]# systemctl restart openstack-keystone
   ```

See also

While these configuration options fit the most common environments, some cases would require making additional settings. You can see complete reference for the Keystone configuration file at `http://docs.openstack.org/developer/keystone/configuration.html`.

Configuring Keystone caching with Memcached

Large OpenStack environments usually require Keystone to handle a huge amount of authorization and authentication requests as Keystone is invoked on almost every OpenStack operation. To improve the scale Keystone can handle in heavy load environments we can configure the Keystone caching mechanism. The caching mechanism can store Tokens, User Identities, and Roles instead of retrieving them from a remote store. Keystone supports caching all configurable subsystems using a caching backend mechanism.

Getting ready

In this recipe, we configure Keystone to use Memcached caching service as a backend plugin for caching Keystone. We will need to install and configure the Memcached service first.

1. Install the `memcached` service with dependent packages:

   ```
   [root@controller ~]# yum install -y
   ```

Chapter 4

```
memcached memcached-selinux
```

2. Edit the `memcached` configuration file

   ```
   [root@controller ~]# vi /etc/sysconfig/memcached
   ```

3. Make sure of the following settings:

   ```
   PORT="11211"
   USER="memcached"
   OPTIONS="-l 127.0.0.1"
   ```

4. Enable and start the `memcached` service:

   ```
   [root@controller ~]# systemctl enable memcached
   [root@controller ~]# systemctl start memcached
   Test whether memcached is running and functional:
   [root@controller ~]# memcached-tool 127.0.0.1:11211
   ```

How to do it...

Run the following steps to configure Keystone to use Memcached as a caching layer:

1. Use the `openstack-config` command to enable Keystone to use a caching backend:

   ```
   [root@controller ~]# openstack-config --set
   /etc/keystone/keystone.conf cache
   enabled true
   ```

2. Set `memcached` as the backend plugin for caching:

   ```
   [root@controller ~]# openstack-config --set
   /etc/keystone/keystone.conf cache
   backend dogpile.cache.memcached
   ```

3. Set the backend plugin to use the locally installed `memcached` service:

   ```
   [root@controller ~]# openstack-config --set
   /etc/keystone/keystone.conf cache
   backend_argument url:127.0.0.1:11211
   ```

4. Restart the `keystone` service as follows:

   ```
   [root@controller ~]# systemctl restart openstack-keystone
   ```

Keystone Identity Service

There's more...

By default, all Keystone subsystems are enabled for caching, it is possible to disable specific subsystems individually in the subsystems section. For example, we can use `openstack-config` to edit the `assignment` section and disable `caching` for assignments:

```
[root@controller ~]# openstack-config --set
/etc/keystone/keystone.conf assignment     caching false
```

See also

Keystone supports granular configuration for many more parameters. All setting can be found on the Keystone developer documentation guide `http://docs.openstack.org/developer/keystone/configuration.html#caching-layer`.

Securing Keystone with SSL

Keystone is responsible for account authorization and authentication to all OpenStack services, as such, the entire communication transport over the Keystone API is sensitive. Information as Tokens, account credentials, and passwords are sent in clear text over the network. If the communication transport to the Keystone API is compromised, the whole OpenStack environment is at risk. For example, in a **man-in-the-middle** (**MITM**) attack, tokens or user credentials can be stolen resulting full access and control over the whole OpenStack environment.

To reduce the risk of sensitive data being intercepted, it is highly recommended to protect Keystone API communication with SSL/TLS, so all ongoing traffic to the Keystone API is encrypted.

Getting ready

In this recipe, we will configure Keystone to enable the SSL/TLS communication. Configuring **Secure Socket Layer** (**SSL**) requires signed private and public keys, and a certificate signed by a certificate authority.

For testing purposes, the `keystone-manage` command can generate a self-signed certificate and private and public keys.

```
[root@controller ~]# keystone-manage ssl_setup --keystone-user
keystone --keystone-group keystone
```

Chapter 4

How to do it...

Follow these steps to enable Keystone API to use the SSL communication:

1. Using `openstack-config` command enable SSL in the Keystone configuration file:

   `openstack-config --set /etc/keystone/keystone.conf ssl enable True`

2. Set the certificate subject, make sure CN maps to the host's name:

   `[root@controller ~]# openstack-config --set /etc/keystone/keystone.conf ssl cert_subject /C=US/ST=Unset/L=Unset/O=Unset/CN=controller.example.com`

3. Point `certfile` to the public certificate, `keyfile` to private certificate, `ca_certs` to the CA trust `authority`, and `ca_key` to private key for the CA:

   `[root@controller ~]# openstack-config --set /etc/keystone/keystone.conf ssl certfile /etc/keystone/ssl/certs/signing_cert.pem`
   `[root@controller ~]# openstack-config --set /etc/keystone/keystone.conf ssl keyfile /etc/keystone/ssl/private/signing_key.pem`
   `[root@controller ~]# openstack-config --set /etc/keystone/keystone.conf ssl ca_certs /etc/keystone/ssl/certs/ca.pem`
   `[root@controller ~]# openstack-config --set /etc/keystone/keystone.conf ssl ca_key /etc/keystone/ssl/certs/cakey.pem`

4. Export `SERVICE_ENDPOINT` to point to the Keystone API:

   `[root@controller ~]# export SERVICE_ENDPOINT=http://controller.example.com:35357/v2.0`
   `[root@controller ~]# export SERVICE_TOKEN=************`

5. If Keystone was previously configured without SSL, you will need to delete the existing `ENDPOINT` and `SERVICE` and recreate them with the new https URL:

   `[root@controller ~]# KEYSTONE_SERVICE=$(keystone service-get keystone | grep ' id ' | awk '{print $4}')`

Keystone Identity Service

```
[root@controller ~]# KEYSTONE_ENDPOINT=$(keystone
endpoint-list | grep $KEYSTONE_SERVICE|awk '{print $2}')
[root@controller ~]# keystone endpoint-delete
$KEYSTONE_ENDPOINT
[root@controller ~]# keystone service-delete
$KEYSTONE_SERVICE
```

6. Create the Keystone catalog service and an Endpoint pointing to the new SSL/TLS-secured transport(https):

   ```
   [root@controller ~]# HOST_NAME=`hostname -f`
   [root@controller ~]# KEYSTONE_SERVICE=$(keystone
   service-create
   --name=keystone \
   --type=identity \
   --description="Keystone Identity Service" \
       | grep ' id ' | awk '{print $4}')
   [root@controller ~]# keystone endpoint-create --region
   RegionOne --service-id $KEYSTONE_SERVICE \
           --publicurl "https://$HOST_NAME:\$(public_port)s/v2.0"
   \       --adminurl "https://$HOST_NAME:\$(admin_port)s/v2.0"
   \       --internalurl
   "https://$HOST_NAME:\$(public_port)s/v2.0"
   ```

7. Edit the OpenStack environment variables' file (usually `keystonerc_admin`) to point to the new https endpoint, and pointing to the CA certificate:

   ```
   export OS_AUTH_URL=https://controller.example.com:35357/v2.0
   export OS_CACERT=/etc/keystone/ssl/certs/ca.pem
   ```

8. Restart the Keystone service and source the edited `keystonerc_admin`:

   ```
   [root@controller ~]# systemctl restart openstack-keystone
   [root@controller ~]# source keystonerc_admin
   ```

There's more...

The configuration in this recipe enables making Keystone API calls over a secure transport layer, which is configured to allow us a secure access to the Keystone API from the public or untrusted network. It is also recommended to configure all OpenStack services consuming Keystone for authentication and authorization, to communicate with Keystone over the SSL/TLS connection.

To enable OpenStack services to communicate with Keystone over SSL, edit each of Openstack's configuration files, for example, `/etc/nova/nova.conf` and change the parameter `auth_url` to point to the Keystone's SSL URI, for example, `https://controller.example.com:5000/`.

See also

You can refer to the SSL configuration documentation for additional options Keystone supports `http://docs.openstack.org/developer/keystone/configuration.html#ssl`.

5
Glance Image Service

In this chapter, we will cover the following:

- Configuring Glance with the local file backend
- Configuring Glance with the NFS backend
- Configuring Glance with the Swift backend
- Configuring Glance with the Ceph backend
- Configuring Glance image caching
- Configuring the Glance image size limit and storage quota

Introduction

Glance image service is a project that offers images as a service, it enables users to discover, register, and retrieve operating system disk images from which users can launch OpenStack instances. The image service offers a REST API that enables users to query virtual machine disk images and metadata. Virtual machine disk images can be stored on various datastore backends, such as local filesystem, NFS, Ceph, Swift, and others.

Glance consists of the following two services:

- `glance-api` accepts REST API calls for image discovery, retrieval, and creation. It stores and retrieves disk images from storage backend. The Image Service supports a variety of backends, including local filesystems, object storage, Ceph RADOS block devices, HTTP, and Amazon S3.

Glance Image Service

> ▸ `glance-registry` stores, processes, and retrieves metadata of disk images from the backend datastore storage device. Metadata includes some items, such as size and type.

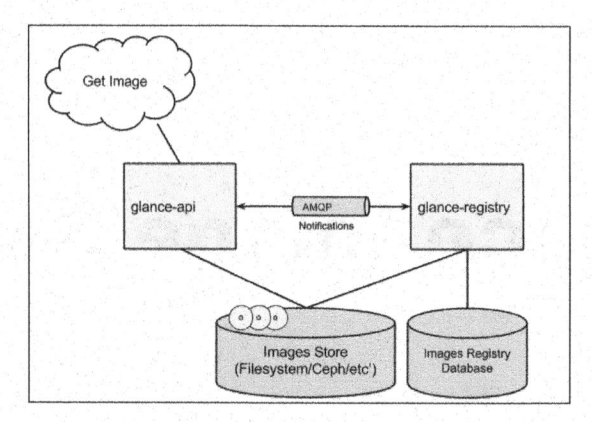

Configuring Glance with the local file backend

In this recipe, we will configure Glance backend to use local storage driver to store image files on the local disk.

Getting ready

Before getting started with configuring the Glance backend driver, we need to make sure that the database, message broker, and Keystone are set for Glance, and both `glance-api.conf` and `glance-registory.conf` are configured correctly to use them.

How to do it...

Perform the following steps to configure Glance with the local file backend:

1. Using the `openstack-config` command, edit the `glance-api` configuration file, and under the default section, set `default_store` to file as follows:

   ```
   [root@controller ~]# openstack-config --set /etc/glance/glance-api.conf default default_store file
   ```

2. Make sure that stores option includes `filesystem store`, under `glance_store` section:

   ```
   [root@controller ~]# openstack-config --set /etc/glance/glance-api.conf glance_store stores glance.store.filesystem.Store
   ```

―― *Chapter 5*

> Note: if you plan to use multiple back-ends, all backend drivers should be specified here.

3. Point `filesystem_store_datadir` to the path that will store Glance disk images:

   `[root@controller ~]# openstack-config --set /etc/glance/glance-api.conf glance_store filesystem_store_datadir /var/lib/glance/images/`

4. Restart the `glance-api` and `glance-registry` services:

   `[root@controller ~]# systemctl restart openstack-glance-api`

   `[root@controller ~]# systemctl restart openstack-glance-registry`

There's More..

Glance also supports configuring of multiple backend stores, allowing to store disk images on multiple paths. While creating a new image, the path is chosen by its priority and disk's capacity, so if the highest priority disk doesn't have the capacity to store an image, the next store is chosen.

Configuring this can be achieved by setting `filesystem_store_datadirs` (Note that this `config` option is plural, that is, with `s` in the suffix) multiple times, each time with a unique `datadir` path and its priority. Higher priority value sets higher priority for the data store.

For example, possible configurations are:

- `[glance_store]`
- `filesystem_store_datadirs=/var/lib/glance/images/disk1/:10`
- `filesystem_store_datadirs=/var/lib/glance/images/disk2/:20`
- `filesystem_store_datadirs=/var/lib/glance/images/disk3/:30`

Verifying the configuration

To verify that Glance was configured correctly, we can try creating a new image as follows:

`[root@controller glance(keystone_admin)]# glance image-create --name="cirros-0.3.2-x86_64" --disk-format=qcow2 --container-format=bare --is-public=true --copy-from http://cdn.download.cirros-cloud.net/0.3.2/cirros-0.3.2-x86_64-disk.img`

Glance Image Service

Configuring Glance with the NFS backend

Glance can use **Network File System** (**NFS**) as a storage backend. Glance does not have an NFS-specific backend store driver. Rather, it uses NFS-mounted directories with the native filesystem store driver. As multiple NFS shares cannot be mounted on a single directory, Glance can use the multiple `datadir` stores option to use several NFS shares. We can specify corresponding priority for each share. While creating new disk images, Glance chooses the location of the new image, based on the priority of the datadir store and the capacity of the share. If several shares have the same priority, the share with maximum available free space is chosen.

Getting ready

Before configuring Glance with multiple datadir stores, we need to make sure that the Database, message broker, and Keystone are set for Glance, and both `glance-api.conf` and `glance-registory.conf` are configured correctly to use them.

We also need to make sure that the NFS shares we want to use as Glance data stores are mounted on server during startup. We need to add the NFS shares and local mount points to server's `/etc/fstab` to automatically mount shares on the server startup:

```
nfs-server1:/share/disk1    /var/lib/glance/images/share1    nfs
nfs-server1:/share/disk2    /var/lib/glance/images/share2    nfs
nfs-server1:/share/disk3    /var/lib/glance/images/share3    nfs
```

How to do it...

Now we will configure Glance with multiple data stores using the previously created mount points:

1. Using the `openstack-config` command, edit the `glance-api` configuration file; under the default section, set `default_store` to file:

   ```
   [root@controller ~]# openstack-config --set /etc/glance/glance-api.conf default default_store file
   ```

2. Make sure that stores option includes filesystem store under the `glance_store` section:

   ```
   [root@controller ~]# openstack-config --set /etc/glance/glance-api.conf glance_store stores glance.store.filesystem.Store
   ```

   > If you plan to use multiple backends, all backend drivers should be specified here.

Chapter 5

3. Edit the Glance API configuration file `/etc/glance/glance-api.conf`, and under `[glance-store]` section, you can add multiple lines of `filesystem_store_datadirs`

   > The configuration option is plural, that is, with `s` in the suffix.

   ```
   [glance_store]
   filesystem_store_datadirs=/var/lib/glance/images/share1/:10
   filesystem_store_datadirs=/var/lib/glance/images/share2/:20
   filesystem_store_datadirs=/var/lib/glance/images/share3/:30
   ```

4. Restart the `glance-api` and `glance-registry` services:

   ```
   [root@controller ~]# systemctl restart openstack-glance-api
   [root@controller ~]# systemctl restart openstack-glance-registry
   ```

There's more...

To verify that Glance was configured correctly, we can try creating a new image:

```
[root@controller glance(keystone_admin)]# glance image-create
--name="cirros-0.3.2-x86_64" --disk-format=qcow2
--container-format=bare --is-public=true --copy-from
http://cdn.download.cirros-cloud.net/0.3.2/cirros-0.3.2-x86_64-
disk.img
```

> Note that store with higher priority will be automatically selected, you can set the data store manually by using the `--store` option, specifying the name of the data store.

Configuring Glance with the Swift backend

If Swift Object Storage is in place, Glance can use the existing Swift cluster as a datastore to store virtual machine images. In this recipe, we will configure the Glance backend driver for swift object storage.

Glance Image Service

Getting ready

Before configuring Glance Swift backend, we need to make sure that the Database, message broker and Keystone are set for Glance, and both `glance-api.conf` and `glance-registry.conf` are configured correctly to use them.

> It is recommended to make sure that the configuration option `filesystem_store_datadir` in `glance-api.conf` is commented out, as it should not be called when filesystem driver is not used.

How to do it...

Follow these steps to configure Glance with the Swift backend:

1. Using the `openstack-config` command, edit the `glance-api` configuration file which is under default section and set `default_store` to swift:

   `default_store = swift`

2. Make sure that the stores option includes swift store under `glance_store` section as follows:

   `[root@controller ~]# openstack-config --set /etc/glance/glance-api.conf glance_store stores glance.store.swift.Store`

   > If you plan to use multiple backends, all backend drivers should be specified here.

3. Under `glance_store` section, set Swift driver to authenticate against Keystone:

   `[root@controller ~]# openstack-config --set /etc/glance/glance-api.conf glance_store swift_store_auth_address  http://controller:35357/v2.0/`

4. Set `glance` service user to authenticate against the Swift authentication service:

   `[root@controller ~]# openstack-config --set /etc/glance/glance-api.conf glance_store swift_store_user services:glance`

5. Set the Swift store key for the user authenticating against the Swift authentication service:

   `[root@controller ~]# openstack-config --set /etc/glance/glance-api.conf glance_store swift_store_key <SWIFT STORE KEY >`

Chapter 5

6. Enable Glance to create a container when it does not exist:

   ```
   [root@controller ~]# openstack-config --set
   /etc/glance/glance-api.conf glance_store
   swift_store_create_container_on_put   True
   ```

7. Restart the `glance-api` and `glance-registry` services:

   ```
   [root@controller ~]# systemctl restart openstack-glance-api
   ```
   ```
   [root@controller ~]# systemctl restart openstack-glance-registry
   ```

There's more...

To verify that Glance was configured correctly, we can try creating a new image as follows:

```
[root@controller glance(keystone_admin)]# glance image-create
--name="cirros-0.3.2-x86_64" --disk-format=qcow2
--container-format=bare --is-public=true --copy-from
http://cdn.download.cirros-cloud.net/0.3.2/cirros-0.3.2-x86_64-
disk.img
```

See also...

Additional configuration options are available for the Swift backend driver, and for more information on the Swift backend documentation refer to `http://docs.openstack.org/developer/glance/configuring.html#configuring-the-swift-storage-backend`.

Configuring Glance with the Ceph backend

Glance can use the existing Ceph pools as a datastore to store virtual machine images. In this recipe, we will configure the Glance backend driver for the Ceph RADOS Block Device.

Getting ready

Before configuring Glance to use the Ceph RBD backend, we need to make sure that the Database, message broker, and Keystone are set for Glance, and both `glance-api.conf` and `glance-registry.conf` are configured correctly to use them. We also need to make sure that a Ceph volume with a corresponding pool for glance was created, and the `ceph.conf` and `key.ring` files were preconfigured.

Glance Image Service

The `CephFS Python` package is also required to use the Ceph RBD backend driver:

`[root@controller ~]# yum install -y python-cephfs`

How to do it...

Follow these steps to configure Glance with the Ceph storage backend:

1. Using the `openstack-config` command, edit the `glance-api` configuration file, and under the default section, set `default_store` to `rdb`:

    `[root@controller ~]# openstack-config --set /etc/glance/glance-api.conf default default_store rbd`

2. Make sure that stores option includes `rbd Store` under `glance_store` section:

    `[root@controller ~]# openstack-config --set /etc/glance/glance-api.conf glance_store stores glance.store.rbd.Store`

    > If you plan to use multiple back-ends, all back-end drivers should be specified here.

3. Point `rbd_store_ceph_conf` to the `ceph.conf` configuration file:

    `[root@controller ~]# openstack-config --set /etc/glance/glance-api.conf glance_store rbd_store_ceph_conf /etc/ceph/ceph.conf`

4. Select which pool to use to store Glance images:

    `[root@controller ~]# openstack-config --set /etc/glance/glance-api.conf glance_store stores rbd_store_pool images`

5. Set the RADOS user to authenticate as if the user was configured in Ceph.conf; this can be skipped:

    `[root@controller ~]# openstack-config --set /etc/glance/glance-api.conf glance_store rbd_store_user glance`

6. The images will be chunked into multiple objects, set the RBD object chunk size:

    `[root@controller ~]# openstack-config --set /etc/glance/glance-api.conf glance_store rbd_store_chunk_size 8`

7. Restart the `glance-api` and `glance-registry` services:

    `[root@controller ~]# systemctl restart openstack-glance-api`

    `[root@controller ~]# systemctl restart openstack-glance-registry`

There's more...

To verify that Glance was configured correctly, we can try creating a new image as follows:

```
[root@controller glance(keystone_admin)]# glance image-create
--name="cirros-0.3.2-x86_64" --disk-format=qcow2 --container-format=bare
--is-public=true --copy-from  http://cdn.download.cirros-cloud.net/0.3.2/
cirros-0.3.2-x86_64-disk.img
```

See Also...

Additional configuration options are available for the Ceph RBD backend driver, more information can be found on the RBD backend documentation at `http://docs.openstack.org/developer/glance/configuring.html#configuring-the-rbd-storage-backend`.

Additional information for creating and configuring Ceph for Glance can be found in Ceph's documentation at `http://ceph.com/docs/master/rbd/rbd-openstack/`.

Configuring Glance image caching

The `glance-api` service can be configured to cache images to local machine's disk. Once configured, the local cache automatically stores copies of images that are successfully retrieved and served. In this configuration, `glance-api` can run on multiple hosts without retrieving the same image from remote storage multiple times, leading the OpenStack environment to handle better scalability. Using Glance image caching is transparent to the user and doesn't change any of Glance's operations. The user does not know of the images are served from the backend storage or from `glance-api` caching mechanism.

Getting Ready

Before enabling and configuring Glance image caching, make sure that glance is configured and can successfully serve images.

How to do it...

We can configure Glance image caching by following these steps:

1. Using the command `openstack-config`, edit `glance-api` configuration file, and set `flavor` to include `cachemanagement` using the `paste_deploy` section:

   ```
   [root@controller ~]# openstack-config --set
   /etc/glance/glance-api.conf  paste_deploy flavor
   keystone+cachemanagement
   ```

Glance Image Service

2. Make the same change on `glance-cache.conf` configuration file:

   `[root@controller ~]# openstack-config --set /etc/glance/glance-cache.conf paste_deploy flavor keystone+cachemanagement`

3. You may set the path in which Glance will keep the cached image files:

   `[root@controller ~]# openstack-config --set /etc/glance/glance-cache.conf default image_cache_dir /var/lib/glance/image-cache/`

4. The maximum size of cache can also be set, and the value is in bytes:

   `[root@controller ~]# openstack-config --set /etc/glance/glance-cache.conf default image_cache_max_size 10737418240`

5. Make sure that glance paste file, `/usr/share/glance/glance-api-dist-paste.ini`, is configured appropriately and `cachemanage` occurs after the context middleware in the application pipeline:

   `[pipeline:glance-api-keystone+cachemanagement]`

   `pipeline = versionnegotiation osprofiler authtoken context cache cachemanage rootapp`

6. Also make sure that `cachemanage` middleware is located in its filter section:

   `[filter:cachemanage]`

   `paste.filter_factory = glance.api.middleware.cache_manage:CacheManageFilter.factory`

7. Restart the `glance-api` service

   `[root@controller ~]# systemctl restart openstack-glance-api`

There's More..

Glance caches image files automatically to local disk, but it does not automatically purge unused images, thus requiring you to maintain it occasionally.

Using `glance-cache-manage`, you can manage and maintain the stored cache files, for example, the following command lists all cached files:

`[root@controller ~]# glance-cache-manage list-cached`

The following command removed an image from the cache:

`[root@controller ~]# glance-cache-manage delete-cached-image <image-id>`

See Also

You can read more about additional configuration options on the Cache section under glance configuration documentation at `http://docs.openstack.org/developer/glance/configuring.html#configuration-options-affecting-the-image-cache`.

Configuring the Glance image size limit and storage quota

The `glance-api` and `glance-registry` services are commonly configured to use `/var` filesystem to store locally Glance images and to cache images locally. It is possible to limit the maximum image size that can be uploaded to glance to avoid filling the `/var` filesystem or abusing the service.

> The maximum possible should be set to a value under 8 exabyte (9223372036854775808).

How to do it...

To limit the size of glance images, follow these steps:

1. Set the maximum image size, in bytes, that can be uploaded through the `glance-api` service to *1* TB:

   `[root@controller ~]# openstack-config --set /etc/glance/glance-api.conf default image_size_cap 1099511627776`

2. Restart the `glance-api` service:

   `[root@controller ~]# systemctl restart openstack-glance-api`

   `[root@controller ~]# systemctl restart openstack-glance-registry`

There's more...

It is also possible to specify the maximum amount of storage that each user can use across all storage stores.

`[root@controller ~]# openstack-config --set /etc/glance/glance-api.conf default user_storage_quota 50GB`

Values are accepted in **B**, **KB**, **MB**, **GB**, or **TB**, which are for **Bytes**, **KiloBytes**, **MegaBytes**, **GigaBytes**, and **TeraBytes**, respectively when the default unit is Bytes.

6
Cinder Block Storage Service

In this chapter, we will cover the following:

- Configuring Cinder with the logical volume management backend driver
- Configuring Cinder with the Ceph RADOS block device backend driver
- Configuring Cinder with the network file system backend driver
- Configuring Cinder with the Ceph RBD backup driver
- Configuring Cinder with multiple backends
- Configuring Cinder scheduler filters and weighers

Introduction

The Cinder block storage service provides block storage volumes as a service. Cinder allows creating block-device volumes and attaches them to Nova virtual machine instances. Cinder supports multiple vendors backend drivers which allows utilizing various storage devices, such as local **logical volume management** (**LVM**), NetApp, EMC storage arrays, and others. Cinder accesses the storage device via its management access and lets a Nova virtual machine instance access volumes directly via the storage path. The storage path depends on the implementation of the storage array and could be an iSCSI target, fiber channel, or other.

It is important to note that Cinder is not a shared storage solution such as a **storage area network** (**SAN**) that allows attaching a volume to multiple servers. Cinder allows attaching a volume to only one instance at a time.

Cinder Block Storage Service

Native cloud applications are stateless by nature; thus, the Nova virtual machine instance does not save any data on the ephemeral disk created for the instance, as the data would get lost when instances are terminated; Cinder volumes can be attached to the virtual machine instances to save persistent data.

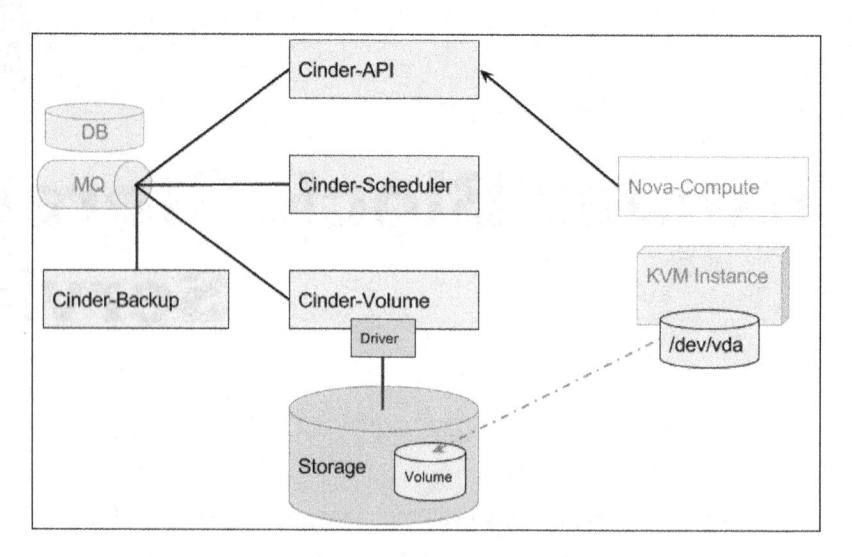

Cinder consists of the following Linux services:

- Cinder-API handles Cinder's API requests and responses, and places them in message queue.
- A Cinder-Scheduler service gathers volume requests and determines which cinder-volume server should provision the requests volume, based on storage's capabilities, capacity, and other weighting metrics.
- A Cinder-Volume service interacts with storage devices via backend drivers.
- A Cinder-Backup service provides ability to back up volumes to an external storage.

Configuring Cinder with the logical volume management backend driver

Cinder's default backend storage provider is LVM. When cinder LVM backend driver is configured, a Cinder-volume service consumes a preconfigured volume group of the host Cinder-volume runs on. Cinder-volume manages the logical volumes of the configured volume group and uses an iSCSI target helper to provide a direct connection path to the volume.

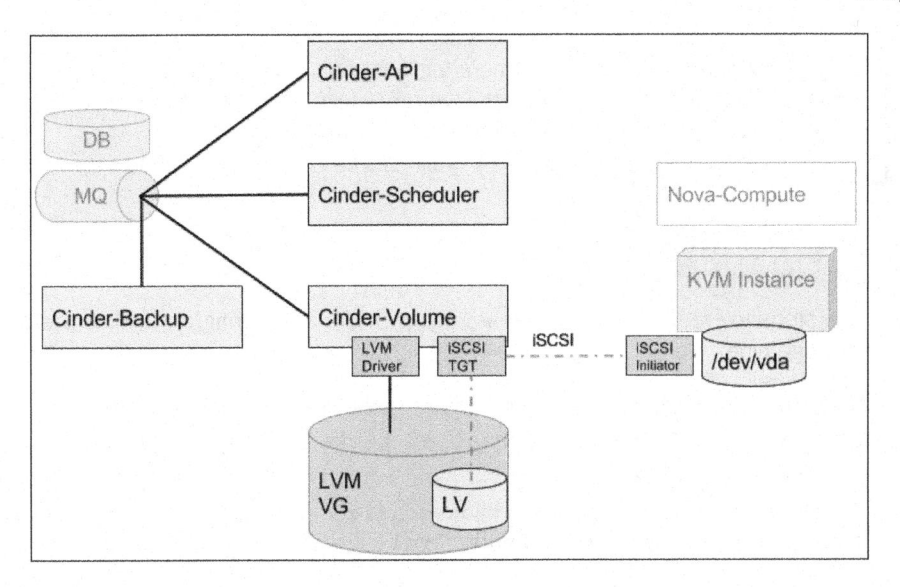

Getting ready

In this recipe, we will configure LVM Cinder backend storage provider. A cinder-volume service will utilize a volume group of the host cinder-volume service runs on. Before getting started with configuring the Cinder backend driver, we need to make sure that the database, message broker, and Keystone are set for Cinder.

Additionally, make sure that the Nova-compute hosts are set to consume Cinder API.

```
[root@controller ~]# grep cinder.API /etc/nova/nova.conf
volume_api_class=nova.volume.cinder.API
```

To create an LVM volume group to be consumed by the cinder-volume service, first prepare a physical volume to be used by LVM:

```
# pvcreate /dev/sdX
```

> Make sure that there's no needed data on /dev/sdX and it is an available block device to be used by LVM.

Create a new volume group named cinder-volumes on the physical volume used in the previous step:

```
[root@controller ~]# vgcreate cinder-volumes /dev/sdX
Volume group "cinder-volumes" successfully created
```

Cinder Block Storage Service

> CentOS 7 and RHEL 7 operating systems use a LioAdm iSCSI target helper and require its Python library. Make sure that the package `python-rtslib` is installed:
>
> `[root@controller ~]# yum install python-rtslib`

How to do it...

Follow these steps to create a new Cinder storage provider and configure LVM as the driver backend storage type:

1. Using the `openstack-config` command, edit the `cinder` configuration file. Under the `DEFAULT` section, set `enabled_backends` to `lvm1` to enable the new storage provider:

    `[root@controller ~]# openstack-config --set /etc/cinder/cinder.conf DEFAULT enabled_backends lvm1`

2. Enable the LVM and iSCSI storage backend driver for the `lvm1` provider. Set the `LVMISCSIDriver` backend volume driver under the `lvm1` section:

    ```
    # openstack-config --set /etc/cinder/cinder.conf \
    lvm1 volume_driver cinder.volume.drivers.lvm.LVMISCSIDriver
    ```

3. Choose which volume group to be used for Cinder volumes:

    ```
    # openstack-config --set /etc/cinder/cinder.conf \
    lvm1 volume_group cinder-volumes
    ```

4. Set a name for the new storage backend provider:

    ```
    # openstack-config --set /etc/cinder/cinder.conf \
    lvm1 volume_backend_name lvm
    ```

5. Set an iSCSI helper to use a LioAdm helper:

    ```
    # openstack-config --set /etc/cinder/cinder.conf \
    lvm1 iscsi_helper lioadm
    ```

    > CentOS 6 and RHEL 6 use a tgtadm iSCSI helper instead of LioAdm.

6. Set the parameter `iscsi_ip_address` with the IP address of the host running cinder-volume service:

    ```
    # openstack-config --set /etc/cinder/cinder.conf \
    lvm1 iscsi_ip_address 192.168.10.100
    ```

7. Restart the `cinder-volume` service:

   ```
   [root@controller ~]# systemctl restart openstack-cinder-volume
   ```

Configuring Cinder with the Ceph RADOS block device backend driver

Ceph is an open source, software-defined storage system that runs on commodity x86 hardware. Ceph provides block storage volumes that can be attached as virtual disks. Ceph utilizes multiple hosts' local disks to create a unified virtual disk pool. Ceph can scale massively to petabyte storage pools and takes care of disk replication, rebalancing, and other storage maintenance operations.

Cinder implements an **rbd** (**RADOS block devices**) backend storage driver that can utilize the existing Ceph storage pool, manage volumes, and attach volumes to VM instances.

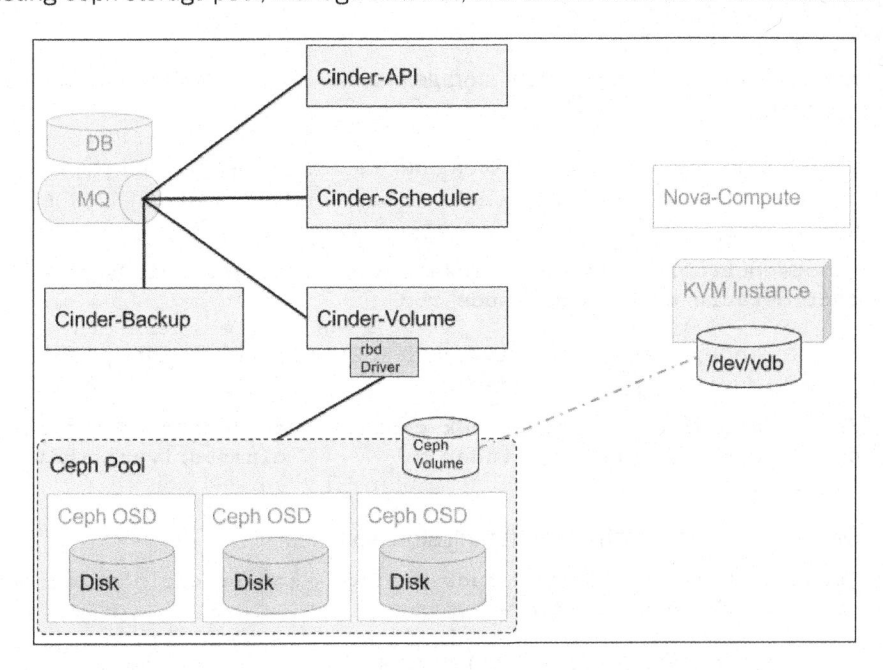

Getting ready

Before getting started with configuring a Ceph rbd backend driver, make sure to install Ceph client packages and the Python rbd binding library on all OpenStack nodes, including controller and compute nodes:

```
[root@controller ~]# yum install -y python-rbd ceph
[root@compute1 ~]# yum install -y python-rbd ceph
```

Cinder Block Storage Service

We will need to prepare a storage `pool` named `cinder-volumes` for Cinder to use:

`[root@ceph-node1 ~]# ceph osd pool create cinder-volumes 128`

Also, we will need a copy of `ceph.conf` and Ceph keyring files with appropriate permissions on all controller nodes running cinder-volume and compute nodes running nova-compute. We have the following code:

`[root@ceph-node1 ~]# ceph auth get-or-create client.cinder mon 'allow r' osd 'allow class-read object_prefix rbd_children, allow rwx pool=cinder-volumes`

`[root@ceph-node1 ~]# ceph auth get-or-create client.cinder | ssh conotroller sudo tee /etc/ceph/ceph.client.cinder.keyring`

`ssh controller sudo chown cinder:cinder /etc/ceph/ceph.client.cinder.keyring`

How to do it...

Follow these steps to create a new Cinder storage provider and configure rbd as the driver backend storage type:

1. Using the `openstack-config` command, edit the `cinder` configuration file; under the `default` section, set `enabled_backends` to `rbd` to enable the new storage provider:

    `[root@controller ~]# openstack-config --set /etc/cinder/cinder.conf default enabled_backends rbd`

2. Set the `cinder.volume.drivers.rbd.RBDDriver` driver as the volume backend driver for the `rbd` provider:

    `[root@controller ~]# openstack-config --set /etc/cinder/cinder.conf rbd volume_driver cinder.volume.drivers.rbd.RBDDriver`

3. Set the pool name in which Cinder will store volumes:

    `[root@controller ~]# openstack-config --set /etc/cinder/cinder.conf rbd rbd_pool cinder-volumes`

4. Set the path of the `ceph.conf` configuration file:

    `[root@controller ~]# openstack-config --set /etc/cinder/cinder.conf rbd rbd_ceph_conf /etc/ceph/ceph.conf`

5. Enable the default Ceph settings:

    `[root@controller ~]# openstack-config --set /etc/cinder/cinder.conf rbd rbd_flatten_volume_from_snapshot false`

    `[root@controller ~]# openstack-config --set /etc/cinder/cinder.conf rbd rbd_max_clone_depth 5`

```
[root@controller ~]# openstack-config --set /etc/cinder/cinder.
conf rbd rbd_store_chunk_size  4
[root@controller ~]# openstack-config --set /etc/cinder/cinder.
conf rbd rados_connect_timeout  -1
[root@controller ~]# openstack-config --set /etc/cinder/cinder.
conf rbd glance_api_version  2
```

6. Set user Ceph user and secret UUID if Ceph authentication is in place:

   ```
   [root@controller ~]# openstack-config --set /etc/cinder/cinder.
   conf rbd rbd_user  cinder
   [root@controller ~]# openstack-config --set /etc/cinder/cinder.
   conf rbd rbd_secret_uuid <UUID>
   ```

7. In order for the nova-compute virtual machine instances to be able to attach Ceph Cinder volumes, nova-compute needs to be configured:

   ```
   [root@controller ~]# openstack-config --set /etc/nova/nova.conf
   libvirt rbd_user  cinder
   [root@controller ~]# openstack-config --set /etc/nova/nova.conf
   libvirt rbd_user  rbd_secret_uuid <UUID>
   ```

8. Make sure that Ceph uses caching on all compute nodes, edit `ceph.conf`, and enable the following:

   ```
   [client]
   rbd cache = true
   rbd cache writethrough until flush = true
   admin socket = /var/run/ceph/$cluster-$type.$id.$pid.$cctid.asok
   ```

9. Restart cinder-volume service:

   ```
   [root@controller ~]# systemctl restart openstack-cinder-volume
   ```

10. On all compute nodes, restart nova-compute service:

    ```
    [root@compute1 ~]# systemctl restart openstack-nova-compute
    ```

Configuring Cinder with the Network File System (NFS) backend driver

Cinder can use **network file system** (**NFS**) shares as a storage backend driver using an NFS driver implementation. A Cinder-volume service takes care of mounting the NFS shares and creates volumes on the shares. The NFS driver works differently than other Cinder block storage drivers. The NFS driver does not allow an instance to access a storage block device, instead files are created on an NFS share and mapped to instances, which emulates a block device.

Cinder Block Storage Service

Getting ready

Cinder-volume utilizes the NFS client utilities. Make sure that the `nfs-utils` packages are installed on the hosts running cinder-volume and nova-compute:

```
[root@controller ~]# yum install nfs-utils nfs-utils-lib
[root@compute1 ~]# yum install nfs-utils nfs-utils-lib
```

Make sure that the NFS shares are exported with appropriate file permissions, so the cinder-volume service has read and write access.

How to do it...

Proceed with the following steps:

1. On the host running a cinder-volume service, create a shares file with an NFS server and path details:

    ```
    [root@controller ~]# echo "nfs-server1:/nfs/share/path" > /etc/cinder/nfs_share
    ```

2. Set ownership and file permissions, so the cinder-volume service can access the shares file:

    ```
    [root@controller ~]# chown root:cinder /etc/cinder/nfs_share
    [root@controller ~]# chmod 0640 /etc/cinder/nfs_share
    ```

3. Using the `openstack-config` command, edit the cinder configuration file; under the `default` section, set `enabled_backends` to `nfs` to enable the new NFS storage provider:

    ```
    [root@controller ~]# openstack-config --set /etc/cinder/cinder.conf default enabled_backends nfs
    ```

4. Set `cinder.volume.drivers.nfs.NfsDriver` driver as the volume backend driver for the `nfs` provider:

    ```
    [root@controller ~]# openstack-config --set /etc/cinder/cinder.conf nfs volume_driver  cinder.volume.drivers.nfs.NfsDriver
    ```

5. Set the path for the `nfs_shares` file to the newly created NFS share file:

    ```
    [root@controller ~]# openstack-config --set /etc/cinder/cinder.conf nfs nfs_shares_config /etc/cinder/nfs_share
    ```

6. Restart the cinder-volume service:

    ```
    [root@controller ~]# systemctl restart openstack-cinder-volume
    ```

Configuring Cinder with the Ceph RBD backup driver

Cinder supports a backup mechanism to back up Cinder volumes on external storage devices. Cinder has a Ceph rbd backup driver implementation allowing you to back up Cinder volumes to a dedicated backup Ceph pool.

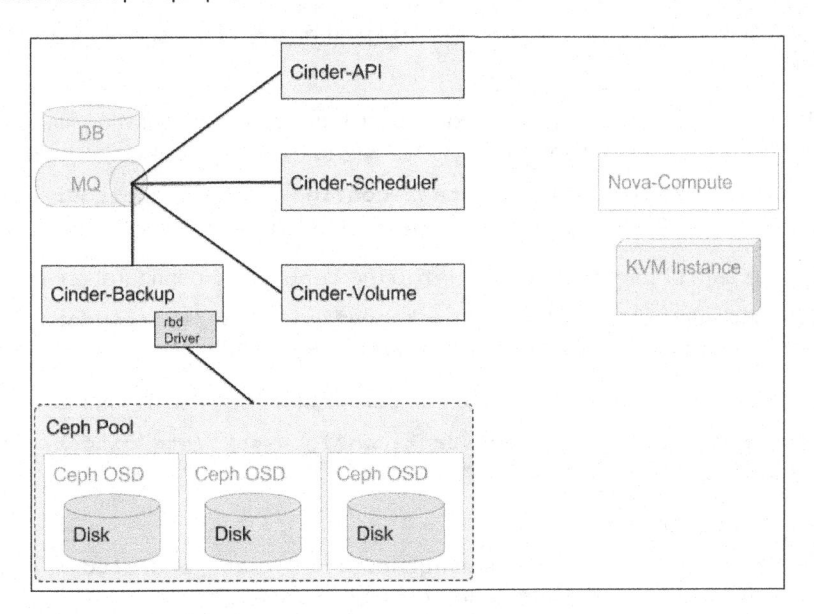

Getting ready

Before getting started with configuring the Ceph rbd backup driver, make sure to install Ceph client packages and Python rbd binding library on node running cinder-backup service:

`[root@controller ~]# yum install -y python-rbd ceph`

We will need to prepare a storage `pool` named `cinder-backups`:

`[root@ceph-node1 ~]# ceph osd pool create cinder-backups 128`

Also, we will need a copy of `ceph.conf` and Ceph keyring files with appropriate permissions on all controller nodes running the cinder-backup service:

`[root@ceph-node1 ~]# ceph auth get-or-create client.cinder-backup mon 'allow r' osd 'allow class-read object_prefix rbd_children, allow rwx pool=cinder-backups'`

Cinder Block Storage Service

```
[root@ceph-node1 ~]# ceph auth get-or-create client.cinder-backup | ssh controller sudo tee /etc/ceph/ceph.client.cinder-backup.keyring
```

```
[root@controller ~]# chown cinder:cinder /etc/ceph/ceph.client.cinder-backup.keyring
```

How to do it...

Perform the following steps to configure Ceph rbd as the backup storage type for Cinder-backup:

1. Using the `openstack-config` command, edit cinder configuration file; under the `default` section, and set `backup_driver` to `cinder.backup.drivers.ceph`:

    ```
    [root@controller ~]# openstack-config --set /etc/cinder/cinder.conf default backup_driver cinder.backup.drivers.ceph
    ```

2. Set the path of `backup_ceph_conf` to the `ceph.conf` configuration file path:

    ```
    [root@controller ~]# openstack-config --set /etc/cinder/cinder.conf default backup_ceph_conf /etc/ceph/ceph.conf
    ```

3. Set the backup pool name in which Cinder will store backed up volumes:

    ```
    [root@controller ~]# openstack-config --set /etc/cinder/cinder.conf default backup_ceph_pool cinder-backups
    ```

4. Set the Ceph backup user:

    ```
    [root@controller ~]# openstack-config --set /etc/cinder/cinder.conf default backup_ceph_user cinder-backup
    ```

5. Enable the default Ceph settings:

    ```
    [root@controller ~]# openstack-config --set /etc/cinder/cinder.conf default backup_ceph_chunk_size 134217728
    ```

    ```
    [root@controller ~]# openstack-config --set /etc/cinder/cinder.conf default backup_ceph_stripe_unit 0
    ```

    ```
    [root@controller ~]# openstack-config --set /etc/cinder/cinder.conf default backup_ceph_stripe_count 0
    ```

    ```
    [root@controller ~]# openstack-config --set /etc/cinder/cinder.conf default restore_discard_excess_bytes true
    ```

6. Restart the cinder-backup service:

    ```
    [root@controller ~]# systemctl restart openstack-cinder-backup
    ```

Configuring Cinder with multiple backends

Previous parts of this chapter discussed configuring various backend storage drivers with the cinder-volume service. Cinder allows configuring and utilizing multiple storage backends simultaneously. While configuring multiple storage backends with Cinder, a cinder-volume process is launched for each storage backend. We can choose a name for each storage backend that can be specified while creating new Cinder volumes. Cinder also supports setting identical names for several storage backends. In this scenario, Cinder-Scheduler decides where to place new volumes when created, based on weighing of the scheduler. This will be discussed further in the next section.

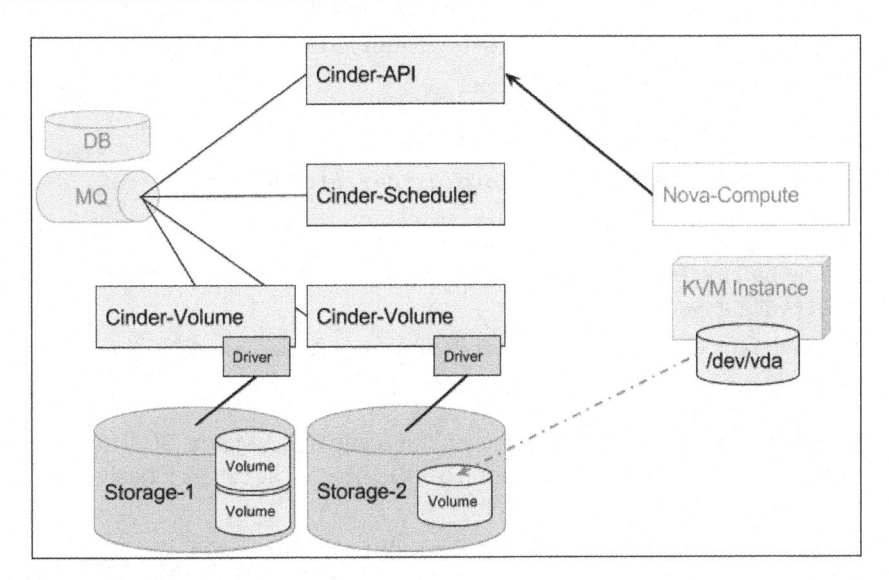

Getting ready

In this section, we will configure cinder to use two separate LVM volume groups as storage backends. Under the default section, we will specify two storage provider names separated by commas, and we will configure each of the storage providers and name them.

How to do it...

Follow these steps to configure two LVM storage provider backends:

1. Using the `openstack-config` command, edit cinder configuration file; under the `default` section, set `enabled_backends` to `lvm1,lvm2` to enable the two LVM providers:

   ```
   [root@controller ~]# openstack-config --set /etc/cinder/cinder.conf default enabled_backends lvm1,lvm2
   ```

Cinder Block Storage Service

2. Configure the first LVM provider `lvm1`. Enable the LVM and iSCSI storage backend driver for the `lvm1` provider; set the `LVMISCSIDriver` backend volume driver under the `lvm1` section:

   ```
   # openstack-config --set /etc/cinder/cinder.conf \
   lvm1 volume_driver cinder.volume.drivers.lvm.LVMISCSIDriver
   ```

3. Choose which volume group to be used with the `lvm1` provider:

   ```
   # openstack-config --set /etc/cinder/cinder.conf \
   lvm1 volume_group cinder-volumes-1
   ```

4. Choose a name for the new storage backend provider:

   ```
   # openstack-config --set /etc/cinder/cinder.conf \
   lvm1 volume_backend_name lvm1
   ```

5. Set an iSCSI helper to use a LioAdm helper:

   ```
   # openstack-config --set /etc/cinder/cinder.conf \
   lvm1 iscsi_helper lioadm
   ```

6. Set the parameter `iscsi_ip_address` with the IP address of the host running cinder-volume service:

   ```
   # openstack-config --set /etc/cinder/cinder.conf \
   lvm1 iscsi_ip_address 192.168.10.100
   ```

7. Configure the second LVM provider `lvm2`. Enable the LVM and iSCSI storage backend driver for the `lvm2` provider, set the `LVMISCSIDriver` backend volume driver under the `lvm2` section:

   ```
   # openstack-config --set /etc/cinder/cinder.conf \
   lvm2 volume_driver cinder.volume.drivers.lvm.LVMISCSIDriver
   ```

8. Choose volume group name to be used with the `lvm2` provider:

   ```
   # openstack-config --set /etc/cinder/cinder.conf \
   lvm2 volume_group cinder-volumes-2
   ```

9. Choose a name for the new storage backend provider:

   ```
   # openstack-config --set /etc/cinder/cinder.conf \
   lvm2 volume_backend_name lvm2
   ```

> The parameter `volume_backend_name` doesn't have to be a unique name. If an identical name is chosen for several storage providers, Cinder-scheduler will weigh and choose where to place new volumes based on weights and filter, this will be further be discussed in the next section.

Chapter 6

10. Set an iSCSI helper to use a LioAdm helper:
    ```
    # openstack-config --set /etc/cinder/cinder.conf \
    lvm2 iscsi_helper lioadm
    ```

11. Set the parameter `iscsi_ip_address` with the IP address of the host running cinder-volume service:
    ```
    # openstack-config --set /etc/cinder/cinder.conf \
    lvm2 iscsi_ip_address 192.168.10.100
    ```

12. Restart the cinder-volume service to load the new configuration.
    ```
    [root@controller ~]# systemctl restart openstack-cinder-volume
    ```

13. At this point, Cinder is configured to use multiple backend drivers. Now we will need to declare the new storage types. Create a new storage type named `lvm_gold`:
    ```
    [root@controller ~(keystone_admin)]# cinder type-create lvm_gold
    ```

> Remember to source the admin project environment variables prior to issuing Cinder commands:
> ```
> [root@controller ~]# source keystonerc_admin
> ```

14. Create a new storage type named `lvm_gold`:
    ```
    [root@controller ~(keystone_admin)]# cinder type-create lvm_gold
    ```

15. Assign the new storage type `lvm_gold` to the LVM backend named `lvm1`:
    ```
    [root@controller ~(keystone_admin)]# cinder type-key lvm_gold set volume_backend_name=lvm1
    ```

16. Create a second storage type named `lvm_silver`:
    ```
    [root@controller ~(keystone_admin)]# cinder type-create lvm_silver
    ```

17. Assign the new storage type `lvm_silver` to the LVM backend named `lvm2`:
    ```
    [root@controller ~(keystone_admin)]# cinder type-key lvm_silver set volume_backend_name=lvm2
    ```

    At this point, the multi backend storage is configured and ready for use.

18. Create a new volume specifying the `volume_type` parameter:
    ```
    cinder create --volume_type lvm_gold --display_name vol_gold 1
    ```

    This will create a new volume on `lvm_gold`, which is assigned to backend named `lvm1`.

Configuring Cinder scheduler filters and weighers

Cinder supports configuring multiple storage backends with identical `volume_backend_name`. In this configuration, Cinder-scheduler automatically schedules the placement of new volumes based on scheduler, which filter out storage backends that don't fit the filter policy, when multiple backends fit the filter policy, the backend storage is chosen, based on scheduler weighers.

`CapacityFilter` and `CapacityWeigher` are the default filter and weigher, respectively. When they are enabled, cinder-scheduler assigns the highest weight to the backend with the most available capacity.

`VolumeNumberWeigher` spreads volumes evenly across all storage backends that passed the filters, so for example, if two storage providers share the same `volume_backend_name`, and 10 volumes are created, each provider backend would host five volumes. This weigher provides another means of balancing workloads across multiple backend providers.

`DriverFilter` and `GoodnessWeigher` give better control of how the scheduler chooses the storage backend. `DriverFilter` and `GoodnessWeigher` allow configuring filters and weighers based on specific provider or volume properties, for example, placing new volumes larger than 5G on one storage provider and smaller on another, or choosing the provider based on the available capacity size of the provider. The `GoodnessWeigher` is configured by the parameter `goodness_function`, which is an equation that rates the quality of the potential provider with the following format "(rule)? potential1 : potential2 ".

If the rule is true, the provider is weighed with potential1, and if the rule is false, the provider is weighed with potential2. The potential of 0 is the lowest to potential of 100, which is the highest potential to schedule the creation of a new volume.

Getting ready

This section assumes that two Cinder providers were configured—as described in the previous section—both configured with the identical `volume_backend_name` LVM. So `/etc/cinder/cinder.conf` would contain a similar configuration to the following:

```
[default]
enabled_backends=lvm-1,lvm-2
[lvm-1]
volume_group=cinder-1
volume_driver=cinder.volume.drivers.lvm.LVMISCSIDriver
volume_backend_name=LVM
```

```
[lvm-2]
volume_group=cinder-2
volume_driver=cinder.volume.drivers.lvm.LVMISCSIDriver
volume_backend_name=LVM
```

How to do it...

Proceed with the following steps:

Enabling capacity filter and weigher

To enable capacity filter and weigher, set `scheduler_default_filters` to `CapacityFilter` and `scheduler_default_weighers` to `CapacityWeigher`, respectively, under the `default` section:

```
[root@controller ~]# openstack-config --set /etc/cinder/cinder.conf default scheduler_default_filters CapacityFilter

[root@controller ~]# openstack-config --set /etc/cinder/cinder.conf default scheduler_default_weighers CapacityWeigher
```

Enabling VolumeNumberWeigher

To enable VolumeNumberWeigher, set `scheduler_default_weighers` to `VolumeNumberWeigher`:

```
[root@controller ~]# openstack-config --set /etc/cinder/cinder.conf default scheduler_default_weighers VolumeNumberWeigher
```

> Cinder supports enabling multiple filters and weighers simultaneously. Simply specify multiple comma separated filters and weighers as in the following example:
> ```
> openstack-config --set /etc/cinder/cinder.conf default cheduler_default_weighers CapacityWeigher,VolumeNumberWeigher
> ```

Enabling and configuring DriverFilter and GoodnessWeigher

1. Enable the driver filter and GoodnessWeigher:

   ```
   [root@controller ~]# openstack-config --set /etc/cinder/cinder.conf default scheduler_default_filters DriverFilter

   [root@controller ~]# openstack-config --set /etc/cinder/cinder.conf default scheduler_default_weighers GoodnessWeigher
   ```

Cinder Block Storage Service

2. When driver filter is enabled, we can set `filter_function` with filtering rules for each storage provider. For example, set the `lvm-1` provider to filter volumes larger than 5G:

   ```
   [root@controller ~]# openstack-config --set /etc/cinder/cinder.conf lvm-1 filter_function  "volume.size < 5"
   ```

   Set lvm-2 to filter volumes smaller than 5G:

   ```
   [root@controller ~]# openstack-config --set /etc/cinder/cinder.conf lvm-1 filter_function  "volume.size => 5"
   ```

   Volumes larger than 5G will be scheduled on LVM-1 and smaller would be scheduled on LVM-2.

3. When goodness weigher is enabled, we can set `goodness_function` with weighting rules. In this example, if the volume size is smaller than 5G, LVM-1 gets potential of 100, and if the volume size is larger than 5G, the potential of LVM-1 to be selected is 50.

   ```
   [root@controller ~]# openstack-config --set /etc/cinder/cinder.conf lvm-1 goodness_function = "(volume.size < 5) ? 100 : 50"
   ```

   We can set `goodness_function` to each backend provider:

   ```
   [root@controller ~]# openstack-config --set /etc/cinder/cinder.conf lvm-2 goodness_function = "(volume.size >= 5) ? 100 : 25"
   ```

4. After configuring the `cinder.conf` configuration file, restart the `cinder-volume` service to load the new configuration.

   ```
   [root@controller ~]# systemctl restart openstack-cinder-volume
   ```

See also

The `DriverFilter` and `GoodnessWeigher` have many supported operators and available properties, which are documented on the OpenStack Admin Guide at `http://docs.openstack.org/admin-guide-cloud/content/driver_filter_weighing.html`.

7
Neutron Networking Service

In this chapter, we will cover the following topics:

- Configuring Neutron VLAN provider network with ML2 and LinuxBridge
- Configuring Neutron VXLAN and GRE tenant networks using Open vSwitch
- Configuring the L3 agent with Open vSwitch
- Configuring the DHCP service agent
- Configuring LoadBalancer as a Service
- Configuring Firewall as a Service

Introduction

Neutron is a software-defined networking service for OpenStack. OpenStack is responsible for managing virtual machine instances, and Neutron networking service is responsible for the network connectivity between virtual machine instances, tenants, and connectivity to external public networks allowing access to OpenStack virtual machine instances.

To provide the basic network connectivity to virtual machine instances, Neutron uses software-defined virtual switches. Neutron offers three types of capabilities, which are Neutron's core entities:

- Network: Networks are isolated Layer-2 broadcast domains, and they can also be regarded as the hubs that virtual machine instances connect to for interconnectivity.

Neutron Networking Service

- Subnet: A subnet is a block of IPv4 or IPv6 address that is associated with a network. The IP address for a subnet can be assigned to virtual machine instances. Multiple subnets can reside in a single network. A DHCP service can be used to assign the IP address from the address blocks to virtual machine instances.
- Port: These represent virtual switch ports that virtual machine instances can plug into.

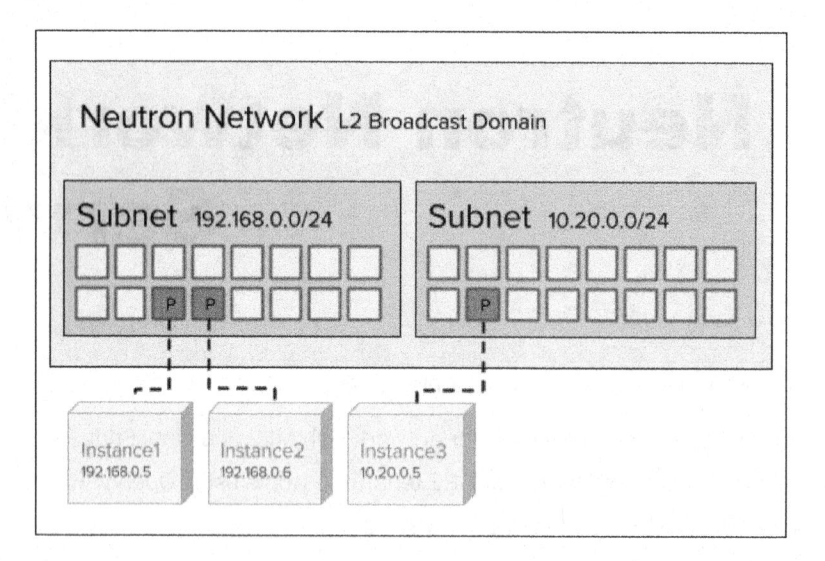

To implement Neutron's basic network switching capabilities, Neutron uses a core plugin mechanism that offers a custom backend implementation for the core networking API. **Modular Layer 2** (**ML2**) is Neutron's core plugin of choice for open source networking solution. ML2 core plugin allows utilizing multiple Layer-2 switching technologies, such as Open vSwitch and LinuxBridges. ML2 also supports multiples networking types that can be used for creating new Neutron-segregated networks. Neutron can create new tenant networks using tunneling technologies, such as VXLAN and VNGRE, to create new networks on top of existing Layer-3 IP networks or use provider networks—usually VLAN networks that are preconfigured on the physical network in the data center.

Neutron has a pluggable service extension framework that allows deploying and managing additional network services, such as routing, load balancing, firewalls, and **virtual private networks** (**VPNs**).

Neutron L3 routing service plugin includes ability to create and configure virtual routers, which can interconnect L2 networks, provide floating IPs to make the ports on private networks accessible from public networks using floating IPs, and interconnect complete L2 networks to external public networks. Neutron Layer-3 routing capabilities can be configured to utilize Open vSwtich or LinuxBridges, using the Linux IP stack and IPTables to perform both L3 forwarding and NAT. To support multiple routers with overlapping IP networks, Neutron L3 uses network namespaces to provide isolated forwarding contexts.

Neutron includes a load balancer service extension that enables Neutron to create virtual **Load Balancer as a Service** (**LBaaS**) via Neutron's API. Neutron load balancing as a service extension uses a HAProxy driver in the default setup and provides the ability to load balance traffic to applications running on virtual machine instances. LBaaS extends Neutron's API to manage virtual IP addresses; create pools, which are groups of virtual machine instances; manage pool members; and set health monitors, which are responsible for periodically checking the health of each member of the pool.

Another service extension that Neutron includes is the **Firewall as a Service** (**FWaaS**) extension. OpenStack provides two methods to secure the network traffic to virtual machine instances. The first method is Security Groups, which utilizes IPTables to filter network traffic to virtual machine instances at the compute hosts' level running the virtual machine instances. The second method, which is complementary to Security Groups, is Firewall as a Service extension, which handles network traffic by filtering network traffic at the perimeter of Neutron's Layer-3 router. FWaaS is commonly configured to utilize the IPTables driver for network traffic filtering.

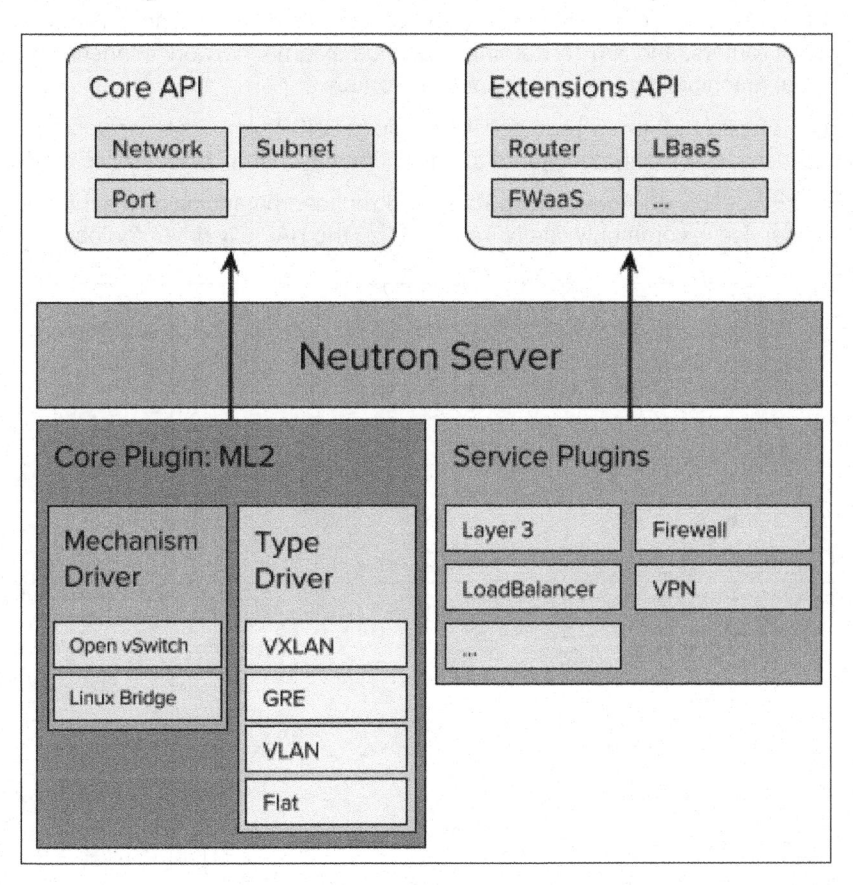

Neutron Networking Service

Neutron consists of several Linux services that implement the various parts of Neutron's capabilities:

- `neutron-server` is the main networking management service controlling the underlying networking mechanisms, plugins, and services. Neutron Server exposes the core networking API and the extension's API. Neutron Server manages the various services via RPC message bus, saves network's configuration and state to a database, which acts as a persistent storage.
- The `neutron-openvswitch-agent` service is responsible for managing the underlaying network provider plugin for Open vSwitch. If Open vSwitch is the chosen mechanism driver, it runs alongside with nova-compute on all compute hypervisor hosts.
- The `neutron-linuxbridge-agent` service is responsible for managing the underlaying network provider plugin for LinuxBridges. If LinuxBridges is the chosen mechanism driver, it runs alongside nova-compute on all compute hypervisor hosts.
- The `neutron-l3-agent` service handles Layer-3 network connectivity, creating virtual routers, and NAT forwarding to provide external network connectivity for virtual machine instances on tenant networks.
- The `neutron-dhcp-agent` service provides DHCP services to virtual machine instances, commonly configured to utilize dnsmasq Linux DNS service driver plugin.
- `neutron-lbaas-agent` OpenStack Neutron load balancing as a service agent. The service is commonly configured to utilize the HAProxy driver for load balancing.

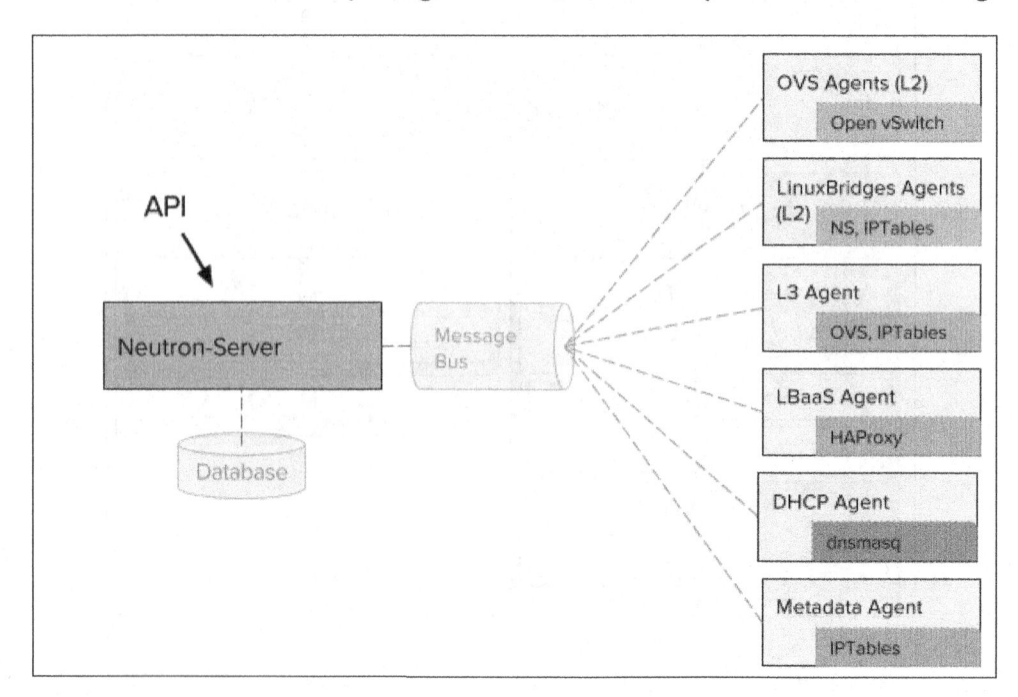

Configuring Neutron VLAN provider network with ML2 and LinuxBridge

Neutron supports utilizing a range of provider network VLANs that were prepared for us beforehand by the network administrator. We will configure Neutron to use the VLAN networks in the range to segregate between different Neutron networks. While creating new Neutron networks, Neutron will dedicate a VLAN from the range for each new network. The hosts use network namespaces for each network to segregate networks between virtual machine instances running on the same host.

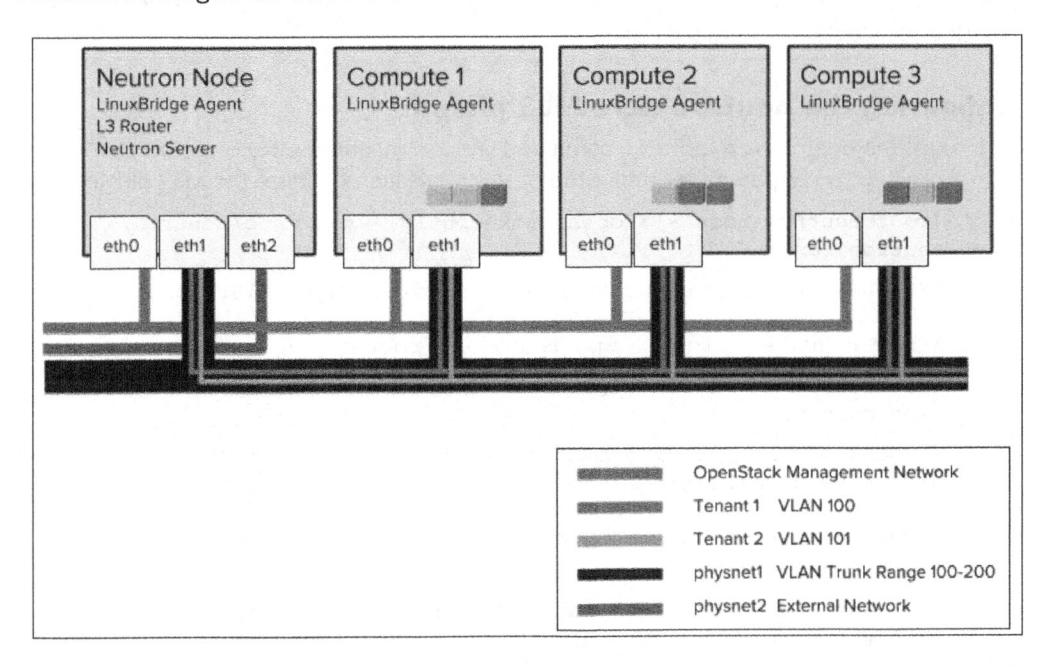

Getting ready

In this recipe, we will configure Neutron to use the **ML2** plugin with the LinuxBridge mechanism driver, and the VLAN tenant network type. We assume all OpenStack services, such as Keystone and nova, and components, such as message broker and database, are installed and configured. Neutron is already set to utilize them.

In this recipe, we will use the VLAN range of 100 to 200, which is preset by the network administrator.

Additionally, make sure that IP forwarding is enabled on the Neutron network node.

Neutron Networking Service

Edit /etc/sysctl.conf and make sure that it includes the following lines:

```
net.ipv4.ip_forward=1
net.ipv4.conf.all.rp_filter=0
net.ipv4.conf.default.rp_filter=0
```

Apply settings by issuing command # sysctl -p.

How to do it...

Follow these steps to configure Neutron with the ML2 plugin to utilize existing provider network VLANs for tenant network traffic.

Configuring the neutron core ML2 plugin

1. Use the openstack-config command line to configure neutron.conf, set the core_plugin parameter under the DEFAULT section to utilize the ML2 plugin:

   ```
   [root@neutron-node ~]# openstack-config --set /etc/neutron/neutron.conf
   
   DEFAULT core_plugin   neutron.plugins.ml2.plugin.Ml2Plugin
   ```

2. Make sure that service_plugin enables l3_router:

   ```
   [root@neutron-node ~]# openstack-config --set /etc/neutron/neutron.conf
   
   DEFAULT service_plugins neutron.services.l3_router.l3_router_plugin.L3RouterPlugin
   ```

3. Create a symbolic link for the core plugin configuration file to the ml2_conf plugin configuration file:

   ```
   [root@neutron-node ~]# # ln -s /etc/neutron/plugins/ml2/ml2_conf.ini /etc/neutron/plugin.ini
   ```

4. In the core plugin configuration file, under the ML2 section, set type_drivers to vlan:

   ```
   [root@neutron-node ~]# openstack-config --set /etc/neutron/plugin.ini \
   
   ml2 type_drivers   vlan
   ```

5. Additionally, set the tenant_network_types parameter to vlan:

   ```
   [root@neutron-node ~]# openstack-config --set /etc/neutron/plugin.ini \
   
   ml2 tenant_network_types   vlan
   ```

Chapter 7

6. Set `mechanism_drivers` to utilize LinuxBridge:

   ```
   [root@neutron-node ~]# openstack-config --set /etc/neutron/plugin.ini \
   ml2 mechanism_drivers linuxbridge
   ```

7. Set a physical network name with VLAN's range to be used for VLANed tenant traffic. In this section, we will also set a name for the external physical name `physnet2`:

   ```
   [root@neutron-node ~]# openstack-config --set /etc/neutron/plugin.ini \
   ml2_type_vlan network_vlan_ranges physnet1:100:200,physnet2
   ```

Configuring the LinuxBridge plugin

1. Now configure the Linux Bridge configuration file, set `tenant_network_type` to `vlans`:

   ```
   [root@neutron-node ~]# openstack-config --set /etc/neutron/plugins/linuxbridge/linuxbridge_conf.ini vlans tenant_network_type vlan
   ```

2. Set the same physical network names and VLAN ranges set in step 6:

   ```
   [root@neutron-node ~]# openstack-config --set /etc/neutron/plugins/linuxbridge/linuxbridge_conf.ini vlans
   network_vlan_ranges physnet1:100:200,physnet2
   ```

3. Set the `physical_interface_mappings` parameter, under the `linux_bridge` section, to map the network names with the physical Network Interfaces on the host:

   ```
   [root@neutron-node ~]# openstack-config --set /etc/neutron/plugins/linuxbridge/linuxbridge_conf.ini linux_bridge
   physical_interface_mappings physnet1:eth1, physnet2:eth2
   ```

Configuring the L3 plugin

1. Set the L3 agent to use the LinuxBridge driver to create Layer-3 connectivity between subnets and external networks:

   ```
   [root@neutron-node ~]# openstack-config --set /etc/neutron/l3_agent.conf
   DEFAULT interface_driver neutron.agent.linux.interface.BridgeInterfaceDriver
   ```

2. Set the value of `external_network_bridge` to blank:

   ```
   [root@neutron-node ~]# openstack-config --set /etc/neutron/l3_agent.conf
   DEFAULT external_network_bridge
   ```

Neutron Networking Service

> The value of parameter `external_network_bridge` has to be set to
> " " [null value] while using the LinuxBridge driver for the L3 agent.

Copy configuration and start services

All Neutron services are installed from a single neutron package and supporting agent packages. Configuration of LinuxBridge takes place in several *.conf files coming from both the Neutron package and LinuxBridge package. Due to the way Neutron is packaged and configured, it is recommended to make sure that all configurations are set on Neutron networking node, and all compute nodes, and start the services based on hosts' role.

1. Copy all Neutron configuration files from the Neutron network node to all compute nodes:

    ```
    [root@neutron-node ~]# scp -rp /etc/neutron/ root@compute-node1:/etc/neutron/

    [root@neutron-node ~]# scp -rp /etc/neutron/ root@compute-node2:/etc/neutron/
    ```

2. Start and enable the services `neutron-server`, `linuxbridge-agent`, `l3-agent`, and `dhcp-agent` on the Neutron node:

    ```
    [root@neutron-node ~]# systemctl start neutron-server
    [root@neutron-node ~]# systemctl enable neutron-server
    [root@neutron-node ~]# systemctl start neutron-l3-agent
    [root@neutron-node ~]# systemctl enable neutron-l3-agent
    [root@neutron-node ~]# systemctl start neutron-linuxbridge-agent
    [root@neutron-node ~]# systemctl enable neutron-linuxbridge-agent
    [root@neutron-node ~]# systemctl start neutron-dhcp-agent
    [root@neutron-node ~]# systemctl enable neutron-dhcp-agent
    ```

    > If the services were previously started, you can issue a `restart` command.

    ```
    [root@neutron-node ~]# systemctl restart neutron-server
    ```

3. Start and enable `linuxbridge-agent` on all compute nodes:

    ```
    [root@compute-node1 ~]# systemctl start neutron-linuxbridge-agent
    [root@compute-node1 ~]# systemctl enable neutron-linuxbridge-agent
    ```

4. Restart the `nova-compute` service on all compute nodes:

   ```
   [root@compute-node1 ~]# systemctl restart openstack-nova-compute
   ```

There's more...

At this point, Neutron is configured and ready to create new Neutron VLAN L2 networks using the existing range of provider network VLANs. Use the `neutron net-create` command to create a new Neutron network by specifying the parameter `segmentation_id`. You can choose which VLAN to be used or let Neutron choose the next available VLAN by not setting `segmentation_id`:

```
[root@neutron-node ~]# neutron net-create --tenant-id <TENANT-ID> net_vlan_101
        --provider:network_type vlan
        --provider:physical_network physnet1
        --provider:segmentation_id 101
[root@neutron-node ~]# neutron subnet-create --tenant-id <TENANT-ID>
--name vlan101_subnet1020 net_vlan_101 10.20.0.0/24
```

> If `segmentation_id` is not specified, Neutron will use the next available VLAN automatically.

To make the network accessible to external networks, we can create a router and connect it to the newly created subnet:

```
[root@neutron-node ~]# neutron router-create router1
[root@neutron-node ~]# neutron net-create --tenant-id <TENANT-ID> public
        --provider:network_type flat
        --provider:physical_network physnet2
        --router:external True
[root@neutron-node ~]# neutron subnet-create --tenant-id <TENANT-ID>
--name subnet1
        --gateway 192.168.100.254 public 192.168.0.0/24 --disable-dhcp
[root@neutron-node ~]# neutron router-gateway-set router1 public
[root@neutron-node ~]# neutron router-interface-add router1 vlan101_subnet1020
```

Neutron Networking Service

Configuring Neutron VXLAN and GRE tenant networks using Open vSwitch

Neutron supports creating layer 2 network overlays for tenant network traffic on top of Layer-3 networks using network tunneling technologies. In this recipe, we will configure Neutron to create GRE and VXLAN network overlays using **Open vSwitch** (**OVS**).

We will configure a topology of Neutron Networking Node that runs the Neutron Server main service, Open vSwitch agent, other Neutron service agents, such as L3 and DHCP. All OpenStack compute nodes run the open vSwitch agent to manage local L2 networks.

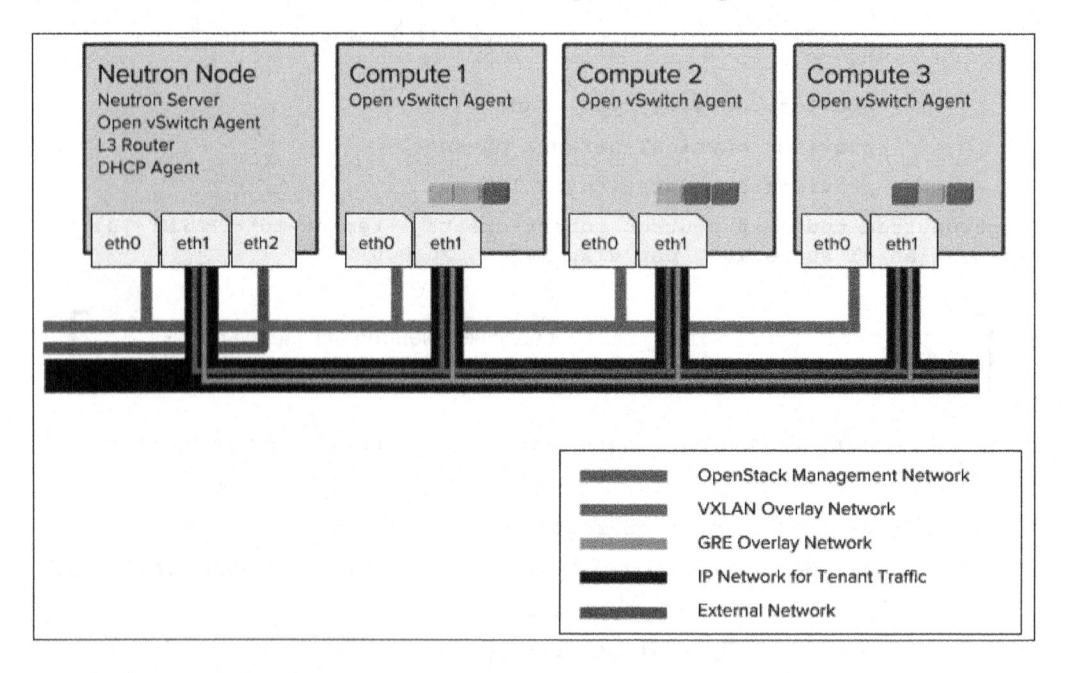

Getting ready

In this recipe, we will configure Neutron to use the ML2 plugin with an Open vSwitch mechanism driver, and tenant network type of VXLAN and GRE. Since the ML2 plugin supports configuring multiple type drivers, we will configure Neutron to support both GRE and VXLAN simultaneously. In this recipe, we assume that all OpenStack services, such as Keystone and nova, and components, such as message broker and database, are installed and Neutron is already configured to use them.

Additionally, make sure that IP forwarding is enabled on the Neutron Network node.

Edit /etc/sysctl.conf and make sure that it includes the following lines:

net.ipv4.ip_forward=1
net.ipv4.conf.all.rp_filter=0
net.ipv4.conf.default.rp_filter=0

Apply settings by issuing the command # sysctl -p.

How to do it...

Follow these steps to configure Neutron with an ML2 core plugin, an Open vSwitch mechanism driver, and GRE and VXLAN network overlays.

Configuring the neutron core ML2 plugin

1. Use the openstack-config command line to configure neutron.conf, set the core_plugin parameter under the DEFAULT section to utilize the ml2 plugin:

    ```
    [root@neutron-node ~]# openstack-config --set /etc/neutron/neutron.conf
    DEFAULT core_plugin   neutron.plugins.ml2.plugin.Ml2Plugin
    ```

2. Create a symbolic link for the core plugin configuration file to the ml2_conf plugin configuration file:

    ```
    [root@neutron-node ~]# ln -s /etc/neutron/plugins/ml2/ml2_conf.ini /etc/neutron/plugin.ini
    ```

3. In the core plugin configuration file, under the ml2 section, set type_drivers to vxlan,gre to load VXLAN and GRE type drivers:

    ```
    [root@neutron-node ~]# openstack-config --set /etc/neutron/plugin.ini \
    ml2 type_drivers   vxlan,gre
    ```

4. Additionally, set the tenant_network_types parameter to vlan,gre to enable VXLAN and GRE for tenant network types:

    ```
    [root@neutron-node ~]# openstack-config --set /etc/neutron/plugin.ini \
    ml2 tenant_network_types   vxlan,gre
    ```

5. Set the Open vSwitch mechanism driver:

    ```
    [root@neutron-node ~]# openstack-config --set /etc/neutron/plugin.ini \
    ml2 mechanism_drivers   openvswitch
    ```

Neutron Networking Service

6. Under the `ml2_type_vxlan` section, set the `vxlan` network identifiers' range:

   ```
   [root@neutron-node ~]# openstack-config --set /etc/neutron/plugin.ini \
   ml2_type_vxlan vni_ranges  10:1000
   ```

7. Set the vxlan multicast group:

   ```
   [root@neutron-node ~]# openstack-config --set /etc/neutron/plugin.ini \
   ml2_type_vxlan vxlan_group 224.0.0.1
   ```

8. Under the section `ml2_type_gre`, set tunnel ID ranges to `1001:2000`:

   ```
   [root@neutron-node ~]# openstack-config --set /etc/neutron/plugin.ini \
   ml2_type_gre tunnel_id_ranges = 1001:2000
   ```

Configuring the Open vSwitch plugin

1. In the OVS configuration file, under the `ovs` section, enable OVS tunneling:

   ```
   [root@neutron-node ~]# openstack-config --set /etc/neutron/plugins/openvswitch/ovs_neutron_plugin.ini ovs enable_tunneling True
   ```

2. Set the integration bridge:

   ```
   [root@neutron-node ~]# openstack-config --set /etc/neutron/plugins/openvswitch/ovs_neutron_plugin.ini ovs integration_bridge br-int
   ```

3. Set the tunnel bridge:

   ```
   [root@neutron-node ~]# openstack-config --set /etc/neutron/plugins/openvswitch/ovs_neutron_plugin.ini ovs tunnel_bridge br-tun
   ```

4. Set the IP address of the **Network Interface Card** (**NIC**) used for tenant network traffic:

   ```
   [root@neutron-node ~]# openstack-config --set /etc/neutron/plugins/openvswitch/ovs_neutron_plugin.ini ovs local_ip 192.168.122.112
   ```

5. Under the `agent` section, set `tunnel_types` to VXLAN, GRE:

   ```
   [root@neutron-node ~]# openstack-config --set /etc/neutron/plugins/openvswitch/ovs_neutron_plugin.ini agent tunnel_types vxlan,gre
   ```

Chapter 7

6. Set the UDP port to use for the `vxlan` packets multicast:

   ```
   [root@neutron-node ~]# openstack-config --set /etc/neutron/plugins/openvswitch/ovs_neutron_plugin.ini agent vxlan_udp_port 4789
   ```

Copy configuration and start services:

All Neutron services are installed from a single neutron package and a supporting agent packages. A configuration of Open vSwitch takes place in several *.conf files coming from both the Neutron package and LinuxBridge package. Due to the way Neutron is packaged and configured, make sure that all configurations are set on Neutron Networking Node, and all compute nodes; and start the services based on the roles of the hosts.

1. Copy all Neutron configuration files from the Neutron Network node to all compute nodes:

   ```
   [root@neutron-node ~]# scp -rp /etc/neutron/ root@compute-node1:/etc/neutron/

   [root@neutron-node ~]# scp -rp /etc/neutron/ root@compute-node2:/etc/neutron/
   ```

2. Start and enable the services `neutron-server`, `neutron-openvswitch-agent`, `l3-agent`, and `dhcp-agent` on the Neutron Node:

   ```
   [root@neutron-node ~]# systemctl start neutron-server
   [root@neutron-node ~]# systemctl enable neutron-server
   [root@neutron-node ~]# systemctl start neutron-l3-agent
   [root@neutron-node ~]# systemctl enable neutron-l3-agent
   [root@neutron-node ~]# systemctl start neutron-openvswitch-agent
   [root@neutron-node ~]# systemctl enable neutron-openvswitch-agent
   [root@neutron-node ~]# systemctl start neutron-dhcp-agent
   [root@neutron-node ~]# systemctl enable neutron-dhcp-agent
   ```

   > If the services were previously started, you can issue a `restart` command.
   > `[root@neutron-node ~]# systemctl restart neutron-server`

3. Start and enable the LinuxBridge agents on all compute nodes:

   ```
   [root@compute-node1 ~]# systemctl start neutron-openvswitch-agent
   [root@compute-node1 ~]# systemctl enable neutron-openvswitch-agent
   ```

Neutron Networking Service

4. Restart the `nova-compute` service on all compute nodes:

   ```
   [root@compute-node1 ~]# systemctl restart openstack-nova-compute
   ```

There's more...

At this point, Neutron is configured and ready to create new tenant VXLAN and GRE overlay networks. Use the `neutron net-create` command to create a new Neutron tenant networks when multiple overlay network types are enabled. Neutron chooses the first configured type as the default overlay type, for example, when `tenant_network_types` is set to `vxlan,gre`, the default network type is `vxlan` since it appears first.

The `net-create` command supports specifying the provider network type:

```
[root@neutron-node ~]# neutron net-create NAME --tenant_id TENANT_ID --provider:network_type gre
```

Configuring the L3 agent with Open vSwitch

The Neutron Layer-3 agent is responsible for creating and managing virtual routers on the Neutron Network node and creating floating IP address that can be attached to virtual machine instances. It is responsible for tenant network connectivity to external public networks. Neutron supports using either LinuxBridge or Open vSwitch as an implementation driver for Layer-3 routing services.

In this recipe, we will configure Neutron L3 agent with Open vSwitch to allow external network connectivity from an existing tenant network.

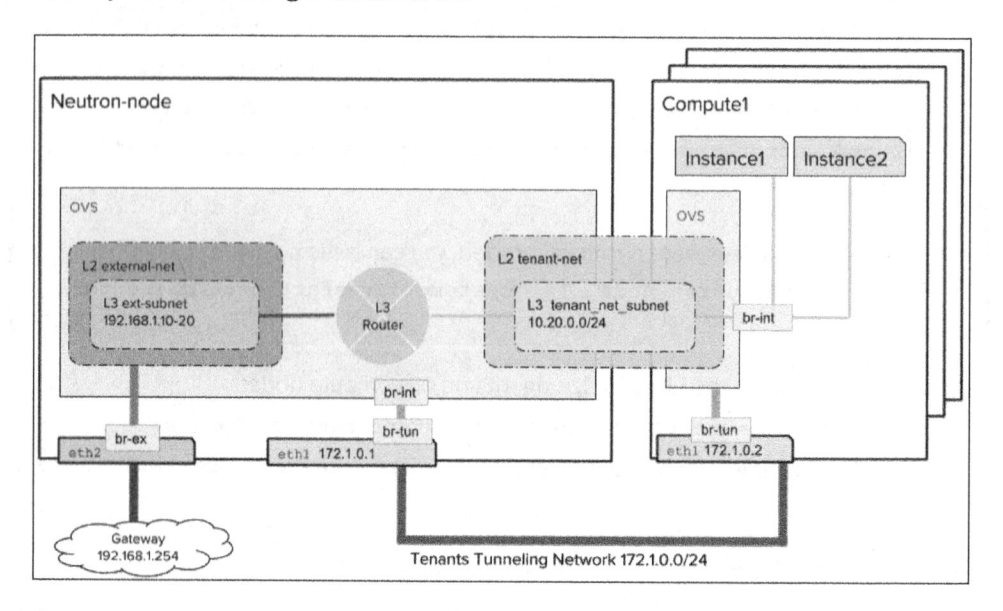

Chapter 7

Getting ready

First, make sure that IP forwarding is enabled on the Neutron network node. Edit the /etc/sysctl.conf file to contain the following parameters:

    net.ipv4.ip_forward=1

Run the command # sysctl -p to amend the changes.

How to do it...

Proceed with the following steps:

1. Using the openstack-config command, edit the main neutron configuration file, and under the DEFUALT section, enable the L3 service plugin:

    [root@neutron-node ~]# openstack-config --set /etc/neutron/neutron.conf DEFAULT service_plugins neutron.services.l3_router.l3_router_plugin.L3RouterPlugin

2. Now edit the L3 agent configuration file /etc/neutron/l3_agent.ini and set the Open vSwitch implementation driver:

    [root@neutron-node ~]# openstack-config --set /etc/neutron/l3_agent.ini DEFAULT interface_driver neutron.agent.linux.interface.OVSInterfaceDriver

3. Enable the use of network namespaces as follows:

    [root@neutron-node ~]# openstack-config --set /etc/neutron/l3_agent.ini DEFAULT use_namespaces True

4. Set the external network bridge name to br-ex (we will create the OVS bridge manually on a later stage):

    [root@neutron-node ~]# openstack-config --set /etc/neutron/l3_agent.ini DEFAULT external_network_bridge br-ex

5. Set router_delete_namespaces to True to delete namespaces of deleted routers:

    [root@neutron-node ~]# openstack-config --set /etc/neutron/l3_agent.ini DEFAULT router_delete_namespaces True

6. Start and enable the Open vSwitch service:

    [root@neutron-node ~]# systemctl enable openvswitch
    [root@neutron-node ~]# systemctl start openvswitch

Neutron Networking Service

7. Create a bridge for L3 agent to route external traffic to:

   `[root@neutron-node ~]# ovs-vsctl add-br br-ex`

8. Add a port to the external bridge, specify the name of the NIC you would like to use to external traffic:

   `[root@neutron-node ~]# ovs-vsctl add-port br-ex eth2`

9. Start and enable the L3 agent and `neutron-ovs-cleanup` service:

   `[root@neutron-node ~]# systemctl enable neutron-l3-agent neutron-ovs-cleanup`

   `[root@neutron-node ~]# systemctl Start neutron-l3-agent neutron-ovs-cleanup`

There's more...

At this point, the Layer-3 agent is configured and we can create new routers and connect them to external networks to provide tenants with connectivity to the public network.

First, we will create a new network and set it as an external network:

`[root@neutron-node ~]# neutron net-create ext-net --router:external True --provider:physical_network external`

Now create a subnet within the range on the external network gateway, and make sure to disable DHCP since DHCP services could be managed by the external network. Additionally, you can specify the range of floating IPs:

`[root@neutron-node ~]# neutron subnet-create ext-net --name ext-subnet --allocation-pool start=192.168.1.100 ,end=192.168.1.200 --disable-dhcp --gateway 192.168.1.254 192.168.1.254/24`

Create a new router named `router-ext` to route external traffic:

`[root@neutron-node ~]# neutron router-create router-ext`

Connect the new router to an existing subnet:

`[root@neutron-node ~]# neutron router-interface-add router-ext subnet1`

Now, we can make the external network as our router's gateway:

`[root@neutron-node ~]# neutron router-gateway-set router-ext ext-net`

Configuring the DHCP service agent

Neutron can provide DHCP services to the virtual machine instances using the `neutron-dhcp-agent` service. In this recipe, we will configure the DHCP agent to utilize `dnsmasq`—a free, lightweight DNS forwarder—and DHCP server that is used to provide DHCP services to networks. The DHCP agent is responsible for spawning and controlling dnsmasq processes for each network that leverages DHCP.

How to do it...

Follow these steps to configure the DHCP service agent:

1. Using the `openstack-config` command, edit the `dhcp` agent configuration file, and under the default section, set OVS as the interface driver:

   ```
   [root@neutron-node ~]# openstack-config --set /etc/neutron/dhcp_agent.ini DEFAULT interface_driver neutron.agent.linux.interface.OVSInterfaceDriver
   ```

2. Choose `dnsmaq` as the `dhcp` driver:

   ```
   [root@neutron-node ~]# openstack-config --set /etc/neutron/dhcp_agent.ini DEFAULT dhcp_driver   neutron.agent.linux.dhcp.Dnsmasq
   ```

3. Enable the use of network namespaces for DHCP services as follows:

   ```
   [root@neutron-node ~]# openstack-config --set /etc/neutron/dhcp_agent.ini DEFAULT use_namespaces True
   ```

4. Enable the deletion of namespaces when the `dhcp` service is disabled:

   ```
   [root@neutron-node ~]# openstack-config --set /etc/neutron/dhcp_agent.ini DEFAULT dhcp_delete_namespaces True
   ```

5. Optionally, set the domain name as follows:

   ```
   [root@neutron-node ~]# openstack-config --set /etc/neutron/dhcp_agent.ini DEFAULT dhcp_domain openstack.local
   ```

6. Start and enable the DHCP agent:

   ```
   [root@neutron-node ~]# systemctl enable neutron-dhcp-agent
   [root@neutron-node ~]# systemctl Start neutron-dhcp-agent
   ```

Configuring LoadBalancer as a service

The Neutron LBaaS extension allows us to create virtual load balancers that can balance incoming application traffic between running virtual machine instances. The extension introduces additional Neutron API calls to create and manage virtual IP addresses, pools, pool members, and health monitors.

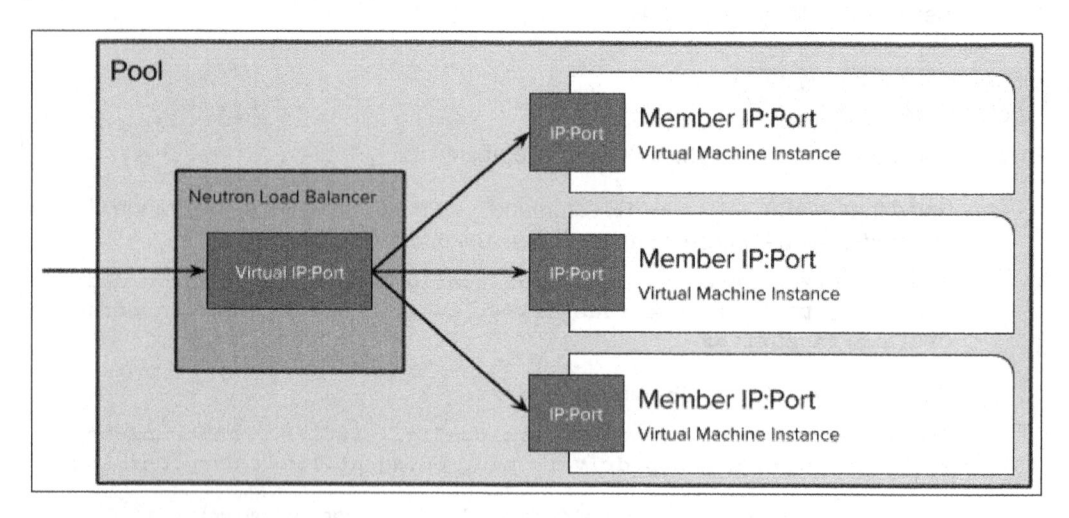

Getting ready

Neutron LBaaS service relies on an HAProxy implementation driver. Before getting started with configuring Neutron LBaaS, make sure that the HAProxy service is installed on the neutron network node running L3 service:

```
[root@neutron-node ~]# yum -y install haproxy
```

> If Neutron LBaaS is installed on same node with Keystone, you will need to change the default HAProxy port, since Keystone uses port 5000 for public endpoint. Edit the file /etc/haproxy/haproxy.cfg and change the line frontend main *:5000 to frontend main *:5001.

How to do it...

Follow these steps to configure Neutron LBaaS:

1. In Neutron's main configuration file, under the `DEFAULT` section, set the `service_plugins` parameter to point the LBaaS plugin:

   ```
   [root@neutron-node ~]# openstack-config --set /etc/neutron/neutron.conf DEFAULT service_plugins neutron.services.loadbalancer.plugin.LoadBalancerPlugin
   ```

   > If additional services are configured, you will need to manually edit the file `/etc/neutron/neutron.conf`, separate the existing value with a comma, and add `neutron.services.loadbalancer.plugin`. The LoadBalancer plugin, for example, loading both L3 and LBaaS, would result in the following code:
   >
   > ```
   > service_plugins = neutron.services.l3_router.
   > l3_router_plugin.L3RouterPlugin, neutron.services.
   > loadbalancer.plugin.LoadBalancerPlugin
   > ```

2. Edit `/etc/neutron/neutron.conf`, and under the `service_providers` section, add HAProxy LBaaS service provider:

   ```
   [root@neutron-node ~]# openstack-config --set openstack-config --set /etc/neutron/neutron.conf service_providers service_provider LOADBALANCER:Haproxy:neutron.services.loadbalancer.drivers.haproxy.plugin_driver.HaproxyOnHostPluginDriver:default
   ```

3. In the LBaaS agent configuration file `lbaas_agent.ini`, set Open vSwitch as the interface driver:

   ```
   [root@neutron-node ~]# openstack-config --set /etc/neutron/lbaas_agent.ini DEFAULT interface_driver neutron.agent.linux.interface.OVSInterfaceDriver
   ```

4. Then, set HAProxy as the device driver:

   ```
   [root@neutron-node ~]# openstack-config --set /etc/neutron/lbaas_agent.ini DEFAULT device_driver neutron.services.loadbalancer.drivers.haproxy.namespace_driver.HaproxyNSDriver
   ```

5. Under the `haproxy` section, set `user_group` to `haproxy`:

   ```
   [root@neutron-node ~]# openstack-config --set /etc/neutron/lbaas_agent.ini haproxy user_group haproxy
   ```

Neutron Networking Service

6. Restart the Neutron-server service:

   `[root@neutron-node ~]# systemctl restart neutron-server`

7. Start and enable the `lbaas-agent` service:

   `[root@neutron-node ~]# systemctl start neutron-lbaas-agent`

   `[root@neutron-node ~]# systemctl enable neutron-lbaas-agent`

There's more...

LBaas can be enabled in Horizon Dashboard. To enable it, set the `enable_lb` setting in the `/etc/openstack-dashboard/local_settings` file to `True` and restart the Apache HTTPD service:

`[root@controller ~]# sed -i "/'enable_lb': False,/c\'enable_lb': True," /etc/openstack-dashboard/local_settings # service`

`[root@controller ~]# systemctl restart httpd`

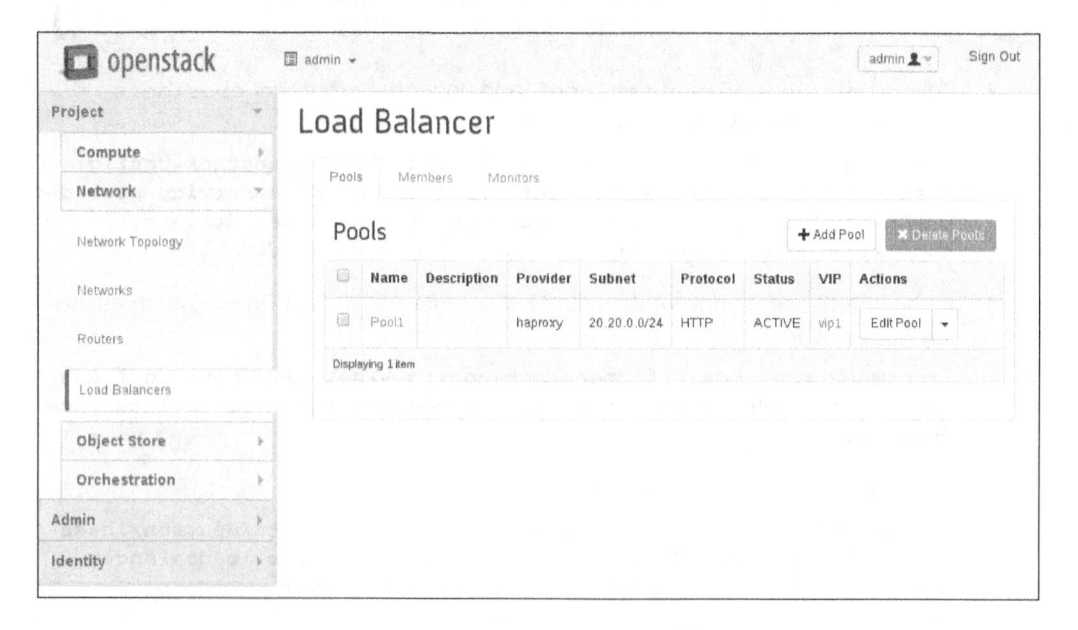

	Name	Description	Provider	Subnet	Protocol	Status	VIP	Actions
	Pool1		haproxy	20.20.0.0/24	HTTP	ACTIVE	vip1	Edit Pool

Displaying 1 item

Configuring Firewall as a Service

The Neutron **Firewall as a Service** (**FWaaS**) plugin adds perimeter firewall management to networking. FWaaS uses IPTables to apply firewall policy to all Networking routers within a project. FWaaS uses IPTables on the node running Layer-3 agent.

How to do it...

Follow these steps to configure Neutron FWaaS:

1. In Neutron's main configuration file, under the DEFAULT section, set the service_plugins parameter to point the FWaaS plugin:

   ```
   [root@neutron-node ~]# openstack-config --set /etc/neutron/neutron.conf DEFAULT service_plugins neutron.services.firewall.fwaas_plugin.FirewallPlugin
   ```

   > If additional services are configured, you will need to manually edit the file /etc/neutron/neutron.conf, separate the existing value with a comma, and add neutron.services.loadbalancer.plugin.LoadBalancerPlugin, for example, loading both L3 and LBaaS would result in the following code:
   >
   >   service_plugins = neutron.services.l3_router.
   >   l3_router_plugin.L3RouterPlugin, neutron.services.
   >   firewall.fwaas_plugin.FirewallPlugin

2. In the FWaaS configuration file /etc/neutron/fwaas_driver.ini, under fwaas section, set the IPTables driver:

   ```
   [root@neutron-node ~]# openstack-config --set /etc/neutron/fwaas_driver.ini fwaas driver neutron.services.firewall.drivers.linux.iptables_fwaas.IptablesFwaasDriver
   ```

3. Set the fwaas service to enable:

   ```
   [root@neutron-node ~]# openstack-config --set /etc/neutron/fwaas_driver.ini fwaas enabled true
   ```

4. Restart the Neutron Server and L3-Agent services:

   ```
   [root@neutron-node ~]# systemctl restart neutron-server
   [root@neutron-node ~]# systemctl restart neutron-l3-agent
   ```

Neutron Networking Service

There's more...

FwaaS can be enabled in Horizon Dashboard. To enable it, set the `enable_firewall` setting in the `/etc/openstack-dashboard/local_settings` file to `True` and restart the Apache HTTPD service:

```
[root@controller ~]# sed -i "/'enable_firewall': False,/c\'enable_firewall': True," /etc/openstack-dashboard/local_settings
[root@controller ~]# systemctl restart httpd
```

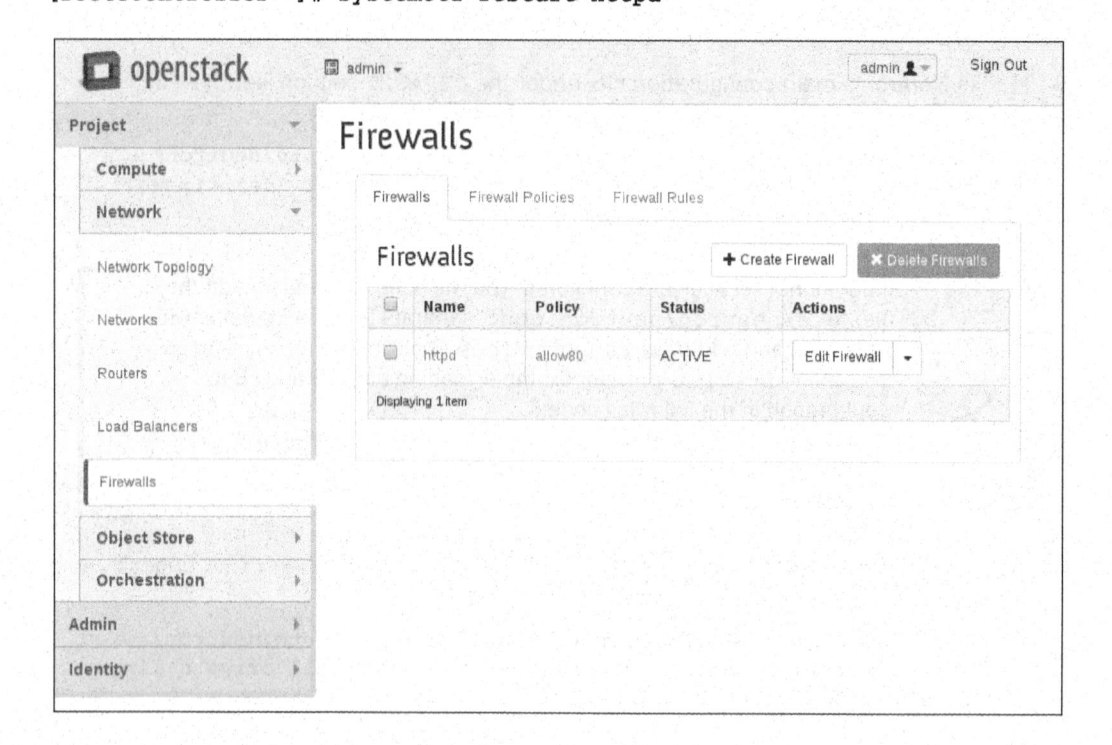

8
Nova-Compute Service

In this chapter, we will cover the following topics:

- Configuring Nova-compute with KVM Hypervisor
- Configuring Nova-compute with a QEMU Hypervisor emulation
- Configuring Nova scheduler filters
- Configuring Nova host aggregates
- Configuring Nova host aggregates filters
- Configuring Nova scheduler weights

Introduction

The front and center of **Infrastructure as a Service** (**IaaS**) solution is the compute service that runs the Cloud application workloads. OpenStack Compute, named project Nova, is responsible for providing computing as a Service framework for OpenStack that enables provisioning and managing the life cycle of instances of virtual machines at a large scale. Nova allows us to create, manage, and destroy virtual machine instances using API calls. Nova also has a complete command-line tool interacting with the API.

Nova-Compute Service

Nova's architecture is designed to scale horizontally on standard hardware, which allows us to create a highly scalable Cloud environment.

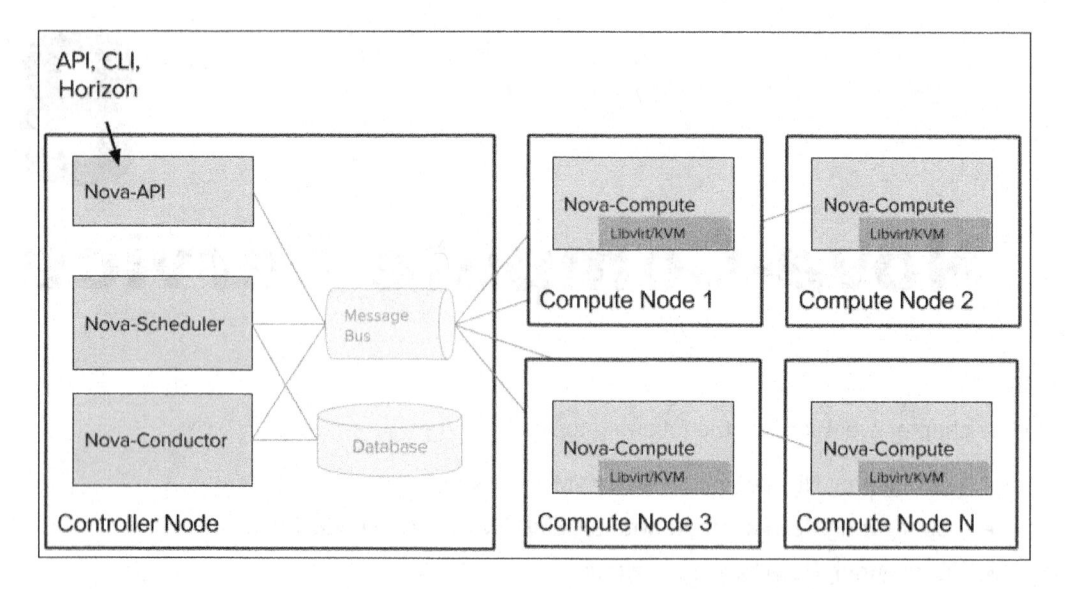

To implement Compute as a Service and manage large amount of virtual machine instances that can rapidly scale out, Nova uses several Linux services that fall under the following categories:

Nova access services

- The `nova-api` service provides an API that the user interacts with. Nova-API supports an OpenStack native Compute API and Amazon EC2 API compatibility. The service also accepts Admin API requests for privileged users to perform administrative actions. The Nova-API service communicates with other services via the RPC message broker.

- The `openstack-nova-novncproxy` service provides a proxy to access running instances through a VNC connection that supports browser-based noVNC clients.

- The `nova-consoleauth` service authorizes tokens for users that console proxies provide. The `nova-consoleauth` services should run on a network that is accessible to the web browser trying to reach the console.

Nova management services

- The `nova-scheduler` service takes a virtual machine instance request from the queue and determines on which compute server it should run based on the confined set of filters, weighers, and segregations, such as cells and host aggregates.

- The `nova-conductor` service accepts scheduling calls from the message queue and communicates with the database. The service aims to eliminate direct accesses to the Cloud database made by Nova-compute.
- The `nova-cert` service manages and generates x509 certificates for EC2 API.

Nova-compute worker service

The `nova-compute` service is the main virtual machine management service. It is responsible for managing virtual machines on the host it runs on. `nova-compute` uses a virtualization backend driver, such as `libvirtd` to manage KVM virtual machines or XEN to manage XEN domains. A Nova-compute service can scale horizontally on multiple compute machines. Using a hypervisor driver, Nova-compute creates, destroys, and performs actions on virtual machines. Nova-compute performs operations on virtual machine instances based on commands it reads from the RPC message bus.

Nova network services

Environments that choose to use legacy Nova-network instead of Neutron also have following services that enable network access to the virtual machine instances.

- The `nova-network` service is similar to `nova-compute`; it accepts networking tasks from the queue and performs tasks to manipulate the network, such as setting up bridging interfaces or changing iptables rules.
- The `nova-dhcpbridge` script tracks IP address leases and records them in the database using the `dnsmasq dhcp-script` facility.

Configuring Nova Hypervisors

The nodes running virtual machine instances are commonly referred to as Compute nodes. Nova Compute nodes are running the nova-compute service, which manages the hypervisor it runs on via a hypervisor driver. A Nova-compute service passes commands to the local hypervisor via the driver to spawn or destroy virtual machine instances. The default and most commonly selected hypervisor with OpenStack is KVM; it requires virtualization hardware support by a CPU. CPUs with native support for KVM can be identified by VT-d (`vmx` flag) with Intel CPUs and AMD-v (`svm` flag) with AMD CPUs.

[All supported hypervisors are listed in the OpenStack Wiki page https://wiki.openstack.org/wiki/HypervisorSupportMatrix.]

Configuring Nova-compute with KVM Hypervisor

Kernel-based virtual machine (**KVM**) is the most common and robust open source virtualization Hypervisor, and it is most commonly used with OpenStack. In this recipe, we will configure the Nova-compute service to use the KVM Hypervisor driver, which invokes `libvirt` service commands to control KVM virtual machines on the host running the Nova-compute service.

Getting ready

Before configuring Nova-compute to use KVM, make sure that hardware-assisted virtualization is enabled, and a virtualization flag is present at `/proc/cpuinfo`. Check whether `amd-v` or `intel-vt` is supported:

```
[root@compute1 ~]# grep -E 'svm|vmx' /proc/cpuinfo
```

If the preceding command returns 0, make sure that virtualization is enabled at BIOS.

How to do it...

After verifying that KVM is supported, follow these steps to configure Nova-compute with the KVM hypervisor driver:

1. Install the `kvm` and `libvirt` packages:

   ```
   [root@compute1 ~]# yum install qemu-kvm libvirt libvirt-python libguestfs-tools
   ```

2. Start and enable `libvirt`:

   ```
   [root@compute1 ~]# systemctl start libvirtd
   [root@compute1 ~]# systemctl enable libvirtd
   ```

3. Reboot the host to make sure that KVM modules are loaded at system startup. To check whether the KVM modules are loaded, run the following command:

   ```
   [root@compute1 ~]# lsmod | grep kvm
   ```

   If the modules were not loaded, we can load them manually as follows:

   ```
   [root@compute1 ~]# modprobe -a kvm
   ```

   Load the Intel KVM module if an Intel CPU is used:

   ```
   [root@compute1 ~]# modprobe -a kvm-intel
   ```

   Load the AMD KVM module if an AMD CPU is used:

   ```
   [root@compute1 ~]# modprobe -a kvm-amd
   ```

Chapter 8

4. Then, edit the file `/etc/modules-load.d/kvm.conf` and add the module names to it to ensure that the modules are loaded on system reboot.

5. Using the `openstack-config` command, set the `compute_driver` parameter under the `DEFAULT` section to use the `libvirt` driver:

   `[root@compute1 ~]# openstack-config --set /etc/nova/nova.conf DEFAULT compute_driver = libvirt.LibvirtDriver`

6. Set the `virt_type` parameter to KVM under the `libvirt` section:

   `[root@compute1 ~]# openstack-config --set /etc/nova/nova.conf libvirt`

   `virt_type = kvm`

7. Set the `virt_type` parameter to KVM under the `libvirt` section:

   `[root@compute1 ~]# openstack-config --set /etc/nova/nova.conf libvirt`

   `virt_type = kvm`

8. Restart the Nova-compute service for all changes to take effect:

   `[root@controller ~]# systemctl restart openstack-nova-compute`

Configuring Nova-compute with a QEMU Hypervisor emulation

Not all environments always have virtualization capabilities supported by the CPU, for example, test environments running the Nova Compute nodes on virtual machines. In such cases, we can configure Nova to use a QEMU virtualization hypervisor emulation. This significantly reduces the performance of virtual machine instances running with the QEMU hypervisor emulation, but allows you to run virtual machine instances without virtualization support by the CPU.

How to do it...

Follow these steps to configure Nova-compute with the QEMU emulation:

1. Install QEMU and the `libvirt` packages:

   `[root@compute1 ~]# yum install qemu libvirt libvirt-python libguestfs-tools`

2. Start and enable `libvirt`:

   `[root@compute1 ~]# systemctl start libvirtd`

   `[root@compute1 ~]# systemctl enable libvirtd`

Nova-Compute Service

3. Using the `openstack-config` command, set the `compute_driver` parameter under the `DEFAULT` section to use the `libvirt` driver:

   ```
   [root@compute1 ~]# openstack-config --set /etc/nova/nova.conf
   DEFAULT compute_driver    libvirt.LibvirtDriver
   ```

4. Set the `virt_type` parameter to QEMU under the `libvirt` section:

   ```
   [root@compute1 ~]# openstack-config --set /etc/nova/nova.conf
   libvirt

   virt_type   qemu
   ```

5. Restart the Nova-compute service for all changes to take effect:

   ```
   [root@controller ~]# systemctl restart openstack-nova-compute
   ```

Configuring Nova scheduling

When Nova gets a request to create a new virtual machine instance, `nova-api` passes the instance creation call to nova-scheduler, then nova-scheduler uses filters and weighers to determine which Nova Compute host is tasked to create the virtual machine instance. First, nova-scheduler uses filters to determine which hosts can be considered to run the virtual machine instance and rules out hosts that did not pass the filter.

After eliminating hosts that are not suitable, nova-scheduler uses weights to calculate the priority for each host, so Compute host with the highest priority gets elected to run the virtual machine instance. Nova scheduler calculates the weight by summarizing all the weighers for each host; the host with the largest weight is given the highest priority and gets elected to run the virtual machine instance.

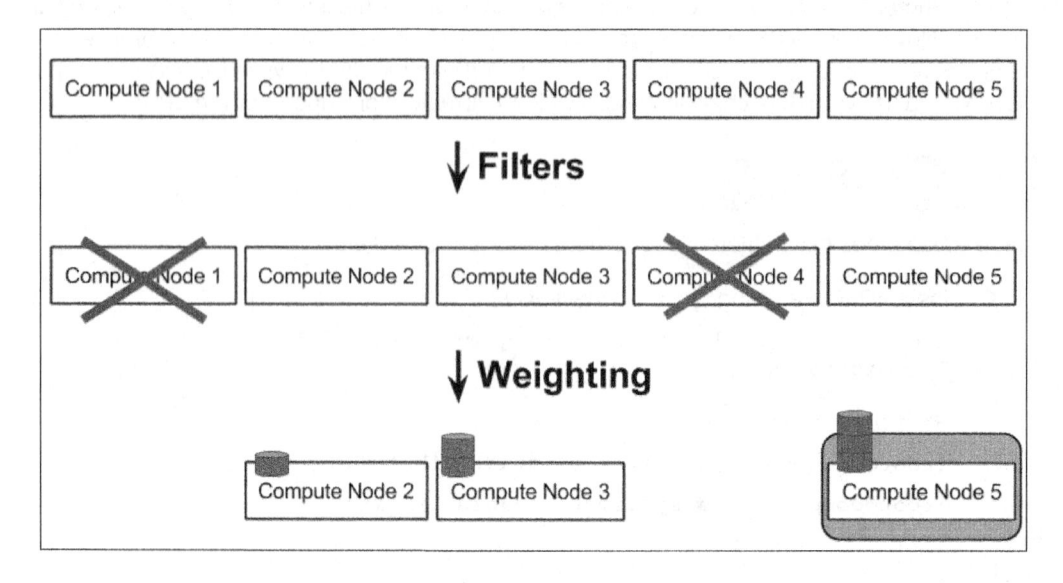

Configuring Nova scheduler filters

First, let's configure Nova scheduler filters, they are configured in Nova's main configuration file `/etc/nova/nova.conf` on the host running a Nova scheduler service, which is most commonly installed on the controller node.

Getting ready

Enable and set the filter scheduler driver under the `DEFAULT` section:

```
[root@controller ~]# openstack-config --set /etc/nova/nova.conf DEFAULT scheduler_driver
```

`nova.scheduler.filter_scheduler.FilterScheduler`

Then, set which filter scheduler should be available:

```
[root@controller ~]# openstack-config --set /etc/nova/nova.conf DEFAULT scheduler_available_filters
```
`nova.scheduler.filters.all_filters`

The parameter `scheduler_default_filters` will enable filters to be used:

```
[root@controller ~]# openstack-config --set /etc/nova/nova.conf DEFAULT scheduler_default_filters RetryFilter, AvailabilityZoneFilter, RamFilter, ComputeFilter, ComputeCapabilitiesFilter, ImagePropertiesFilter, CoreFilter
```

Note that `scheduler_default_filters` allows us to enable multiple comma separated filters.

How to do it...

Configuring Nova-scheduler filters consist of the following steps:

Filter operational and enabled hosts by ComputeFilter

The `ComputeFilter` passes all hosts that are operational and enabled. ComputeFilter is part of the default filters and generally should be enabled while using Nova scheduler filters.

1. Enable and configure `ComputeFilter` by editing Nova's configuration file `/etc/nova/nova.conf`, add the value `ComputeFilter` to the parameter `scheduler_default_filters`:

    `scheduler_default_filters = ComputeFilter`

Nova-Compute Service

2. Restart the Nova-scheduler service for changes to take effect:

   `[root@controller ~]# systemctl restart openstack-nova-scheduler`

Multiple scheduling retries with RetryFilter

The filter `RetryFilter` removes hosts that failed to respond a service request, and it allows the configuration of the number of schedule attempts by setting the parameter `scheduler_max_attempts`.

Enable and configure `RetryFilter` by following these steps:

1. In Nova's configuration file `/etc/nova/nova.conf`, edit the parameter `scheduler_default_filters` and add `RetryFilter` to the list of values.

   `scheduler_default_filters = RetryFilter`

2. To allow two scheduling retries for each host set `scheduler_max_attempts` to 2:

   `[root@controller ~]# openstack-config --set /etc/nova/nova.conf DEFAULT`

   `scheduler_max_attempts 2`

3. Restart the Nova-scheduler service for changes to take effect:

   `[root@controller ~]# systemctl restart openstack-nova-scheduler`

Memory overcommitment with RamFilter

`RamFilter` allows to limit Nova scheduler to only schedule instances on hosts that have sufficient memory available. It also allows the configuration of the allowed memory overcommitment ratio by setting the parameter `ram_allocation_ratio`. If `RamFilter` is not set, the scheduler may overprovision a host with virtual machine instances exceeding the physical memory.

Enable and configure `RamFilter` by following these steps:

1. In Nova's configuration file `/etc/nova/nova.conf`, edit the parameter `scheduler_default_filters` and add `RamFilter` to the list of values:

   `scheduler_default_filters = RamFilter`

2. To allow memory overcommitment by 150 percent, set `ram_allocation_ratio` to `1.5`:

   `[root@controller ~]# openstack-config --set /etc/nova/nova.conf DEFAULT`

   `ram_allocation_ratio 1.5`

   This setting enables instances to consume 1.5 GB of memory on compute nodes with 1 GB of free RAM.

3. Restart the Nova-scheduler service for changes to take effect:

   `[root@controller ~]# systemctl restart openstack-nova-scheduler`

CPU overcommitment with CoreFilter

`CoreFilter` limits the scheduling of virtual machine instances on hosts that have sufficient CPU core available. `CoreFilter` allows us to configure a fixed amount of vCPU overcommitment by using the `cpu_allocation_ratio` parameter in `nova.conf`. If `CoreFilter` is not set, the scheduler can overprovision the host with virtual machine instances CPU cores exceeding the physical cores.

Enable and configure `CoreFilter` by following these steps:

1. In Nova's configuration file `/etc/nova/nova.conf`, edit the parameter `scheduler_default_filters` and add `CoreFilter` to the list of values:

   `scheduler_default_filters = CoreFilter`

2. To allow overcommitting CPU, set `cpu_allocation_ratio` to the desired overcommitment ratio:

   `[root@controller ~]# openstack-config --set /etc/nova/nova.conf DEFAULT`

   `cpu_allocation_ratio 10.0`

   This setting allows us to run 10 vCPUs on each physical CPU core.

   To disable CPU overcommitment, set `cpu_allocation_ratio` to 1.

   `[root@controller ~]# openstack-config --set /etc/nova/nova.conf DEFAULT`

   `cpu_allocation_ratio 1.0`

3. Restart the Nova-scheduler service for changes to take effect:

   `[root@controller ~]# systemctl restart openstack-nova-scheduler`

Ephemeral disk overcommitment with DiskFilter

`DiskFilter` allows us to set the disk overcommitment ratio that the scheduler should allow. It filters out hosts when the free disk space available is smaller than the configured ratio. `DiskFilters` allows the configuration of maximum disk overcommitment ratio by using the `disk_allocation_ratio` configuration option in the `/etc/nova/nova.conf` configuration file. By default, disk overcommitment is disabled. It is useful to set disk overcommitment when SPARSE image format is in use, and disk image sizes are usually smaller than the virtual disk size.

Nova-Compute Service

Enable and configure `DiskFilter` by following these steps:

1. In Nova's configuration file `/etc/nova/nova.conf`, edit the parameter `scheduler_default_filters` and add `DiskFilter` to the list of values.

    `scheduler_default_filters = DiskFilter`

2. To allow overcommitting disk, set `disk_allocation_ratio` to the desired overcommitment ratio:

    ```
    [root@controller ~]# openstack-config --set /etc/nova/nova.conf DEFAULT
    disk_allocation_ratio  1.3
    ```

3. Restart the Nova-scheduler service for changes to take effect:

    `[root@controller ~]# systemctl restart openstack-nova-scheduler`

ImagePropertiesFilter

`ImagePropertiesFilter` allows the filtering of hosts by properties defined on the instance's glance image. `ImagePropertiesFilter` passes hosts that support properties specified by the image contained in the instance. `ImagePropertiesFilter` supports filtering by architecture, which includes `x86_64`, i686, arm, and ppc64. `ImagePropertiesFilter` also supports filtering by hypervisor type, which includes `qemu` (used both for KVM and QEMU emulation), XEN, and XENAPI.

Enable and configure `ImagePropertiesFilter` by following these steps:

1. In Nova's configuration file `/etc/nova/nova.conf`, edit the parameter `scheduler_default_filters` and add `ImagePropertiesFilter` to the list of values.

    `scheduler_default_filters = ImagePropertiesFilter`

2. Update the properties to glance image, add architecture property `x86_64`, and KVM Hypervisor:

    ```
    [root@controller ~]# glance image-update img-uuid --property architecture=x86_64 --property hypervisor_type=qemu
    ```

3. Restart the Nova-scheduler service for changes to take effect:

    `[root@controller ~]# systemctl restart openstack-nova-scheduler`

Configuring instances affinity group with ServerGroupAffinityFilter

Nova includes the `ServerGroupAffinityFilter` filter, which allows the scheduling of virtual machine instances provisioning on physical nova compute hosts with affinity to each other. This allows virtual machine instances to run, of the same Cloud application, for example, run with affinity to each other on the same host. This is desired for a variety of reasons, for example, to gain performance of intercommunication between virtual machine instances. To use `ServerGroupAffinityFilter` filter, create a Nova server group with an affinity policy, when launching a new virtual machine instance pass a scheduler hint, using group as the key and the server group UUID as the value.

Enable and configure `ServerGroupAffinityFilter`, as described in the following steps:

1. In Nova's configuration file `/etc/nova/nova.conf`, edit the parameter `scheduler_default_filters` and add `ServerGroupAffinityFilter` to the list of values.

   ```
   scheduler_default_filters = ServerGroupAffinityFilter
   ```

2. Create a new server group with affinity policy as follows:

   ```
   [root@controller ~]# nova server-group-create --policy affinity AffinityGroup1
   ```

3. Boot the virtual machine instance with the `--hint` flag that points to the UUID of the affinity group:

   ```
   [root@controller ~]# nova boot --image <GLANCE_IMAGE_ID> --flavor <FLAVOR> --hint group=<AffinityGroup1-UUID> new_instance_1
   ```

4. Restart the Nova-scheduler service for changes to take effect:

   ```
   [root@controller ~]# systemctl restart openstack-nova-scheduler
   ```

Configuring instances anti-affinity group with ServerGroupAntiAffinityFilter

In contrast to affinity group, the anti affinity filter `ServerGroupAntiAffinityFilter` ensures that each virtual machine instance in a group is on a different host. `ServerGroupAntiAffinityFilter` is configured by creating a server group with an anti-affinity policy, and pass a scheduler hint with the anti-affinity group UUID.

1. In Nova's configuration file `/etc/nova/nova.conf`, edit the parameter `scheduler_default_filters` and add `ServerGroupAntiAffinityFilter` to the list of values.

   ```
   scheduler_default_filters = ServerGroupAntiAffinityFilter
   ```

Nova-Compute Service

2. Create a new server group with the anti-affinity policy:

   ```
   [root@controller ~]# nova server-group-create --policy anti-affinity AntiAffinityGroup1
   ```

3. Boot the virtual machine instance with a flag that is pointing to the UUID of the anti-affinity group:

   ```
   [root@controller ~]# nova boot --image <GLANCE_IMAGE_ID> --flavor <FLAVOR> --hint group=<AntiAffinityGroup-UUID> new_instance_1
   ```

4. Restart the Nova-scheduler service for changes to take effect:

   ```
   [root@controller ~]# systemctl restart openstack-nova-scheduler
   ```

Configuring Nova host aggregates

In some cases, OpenStack users require their virtual machine instances to run with a specific underlying hardware or hypervisor characteristics, for example, to guarantee certain behavior like disk or CPU performance. Nova the grouping of hypervisor hosts with specific characteristics into hypervisor host aggregates. Nova host aggregates are nova-compute nodes grouped by a certain characteristics they share; flavors can be restricted to be launched on host aggregates featuring matched characteristics.

Nova host aggregates allow to partition compute hypervisors into logical groups, for example, the partitioning of hosts by common infrastructure, such as shared storage devices, hosts sharing a similar CPU, trusted compute hardware, or other types of hardware. This is preferred mostly to ensure consistent performance when launching instances of certain flavors. Another common use of host aggregates is categorizing hosts by class of service, such as Gold and Silver, where hosts assigned to Gold host aggregate are hosts with higher performing characteristics than Silver.

Each node is allowed to be assigned to one or more host aggregates, which allows to include hosts in several host aggregates base on different characteristics.

In the following example, Nova compute node 1 and Nova compute node 2 are running with solid-state drivers and are in a host aggregate identified by their disk type, but Nova compute node 2 also shares the same CPU type with the host aggregate identified by the CPU type.

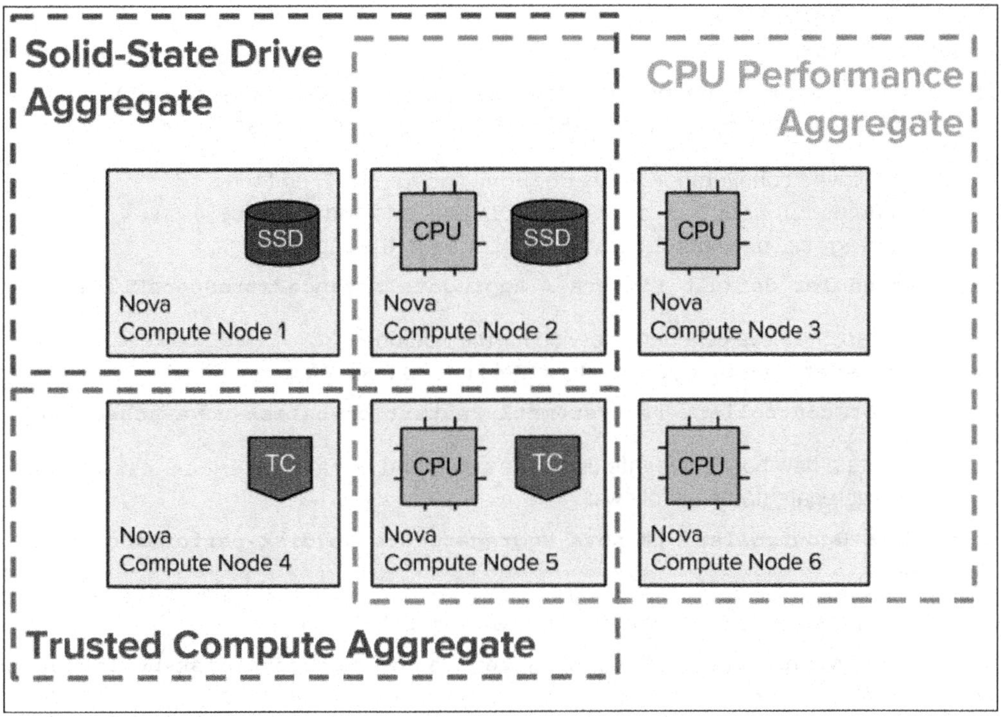
Solid-State Drive
Aggregate
CPU Performance
Aggregate
SSD
CPU
SSD
CPU
Nova
Compute Node 1
Nova
Compute Node 2
Nova
Compute Node 3
TC
CPU
TC
CPU
Nova
Compute Node 4
Nova
Compute Node 5
Nova
Compute Node 6
Trusted Compute Aggregate

Getting ready

Nova host aggregates are configured by enabling `AggregateInstanceExtraSpecsFilter` in the filter scheduler, then assigning key-value pairs in the aggregate metadata and matching key-value pairs in flavor's `extra_specs` metadata.

Users are not required to specify the host aggregate while launching a virtual machine instance, and flavors are mapped to host aggregates with matching key-value metadata pairs to. On virtual machine instance's launch, Nova scheduler matches flavor's key-value pairs to the host aggregate's metadata and filters out hosts without matching metadata key-value pairs.

Nova-Compute Service

How to do it...

In this example, we will create the host aggregate of fast solid-state drivers. Also, we will create a new flavor and bound it to the SSD host aggregate. Follow these steps:

1. Edit Nova's configuration file /etc/nova/nova.conf, edit the parameter scheduler_default_filters, and add the value AggregateInstanceExtraSpecsFilter to the list of values:

   ```
   scheduler_default_filters = AggregateInstanceExtraSpecsFilter
   ```

2. Restart the Nova-scheduler service for the addition of AggregateInstanceExtraSpecsFilter to take effect:

   ```
   [root@controller ~]# systemctl restart openstack-nova-scheduler
   ```

3. Create a new host aggregate using the command nova aggregate-create with an aggregate name as follows:

   ```
   [root@controller ~]# nova aggregate-create disk-performance-ssd nova
   ```

4. Add metadata to the newly created host aggregate:

   ```
   [root@controller ~]# nova aggregate-set-metadata disk-performance-ssd ssd=true
   ```

5. Assign nova-compute hypervisor host's compute-node1 and compute-node2 to the host aggregate:

   ```
   [root@controller ~]# nova aggregate-add-host 1 nova-compute-node1
   [root@controller ~]# nova aggregate-add-host 1 nova-compute-node2
   ```

6. Create a new flavor that will be bound to launch instances on the host aggregate; this will create a flavor with 8 GB of memory, 80 GB of disk, and 4 VCPUs:

   ```
   [root@controller ~]# nova flavor-create ssd.large 6 8192 80 4
   ```

   > Make sure that the flavor ID is not already used in your environment.

7. Set aggregate_instance_extra_specs of the flavor to match the SSD key-value pair:

   ```
   [root@controller ~]# nova flavor-key ssd.large set aggregate_instance_extra_specs:ssd=true
   ```

8. At this point, OpenStack users can launch virtual machine instances of the flavor, which will be scheduled on the SSD host aggregate:

   ```
   [root@controller ~]# nova boot --flavor 6 --image 17a34b8e-c573-48d6-920c-b4b450172b41 New-Instance-1
   ```

Configuring Nova host aggregates filters

Nova scheduler supports the configuring filters for individual host aggregates, and each host aggregate is configured with filters that are applied only when instances are to be scheduled within that host aggregate.

The host aggregate filters are enabled in the `/etc/nova/nova.conf` configuration file, the specific settings can be done for each host aggregate, and settings are set as metadata assigned to the host aggregate. When a filter is not set or the metadata value is not found for the host aggregate, the filter falls back to the default global value set in `nova.conf`.

How to do it...

Proceed with the following steps to configure Nova host aggregates filters:

AggregateCoreFilter

`AggregateCoreFilter` limits the scheduling of virtual machine instances on hosts that have sufficient CPU core available. `AggregateCoreFilter` allows the configuration of a fixed amount of vCPU overcommitment for each host aggregate, by setting the aggregate with the metadata key `cpu_allocation_ratio` with the number of cores as the value. If the per-aggregate value is not found, the value falls back to the global `CoreFilter` option. If the host is in more than one aggregate and more than one value is found, the minimum value will be used.

1. Enable and configure `AggregateCoreFilter` by editing Nova's configuration file `/etc/nova/nova.conf`. Add to the parameter `scheduler_default_filters` the value `AggregateCoreFilter`:

   ```
   scheduler_default_filters = AggregateCoreFilter
   ```

2. Restart the Nova-scheduler service for changes to take effect:

   ```
   [root@controller ~]# systemctl restart openstack-nova-scheduler
   ```

3. Set the host aggregate with the metadata key `cpu_allocation_ratio` with the number of cores as value:

   ```
   [root@controller ~]# nova aggregate-set-metadata host-aggr-1 cpu_allocation_ratio=6
   ```

AggregateDiskFilter

`AggregateDiskFilter` allows us to set the disk overcommitment ratio the scheduler should allow each host aggregate, and it filters out hosts when the free disk space available is smaller than the configured ratio. `AggregateDiskFiltes` allows the configuration of maximum disk overcommitment ratio by using the `disk_allocation_ratio` host aggregate metadata key. By default, disk overcommitment is disabled, it is useful to set disk overcommitment when SPARSE image format is in use, and disk image sizes are usually smaller than the virtual disk size. If the host aggregate metadata key `disk_allocation_ratio` is not set, the value falls back to the global setting. If the host is in more than one aggregate and more than one value is found, the minimum value will be used.

Enable and configure `AggregateDiskFilter` by following these steps:

1. In Nova's configuration file `/etc/nova/nova.conf`, edit the parameter `scheduler_default_filters` and add `AggregateDiskFilter` to the list of values:

   `scheduler_default_filters = AggregateDiskFilter`

2. Restart the Nova-scheduler service for changes to take effect:

   `[root@controller ~]# systemctl restart openstack-nova-scheduler`

3. Set the host aggregate with the metadata key `disk_allocation_ratio`, with the overcommitment ratio as value:

   `[root@controller ~]# nova aggregate-set-metadata host-aggr-1 disk_allocation_ratio = 1.3`

AggregateRamFilter

`AggregateRamFilter` allows us to limit Nova scheduler for each host aggregate to schedule instances only on hosts that have sufficient memory available, it allows the configuration of the allowed memory overcommitment ratio by setting the host aggregate metadata key `ram_allocation_ratio` with the overcommitment allocation ratio. If the per-aggregate host aggregate metadata value is not set, the value falls back to the global setting. If the host is in more than one aggregate and thus more than one value is found, the minimum value will be used.

Enable and configure `AggregateRamFilter` by following these steps:

1. In Nova's configuration file `/etc/nova/nova.conf`, edit the parameter `scheduler_default_filters` and add `AggregateRamFilter` to the list of values.

   `scheduler_default_filters = AggregateRamFilter`

2. Restart the Nova-scheduler service for changes to take effect:

   `[root@controller ~]# systemctl restart openstack-nova-scheduler`

3. To allow memory overcommitment of 150 percent within `host-aggr-1`, set the `ram_allocation_ratio` key to the value of `1.5`:

   `[root@controller ~]# nova aggregate-set-metadata host-aggr-1 ram_allocation_ratio = 1.5`

   This setting enables instances within the `host-aggr-1` host aggregate to consume 1.5 GB of memory on compute nodes with 1 GB of free RAM.

AggregateNumInstancesFilter

`AggregateNumInstancesFilter` allows us to limit the number of instances on hosts within each host aggregate. It also allows us to configure the maximum allowed instances on hosts within a host aggregate by setting the metadata key `max_instances_per_host` to the value of maximum allowed hosts. If the value is not configured with the host aggregate, the value falls back to the global setting. If the host is in more than one aggregate and thus more than one value is found, the minimum value will be used.

Enable and configure `AggregateNumInstancesFilter` by following these steps:

1. In Nova's configuration file `/etc/nova/nova.conf`, edit the parameter `scheduler_default_filters` and add `AggregateNumInstancesFilter` to the list of values.

   `scheduler_default_filters = AggregateNumInstancesFilter`

2. Restart the Nova-scheduler service for changes to take effect:

   `[root@controller ~]# systemctl restart openstack-nova-scheduler`

3. Limit the maximum allowed instances on each host of the host aggregate to 10 instances. Set the metadata key `max_instances_per_host` to the value of 10:

   `[root@controller ~]# nova aggregate-set-metadata host-aggr-1 max_instances_per_host = 10`

Nova-Compute Service

Configuring Nova scheduler weights

Nova scheduler first evaluates the configured filters, and it compiles a list of hosts that pass the filters and can be tasked with running the virtual machines instances, after filtering out hosts that don't follow the required capabilities. After Nova scheduler compiles a list of valid candidates to execute the nova request, the scheduler uses weights mechanism to determine which host is the most suitable candidate that executes the request and runs the virtual machine instance. Weights are calculated for each host when a virtual machine instance is to be scheduled, the scheduler calculates host's weight by monitoring resource consumptions of the host. We can set a policy to spread the virtual machine instances across the hosts, or to stack them on a host until resources on that host are exhausted and then schedule virtual machine instances to run on the next best suited host.

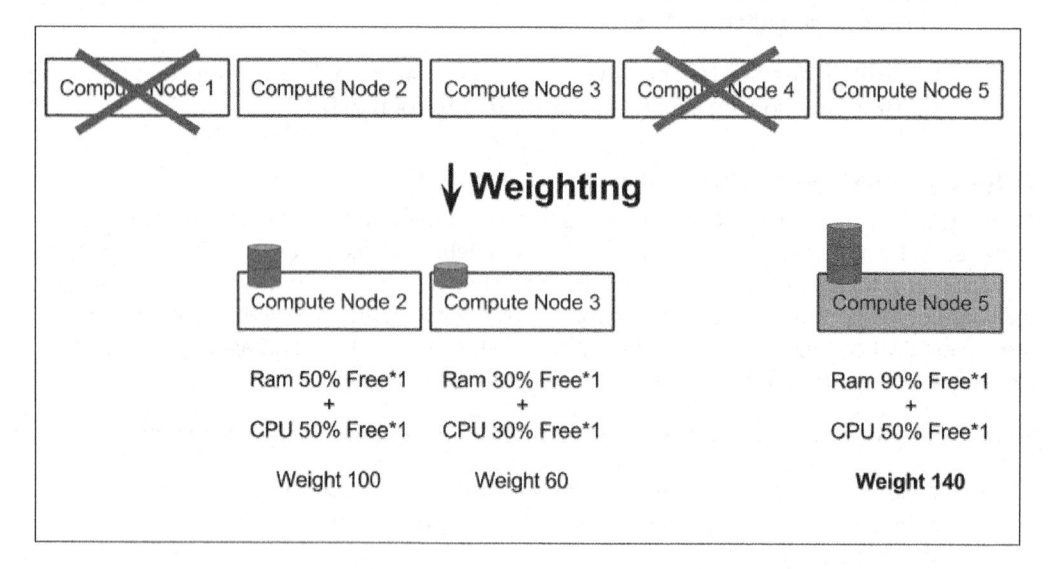

	Compute Node 2	Compute Node 3		Compute Node 5
Ram	50% Free*1	30% Free*1		90% Free*1
CPU	50% Free*1	30% Free*1		50% Free*1
Weight	100	60		**140**

Nova scheduler calculates each weight with a configurable multiplier and then sums up all calculated weights. Hosts with the largest weight are given with a higher priority. By default, the scheduler elects the host with the highest weight. The weights mechanism also allows the configuration of the host subset size, which is a group of a defined number of hosts best matching weights, then the scheduler chooses a random host from the hosts subset group to run the virtual machine instance. The default subset size is 1 host, which effectively allows the scheduler to choose from a list of a single host with the highest weight.

In the following example, Nova scheduler is configured with a subset of two nodes with the highest weights, and the scheduler chooses a random host from the subset list of hosts.

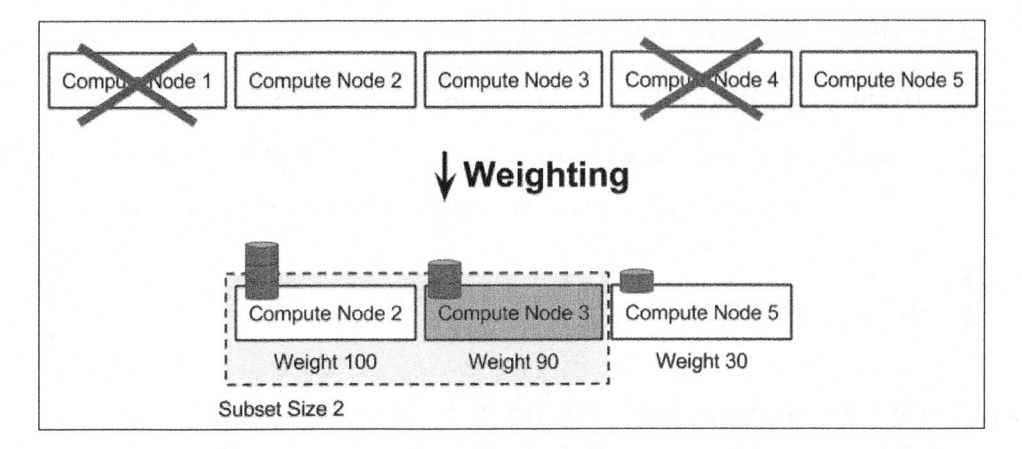

Nova scheduler evaluates the required resources for each individual instance, it virtually consumes those resources, and the following selections are adjusted accordingly. This is useful when a single request requires a large amount of instances, and the weight is computed for each requested instance separately.

Getting ready

Each hypervisor that runs Nova-compute constantly monitors its resources and sends the updates saved in the database, leading the database to hold a concurrent usage state of all monitored metrics of all Nova compute nodes.

First, we will enable the monitoring of the metrics on the compute nodes that allow you to collect usage stats to the database, then we will configure the Nova scheduler weighers by setting the weights multipliers of each metric and its policy. This allows us to choose whether we want to spread instances across suitable Nova compute nodes by configuring a positive value for the multiplier or stacking instances, by setting a negative value to the multiplier.

How to do it...

Run the following commands to enable nova compute to monitor the CPU metrics of the compute nodes and configure the scheduler weighing policy:

Enabling compute metrics monitoring

1. Using the `openstack-config` command, edit Nova's configuration file `/etc/nova/nova.conf`; under the `DEFAULT` section, set the parameter `compute_available_monitors` to `monitors.all_monitors`:

    ```
    [root@compute1 ~]# openstack-config --set /etc/nova/nova.conf DEFAULT compute_available_monitors  nova.compute.monitors.all_monitors
    ```

Nova-Compute Service

2. Set nova compute to monitor the CPU metrics:

   ```
   [root@compute1 ~]# openstack-config --set /etc/nova/nova.conf
   DEFAULT compute_monitors  ComputeDriverCPUMonitor
   ```

3. Restart the Nova-compute service for changes to take effect:

   ```
   [root@controller ~]# systemctl restart openstack-nova-compute
   ```

> Nova introduces a new API get call to gather all collected metrics in the Liberty release.

Enabling and configuring weights scheduling

1. Enable the `weights.all_weighers` class, which enables `RamWeigher` and `MetricsWeigher`:

   ```
   [root@controller ~]# openstack-config --set /etc/nova/nova.conf
   DEFAULT
   
   scheduler_weight_classes   nova.scheduler.weights.all_weighers
   ```

2. Set the host subset size to 1, which makes the scheduler choose the host with the highest weight:

   ```
   [root@controller ~]# openstack-config --set /etc/nova/nova.conf
   DEFAULT
   
   scheduler_host_subset_size   1
   ```

3. Set the ram weight multiplier to 1 to spread the virtual machine instance evenly between hosts with free memory:

   ```
   [root@controller ~]# openstack-config --set /etc/nova/nova.conf
   DEFAULT
   
   ram_weight_multiplier   1.0
   ```

> If stacking virtual machine instances is preferred until all memory is consumed, instead of spreading them across the hosts, set the `ram_weight_multiplier` option to a negative value, for example, -1.0.

4. Set `weight_multiplier`, under the metrics section, to 1.0 to spread virtual machine instance evenly between hosts:

   ```
   [root@controller ~]# openstack-config --set /etc/nova/nova.conf
   metrics
   
   weight_multiplier   1.0
   ```

5. You can set how each of the supported metrics is weighed. Set a positive value for spreading or negative value for stacking:

   `[root@controller ~]# openstack-config --set /etc/nova/nova.conf metrics`

   `weight_setting = cpu.user.percent=1.0, cpu.idle.time=-1.0`

   > Nova scheduler weights include the `ComputeDriverCPUMonitor` class, which supports the following metrics:
   > - `cpu.user.percent`
   > - `cpu.kernel.time`
   > - `cpu.iowait.percent`
   > - `cpu.idle.time`
   > - `cpu.frequency`
   > - `cpu.iowait.time`
   > - `cpu.percent`
   > - `cpu.user.time`
   > - `cpu.idle.percent`
   > - `cpu.kernel.percent`

6. Set the metrics required option to false, for the scheduler weights to treat missing metrics as a negative value, lowering hosts' weight:

   `[root@controller ~]# openstack-config --set /etc/nova/nova.conf metrics`

   `required    false`

7. Set the negative value to use when a metric is reported:

   `[root@controller ~]# openstack-config --set /etc/nova/nova.conf metrics`

   `weight_of_unavailable = -1000.0`

8. Restart Nova-compute service for changes to take effect:

   `[root@controller ~]# systemctl restart openstack-nova-scheduler`

9
Horizon Dashboard Service

In this chapter, we will cover the following topics:

- Securing Horizon with Secure Socket Layer
- Configuring Horizon caching with memcached
- Customizing Horizon dashboard appearance

Introduction

The Horizon dashboard service provides a web-based graphical user interface for OpenStack. This allows users to consume the OpenStack services. Administrators can access the overall view of the size and state of the OpenStack Cloud. Administrators can also access, manage, and provision OpenStack compute, storage, networking, and other services and resources that OpenStack provides.

Horizon dashboard can be used as a self-service portal for OpenStack Cloud users to provision OpenStack resources within the limits and quotas set by the Cloud administrators.

OpenStack dashboard is designed to be extensible. It is easy to plug in and expose third-party products and services within the dashboard, such as billing, monitoring, and additional management tools. The dashboard can also be configured with custom branding for service providers and other vendors who want to make use of it.

Horizon Dashboard Service

The OpenStack Horizon dashboard service interacts with other services' APIs to retrieve data. To create new OpenStack resources, it is built on top of Django Python web framework and runs under a web server, which is commonly Apache HTTPD or NGINX.

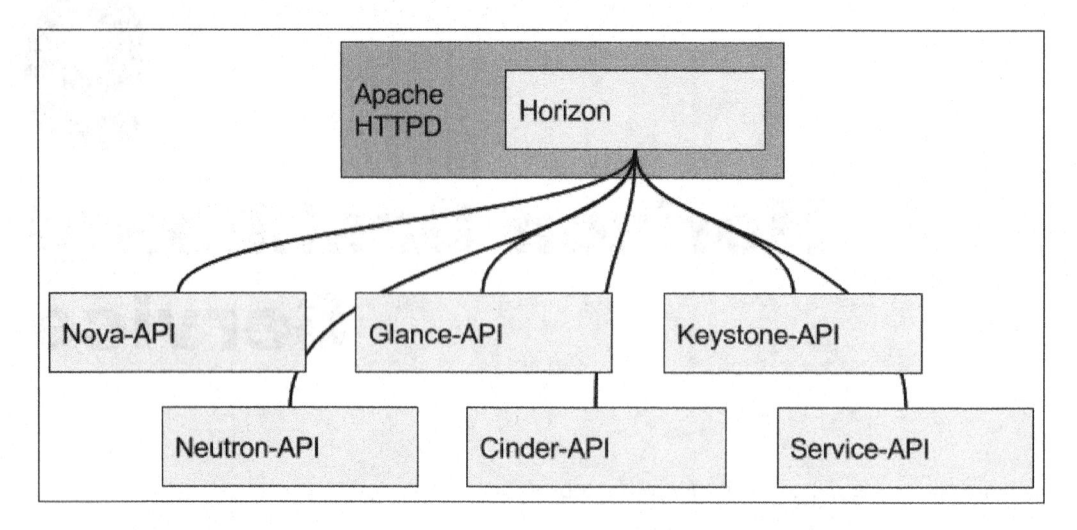

The dashboard consists of the following packages:

- `httpd` is the Apache HTTP service that hosts and serves the web dashboard application.
- The `openstack-dashboard` package provides the dashboard web application running within the Django web framework.

Securing Horizon with Secure Socket Layer

Horizon allows complete control for all the OpenStack resources. The communication that is going back and forth between the user's web browser and the Django web server serving Horizon dashboard contains sensitive information, such as user account passwords and environmental details revealing sensitive user information. The default configuration for Horizon allows an unencrypted, clear text communication channel to the Horizon Django web server. It is highly recommended to configure Horizon to encrypt the data going back and forth using the SSL/TLS protocol.

In this recipe, we will configure the Apache HTTPD server running the Django web service to use the SSL/TLS certificate to encrypt the communication channel, so all information going between the user and Horizon will be encrypted. We will also add a configuration to redirect users from unsecure port 80 to port 443 to use the secured HTTPS protocol.

Getting ready

We will use a self-signed SSL/TLS certificate with a matching key file. It is recommended to obtain a signed SSL/TLS certificate from a trusted **certified authority** (**CA**). If you do not have a signed SSL/TLS certificate, you can generate a self-signed certificate.

> Modern web browsers can detect certificates coming from unauthorized authorities, for example, self-signed certificates, and notify the user with a warning.

Generate a self-signed SSL/TLS certificate using the `openssl` command as follows:

```
[root@controller ~]# openssl req -x509 -nodes -days 365 -newkey rsa:2048 -keyout /etc/httpd/ssl/apache.key -out /etc/httpd/ssl/apache.crt
Generating a 2048 bit RSA private key
......................+++
.+++
writing new private key to 'apache.key'
-----
You are about to be asked to enter information that will be incorporated
into your certificate request.
What you are about to enter is what is called a Distinguished Name or a
DN.
There are quite a few fields but you can leave some blank
For some fields there will be a default value,
If you enter '.', the field will be left blank.
-----
Country Name (2 letter code) [XX]:US
State or Province Name (full name) []:CA
Locality Name (eg, city) [Default City]:San Francisco
Organization Name (eg, company) [Default Company Ltd]:Acme
Organizational Unit Name (eg, section) []:DevOps
Common Name (eg, your name or your server's hostname) []:OpenStack
Email Address []:email@address.com
```

At this point, we have created a self-signed SSL/TLS certificate and a matching key file, which are located at `/etc/httpd/ssl/`. We will use this certificate in this recipe as an example.

Horizon Dashboard Service

How to do it...

Follow these steps to configure the Apache HTTPD server running the Horizon Django web service with SSL/TLS:

1. Install the `mod_ssl` package, which will be used by the `httpd` service:

    `[root@controller ~]# yum install mod_ssl openssl`

2. Edit the dashboard configuration file `/etc/openstack-dashboard/local_settings` and set parameters `CSRF_COOKIE_SECURE` and `SESSION_COOKIE_SECURE` to the value `True`:

    `[root@controller ~]# vim /etc/openstack-dashboard/local_settings`

    ..

    `CSRF_COOKIE_SECURE = True`

    `SESSION_COOKIE_SECURE = True`

    ..

3. Configure the `vhost` section at `/etc/httpd/conf.d/15-horizon_vhost.conf`:

    > This recipe assumes that the `httpd` configuration for Horizon was done using the `PackStack` installer. The `vhost` configuration file name, `15-horizon_vhost.conf`, might be different in your system.

4. Open the `vhost` configuration file for editing:

    `vim /etc/httpd/conf.d/15-horizon_vhost.conf`

5. Change the `VirtualHost` port from port `80` to port `433` as follows:

    `<VirtualHost *:443>`

6. Change the port number in the value of `ServerName` from port `80` to port `443` as follows:

    `ServerName centos7-kilo.berezins.com:443`

7. Make sure that the `mod_ssl` module is loaded, and add the following line:

    `LoadModule ssl_module modules/mod_ssl.so`

8. After loading the `mod_ssl` module, set `SSLEngine` to `on`:

    `SSLEngine on`

9. Specify the certificate and certificate key files:

    `SSLCertificateFile /etc/httpd/ssl/apache.crt`

    `SSLCertificateKeyFile /etc/httpd/ssl/apache.key`

Chapter 9

10. Edit the file `/etc/httpd/conf/ports.conf` and set the `httpd` service to open port `443`:

    vim /etc/httpd/conf/ports.conf

    Listen 443

11. For all changes to take effect, restart the httpd service:

    [root@controller ~]# systemctl restart httpd.service

12. Navigate to your horizon URL using HTTPS protocol:

    https://controller

> Since we are using a self-signed certificate in this recipe, the browser will prompt a warning due to an unrecognized certificate authority.

There's more...

It is recommended to redirect users coming to unsecured HTTP port `80` to the encrypted HTTPS protocol on port `443`, add the following section to the `vhost` configuration file under `/etc/httpd/conf.c/15-horizon_vhost.conf`:

```
<VirtualHost *:80>
ServerName centos7-kilo.berezins.com:80
<IfModule mod_rewrite.c>
RewriteEngine On
RewriteCond %{HTTPS} off
RewriteRule (.*) https://%{HTTP_HOST}%{REQUEST_URI}
</IfModule>
<IfModule !mod_rewrite.c>
RedirectPermanent / https://%{HTTP_HOST}%{REQUEST_URI}
</IfModule>
</VirtualHost>
```

> Make sure that there's no other `vhost` configuration listening to port `80`.

Horizon Dashboard Service

Configuring Horizon caching with memcached

To better address large-scale environments while using the Horizon dashboard service, with a large amount of users, it is recommended to configure a caching layer in front of the dashboard. This reduces the amount of calls `httpd` needs to address and allows Horizon dashboard to serve a larger amount of users.

Getting started

In this recipe, we will configure Horizon to use a memcached caching service. We will need to install and configure the memcached service first.

Install the memcached service with dependent packages:

```
[root@controller ~]# yum install -y memcached memcached-selinux
```

Edit the memcached configuration file:

```
[root@controller ~]# vi /etc/sysconfig/memcached
```

Make sure that the following settings are done:

```
PORT="11211"
USER="memcached"
OPTIONS="-l 127.0.0.1"
```

Enable and start the memcached service:

```
[root@controller ~]# systemctl enable memcached
[root@controller ~]# systemctl start memcached
```

Test if memcached is running and functional as follows:

```
[root@controller ~]# memcached-tool 127.0.0.1:11211
```

How to do it...

1. Edit `/etc/openstack-dashboard/local_settings` and make sure that the CACHES section is not commented out, and the memcached service located at the localhost `127.0.0.1:11211` is set as the backend:

    ```
    [root@controller ~]# vi /etc/openstack-dashboard/local_settings
    ..
    CACHES = {
    ```

```
    'default': {
        'BACKEND': 'django.core.cache.backends.memcached.
MemcachedCache',
        'LOCATION': '127.0.0.1:11211',
    }
}
..
```

2. Restart the HTTPD service:

   `[root@controller ~]# systemctl restart httpd`

Customizing Horizon dashboard appearance

Horizon web dashboard allows us to change its style and customize its look and feel to match the organization's branding language. It allows changing the OpenStack logos on the login landing page and changing the logo of the dashboard itself as well. Additionally, the OpenStack dashboard supports loading custom styling using additional **Cascading Style Sheets** (**CSS**) that Horizon can load and override the default appearance of the dashboard.

Changing the OpenStack Horizon landing page logos

In this recipe, we will upload and configure a new logo for the login landing page, and for the Horizon OpenStack dashboard interface. We will replace the default CSS to a custom CSS file.

The original landing page logo size is 108 x 121 pixels, and the top-left corner logo size is 110x24 pixels. We can customize the logo size and upload logos of different sizes.

How to do it...

Follow these steps to change the default logo on the Horizon login landing page:

1. Copy your custom logo to the static images path `/usr/share/openstack-dashboard/static/dashboard/img/`:

   `[root@controller ~]# cp /root/custom_openstack_logo.png /usr/share/openstack-dashboard/static/dashboard/img/`

2. Set the read permissions for user "other":

   `[root@controller ~]# chmod o+r custom_openstack_logo.png`

   `[root@controller ~]# ls -l custom_openstack_logo.png`

   `-rw-r--r--. 1 root root 35396 Jul 24 17:38 custom_openstack_logo.png`

Horizon Dashboard Service

3. Edit the `splash.scss` file `/usr/share/openstack-dashboard/static/dashboard/scss/_splash.scss`:

   ```
   [root@controller ~]# vi /usr/share/openstack-dashboard/static/dashboard/scss/_splash.scss
   ```

4. Under the section `splash`, set the background image `url` of `.logn` to your custom logo. We have the following section:

   ```
   .login {
     background: url(../img/logo-splash.png) no-repeat center 35px;
     ...
   }
   ```

   Change this to the following:

   ```
   .login {
     background: url(../img/custom_openstack_logo.png) no-repeat center 35px;
     ...
   }
   ```

5. Restart the HTTPD service as follows:

   ```
   [root@controller ~]# systemctl restart httpd
   ```

There's more...

You can also change the page title by setting the parameter `SITE_BRANDING` in the dashboard settings file `/etc/openstack-dashboard/local_settings`:

```
[root@controller ~]#vi /etc/openstack-dashboard/local_settings
..
SITE_BRANDING = "My OpenStack Dashboard Title"
..
```

Then, restart the Apache HTTPD service:

```
[root@controller ~]# systemctl restart httpd
```

Index

A

AggregateCoreFilter
 about 171
 configuring 171
 enabling 171
AggregateDiskFilter
 about 172
 configuring 172
 enabling 172
AggregateNumInstancesFilter
 about 173
 configuring 173
 enabling 173
AggregateRamFilter
 about 172
 configuring 173
 enabling 173
architectural layouts, OpenStack
 about 4
 all-in-one layout 5
 Controller-Neutron-computes layout 5
 custom-distributed layout 6

C

CapacityFilter
 about 132
 enabling 133
CapacityWeigher
 about 132
 enabling 133
Cascading Style Sheets (CSS) 185
Ceph 123
Ceph backend
 Glance, configuring with 113-115

certified authority (CA) 181
Cinder
 configuring, with Ceph RADOS block device backend driver 123-125
 configuring, with Ceph RBD backup driver 127, 128
 configuring, with multiple backends 129-131
 configuring, with NFS backend driver 125, 126
 Linux services 120
Cinder-API 120
Cinder-Backup service 120
Cinder block storage service 119
Cinder scheduler filters
 configuring 132
Cinder-Scheduler service 120
Cinder scheduler weighers
 configuring 132
Cinder-Volume service 120
Cluster Labs
 URL 74
ComputeFilter
 about 163
 configuring 164
 enabling 163
compute node, for Neutron
 configuring 40
 message broker, configuring 41
 Neutron networks, creating 44
 Neutron service, configuring 41-43
compute nodes, Nova
 configuring 29
 database connection, configuring 29
 message broker, configuring 29
 service, configuring 30
 service, enabling 31

service packages, installing 29
service, starting 31
CoreFilter
  about 165
  configuring 165
  enabling 165
core services
  Glance 3
  Keystone 3
  Neutron 3
  Nova 3

D

deployment method, OpenStack
  configuration management tools 7
  deploying, from packages 7, 8
  Foreman with Staypuft plugin 7
  manual deployment, from packages 6
  PackStack 7
DHCP service agent
  configuring 151
DiskFilter
  about 165
  configuring 166
  enabling 166
DriverFilter
  about 132
  configuring 134
  enabling 133

E

environment, for Staypuft
  networks layout 48
  PXE network, provisioning 48
  setting up 48
environment setup, OpenStack 8, 9

F

Firewall as a Service (FWaaS)
  about 137
  configuring 155
Foreman 7

G

Galera cluster
  configuring, for MariaDB 78-81
Glance
  about 21
  configuration, verifying 109
  configuring 24
  configuring, with Ceph backend 113-115
  configuring, with local file backend 108
  configuring, with NFS backend 110, 111
  configuring, with Swift backend 111-113
  database connection, configuring 23
  database, creating 22
  Glance service credentials, creating in Keystone 22
  Glance service endpoint, creating in Keystone 23
  image size limit, configuring 117
  installation, verifying 25
  installing 21
  service configuration 23
  service firewall ports 23
  service packages, installing 23
  storage quota, configuring 117
Glance image caching
  configuring 115-117
Glance image service
  about 107
  glance-api 107
  glance-registry 108
GoodnessWeigher
  about 132
  configuring 134
  enabling 134
GRE tenant networks
  configuring, Open vSwitch used 144

H

HAProxy
  installing 74-77
Horizon
  about 45
  installation, verifying 46

installing 45, 46
securing, with Secure Socket Layer 180-183
Horizon caching
configuring, with memcached 184
Horizon dashboard appearance
customizing 185
landing page logos, changing 185, 186
Horizon dashboard service
about 179
httpd 180
openstack-dashboard package 180
host networking
configuring 66
hosts
allocating, to roles 65, 66
hosts, discovering for provisioning
about 55
Staypuft web user interface, accessing 56-58
hosts prerequisites
configuring 10
firewall service 11
NTP 12
openstack-utils package 11, 12
SELinux 12
Yum repositories 11

I

ImagePropertiesFilter
about 166
configuring 166
enabling 166
Infrastructure as a Service (IaaS) 2, 71

K

kernel-based virtual machine (KVM) 3, 160
Keystone
about 15, 89
administrative token, configuring 17
configuring, with Microsoft Active Directory and LDAP 97-99
database connection, configuring 16
database, creating 15, 16
installation, verifying 21
installing 15
securing, wih SSL 102-104
service basic configuration 17
service firewall ports 16
service packages, installing 16
services 90
Keystone caching
configuring, with Memcached 100-102
Keystone configuration, with MariaDB backend
about 91
administrative token, configuring 93
database connection, configuring 92
Keystone administrator account 96
Keystone database, creating 91
Keystone endpoints, configuring 95
Keystone service firewall ports 92
Keystone user account 96
service basic configuration 93
service, enabling 94
service packages, installing 92
service, starting 94
tokens PKIs, configuring 93, 94
tokens PKIs, generating 93
KVM Hypervisor
Nova-compute, configuring with 160, 161

L

L3 agent
configuring, with Open vSwitch 148-150
L3 plugin
configuring 141
LinuxBridge plugin
configuring 141
Linux services, Neutron
neutron-dhcp-agent service 138
neutron-l3-agent service 138
neutron-linuxbridge-agent service 138
neutron-openvswitch-agent service 138
neutron-server 138
Load Balancer as a Service (LBaaS)
about 137
configuring 152-154
logical volume management (LVM) 119
LVM Cinder backend storage provider
configuring 120-122

M

man-in-the-middle (MITM) attack 102
MariaDB database
 installing 12, 13
Modular Layer 2 (ML2) 31, 136, 139

N

network
 configuring 60, 61
 services configuration 63, 64
Neutron
 about 31, 135
 configuring 33-35
 database connection, configuring 32
 database, creating 31
 Firewall as a Service (FWaaS) 137
 installing 31
 Keystone service credentials, creating 32
 Keystone service endpoint, creating 32
 Linux services 138
 Load Balancer as a Service (LBaaS) 137
 load balancer service extension 137
 message broker, configuring 33
 networks 135
 network switching capabilities, implementing 136
 port 136
 service, enabling 36
 service firewall ports 32
 service packages, installing 32
 service, starting 36
 subnet 136
neutron core ML2 plugin
 configuring 140-146
Neutron network node
 configuring 36
 message broker, configuring 37
 Neutron service, configuring 37-39
 service, enabling 40
 service, starting 40
Neutron VLAN provider network
 configuration, copying 142-148
 configuring, with ML2 and LinuxBridge 139
 services, starting 142-148

Neutron VXLAN
 configuring, Open vSwitch used 144
NFS backend
 Cinder, configuring with 125, 126
 Glance, configuring with 110, 111
Nova
 about 26
 configuring 28
 database connection, configuring 27
 database, creating 26
 installation, verifying 29
 installing 26
 Keystone service credentials, creating 26
 Keystone service endpoint, creating 27
 message broker, configuring 28
 service, enabling 28
 service firewall ports 27
 service packages, installing 27
 service, starting 28
Nova access services
 nova-api service 158
 nova-consoleauth service 158
 openstack-nova-novncproxy service 158
Nova-compute
 configuring, with KVM Hypervisor 160, 161
 configuring, with QEMU Hypervisor emulation 161
Nova-compute worker service 159
Nova host aggregates
 configuring 168-170
Nova host aggregates filters
 AggregateCoreFilter 171
 AggregateDiskFilter 172
 AggregateNumInstancesFilter 173
 AggregateRamFilter 172
 configuring 171
Nova Hypervisors
 configuring 159
Nova management services
 nova-cert service 159
 nova-conductor service 159
 nova-scheduler service 158
Nova network services
 about 159
 nova-dhcpbridge script 159
 nova-network service 159

Nova scheduler filters
  ComputeFilter 163
  configuring 163
  CoreFilter 165
  DiskFilter 165
  ImagePropertiesFilter 166
  RamFilter 164
  RetryFilter 164
  ServerGroupAffinityFilter 167
  ServerGroupAntiAffinityFilter 167
Nova scheduler weights
  compute metrics monitoring, enabling 175
  configuring 174-177
  enabling 176
Nova scheduling
  configuring 162

O

OpenStack
  about 2
  architectural layouts 4
  components 2
  core services 3
  deploying 68, 69
  deployment, creating 58, 59
  deployment, verifying 69
  environment setup 8
  optional services 3
  physical network topology 9, 10
  projects 2
  services, configuring 83-86
  Wiki page 159
Open vSwitch
  configuring 146
  L3 agent, configuring with 148-150
optional services
  Ceilometer 3
  Cinder 3
  Heat 3
  Horizon 3
  Sahara 3
  Swift 3
  Trove 3
  Zaqar 3

P

Pacemaker
  about 71, 72
  installing 73, 74
PackStack 7
physical network topology 9, 10
PXE network, Staypuft
  external public network 49
  provisioning 48
  Staypuft host 49
  Tenant network 49

Q

QEMU Hypervisor emulation
  Nova-compute, configuring with 161

R

RabbitMQ
  installing 14
  installing, with mirrored queues 81-83
  reference 83
RamFilter
  about 164
  configuring 164
  enabling 164
rbd (RADOS block devices) 123
RetryFilter
  about 164
  configuring 164
  enabling 164

S

Secure Socket Layer
  Horizon, securing with 180
ServerGroupAffinityFilter
  about 167
  configuring 167
  enabling 167
ServerGroupAntiAffinityFilter
  about 167
  configuring 167, 168
  enabling 167

Staypuft
   about 7, 47
   configuring, as Internet gateway 49
   environment, setting up 48
   for deploying OpenStack 55
   packages, installing 51-55
   YUM repositories, setting 50
storage area network (SAN) 119
Swift backend
   Glance, configuring with 111-113

T

tokens PKIs
   configuring 17
   generating 17

Keystone administrator account 20
Keystone endpoints, configuring 19
Keystone user account 20
service, enabling 18
service, starting 18

V

virtual private networks (VPNs) 136
VolumeNumberWeigher
   about 132
   enabling 133

W

write set replication (wsrep) API 78

[PACKT] open source
PUBLISHING — community experience distilled

Thank you for buying
Production Ready OpenStack - Recipes for Successful Environments

About Packt Publishing

Packt, pronounced 'packed', published its first book, *Mastering phpMyAdmin for Effective MySQL Management*, in April 2004, and subsequently continued to specialize in publishing highly focused books on specific technologies and solutions.

Our books and publications share the experiences of your fellow IT professionals in adapting and customizing today's systems, applications, and frameworks. Our solution-based books give you the knowledge and power to customize the software and technologies you're using to get the job done. Packt books are more specific and less general than the IT books you have seen in the past. Our unique business model allows us to bring you more focused information, giving you more of what you need to know, and less of what you don't.

Packt is a modern yet unique publishing company that focuses on producing quality, cutting-edge books for communities of developers, administrators, and newbies alike. For more information, please visit our website at `www.packtpub.com`.

About Packt Open Source

In 2010, Packt launched two new brands, Packt Open Source and Packt Enterprise, in order to continue its focus on specialization. This book is part of the Packt open source brand, home to books published on software built around open source licenses, and offering information to anybody from advanced developers to budding web designers. The Open Source brand also runs Packt's open source Royalty Scheme, by which Packt gives a royalty to each open source project about whose software a book is sold.

Writing for Packt

We welcome all inquiries from people who are interested in authoring. Book proposals should be sent to `author@packtpub.com`. If your book idea is still at an early stage and you would like to discuss it first before writing a formal book proposal, then please contact us; one of our commissioning editors will get in touch with you.

We're not just looking for published authors; if you have strong technical skills but no writing experience, our experienced editors can help you develop a writing career, or simply get some additional reward for your expertise.

Implementing Cloud Storage with OpenStack Swift

ISBN: 978-1-78216-805-8   Paperback: 140 pages

Design, implement, and successfully manage your own cloud storage cluster using the popular OpenStack Swift software

1. Learn about the fundamentals of cloud storage using OpenStack Swift.

2. Explore how to install and manage OpenStack Swift along with various hardware and tuning options.

3. Perform data transfer and management using REST APIs.

OpenStack Essentials

ISBN: 978-1-78398-708-5   Paperback: 182 pages

Demystify the cloud by building your own private OpenStack cloud

1. Set up a powerful cloud platform using OpenStack.

2. Learn about the components of OpenStack and how they interact with each other.

3. Follow a step-by-step process that exposes the inner details of an OpenStack cluster.

Please check www.PacktPub.com for information on our titles

Learning OpenStack Networking (Neutron)

ISBN: 978-1-78398-330-8　　　　Paperback: 300 pages

Architect and build a network infrastructure for your cloud using OpenStack Neutron networking

1. Build a virtual switching infrastructure for virtual machines using the Open vSwitch or Linux Bridge plugins.

2. Create networks and software routers that connect virtual machines to the Internet using built-in Linux networking features.

3. Scale your application using Neutron's load-balancing-as-a-service feature using the haproxy plugin.

Mastering Citrix® XenServer®

ISBN: 978-1-78328-739-0　　　　Paperback: 300 pages

Design and implement highly optimized virtualization solutions using Citrix® XenServer® 6.2

1. Master mission-critical aspects of virtualization to develop, deploy, and administer virtual infrastructures.

2. Integrate Citrix XenServer with OpenStack and CloudStack to create a private cloud.

3. Implement automation with command-line Windows PowerShell scripting.

Please check **www.PacktPub.com** for information on our titles

CPSIA information can be obtained
at www.ICGtesting.com
Printed in the USA
LVOW03s1530031115

460925LV00009B/370/P

9 781783 986903